D1261352

Giordano Bruno and the Philosophy of the Ass

NUCCIO ORDINE

Giordano Bruno and the
Philosophy of the Ass

Translated by Henryk Barański in collaboration with Arielle Saiber

Yale University Press New Haven and London

This volume is published under the patronage
of the Istituto Italiano per gli Studi
Filosofici of Naples, Italy.

Original title: *La cabala dell'asino* © 1987 by
Liguori Editore, S.r.l.
English translation copyright © 1996 by Yale University.

All rights reserved.
This book may not be reproduced, in whole or
in part, including illustrations, in any form
(beyond that copying permitted by Sections 107
and 108 of the U.S. Copyright Law and except
by reviewers for the public press), without
written permission from the publishers.

Designed by Sonia L. Scanlon.
Set in Bodoni type by Rainsford Type,
Danbury, Connecticut.
Printed in the United States of America by
BookCrafters, Inc., Chelsea, Michigan.

Library of Congress Cataloging-in-Publication
Data
Ordine, Nuccio, 1958–
    [Cabala dell'asino.   English]
    Giordano Bruno and the philosophy of the
    ass / Nuccio Ordine.
        p.   cm.
    Includes bibliographical references and
    index.
    ISBN 0-300-05852-7 (cloth : alk. paper)
    1. Bruno, Giordano, 1548–1600.
    2. Mental efficiency—History—16th
    century.   3. Donkeys—Miscellanea.
    I. Title.
    B783.Z707313   1996   95–39256
                             CIP

A catalogue record for this book is available
from the British Library.

The paper in this book meets the guidelines
for permanence and durability of the Committee
on Production Guidelines for Book Longevity of
the Council on Library Resources.

10   9   8   7   6   5   4   3   2   1

per enne

"e nulla torna se non forse in questi
disguidi del possibile." (E. Montale)

CONTENTS

Eugenio Garin

The literature of the ass, if we understand thereby the body of writings devoted to the ass, occupies a prominent place in the literature of the sixteenth century, from Machiavelli's poetry to the developments by Cornelius Agrippa, who, precisely by means of a *digressio ad encomium asini*—situated between the chapters *de Verbo Dei* and *de scientiarum magistris* on the one hand and the *operis peroratio* on the other—concludes his famous *declamatio de incertitudine et vanitate scientiarum atque artium*. After having placed the apostles on a level with asses, Agrippa in passing intends to cast light upon the *asini mysteria* to reinforce his conclusion: "From what I have said, it is as clear as day that no other animal is in a better position than the ass to receive the divine. If you do not look to the ass, you will be in no position to receive the divine mysteries."

As irreverent as it is amusing, Agrippa's "digression" came to be part of a framework of symbols that Bruno certainly utilized. At its origin we find, of course, Apuleius's romance, which was widely diffused; we find as well the taste of transgression, the pleasure of toying with a provocative and multifaceted symbol. Machiavelli recalls how, "in the form of an ass," he had "toiled and suffered" to discover "more bad than good" at every level of our world. It was thanks to this experience that he was able to acquaint himself with men's vices and virtues, and then to expose them openly and without shame ("thus one will appreciate how rotten the world is"). The patient, doleful work of the beast of burden transformed itself into revelatory knowledge, through which one had a paradoxical means of exposing *coincidentia oppositorum:* ignorant, but learned; humble, but powerful.

By the end of the century, the theme of the ass, therefore, was no longer original, apart from its being used as a symbol that henceforth was charged with complex meanings. What were original, however, were Giordano Bruno's "exploitation" to excess of this theme, his insistence on this central motif, and the wealth of meaning he takes on in expressing (sometimes with extraordinary effectiveness) certain points essential to his philosophical reflections. Bruno does not invent the theme of the ass, nor the polysemous play to which it lends itself; but by conferring a decisive value upon it, by pushing its possibilities to the extreme, he devotes pages to it where felicitous expression is allied to theoretical depth. Similarly, Nuccio Ordine is certainly not the first to deal with the subject—although his book presents new and often highly pertinent elements; nor is he the first to underline the importance this theme holds for Bruno. But he is the first to collate systematically the theoretical meanings of asininity, to specify its every ambivalence, to analyze its contradictory meanings and to show how this play of opposites leads to the very heart of Bruno's thought. But what is more important, when he illustrates the theme of asininity and proceeds to make a careful comparison with other thinkers and literary figures of the sixteenth century, Nuccio Ordine emphasizes the inimitable flavor of Bruno's prose, brings out its literary value, and evaluates its singular theoretical depth. The novelty of this essay lies in the fact that it does not disassociate the artist from the philosopher. Far from considering in isolation the theme of asininity, he inserts it into the context of a deep meditation. In an image that at first may appear paradoxical, he fixes a nodal point of speculative research.

It is clear that, precisely by choosing the image of the ass, and by exploiting all its possibilities, Bruno was also counting on its shock effect and on instilling a sense of surprise in the reader, by giving free rein to his desire to shock at all costs ("according to cabalistic revelation . . . , the ass or asininity is the symbol of wisdom"; "pray, pray my dearest ones, that God may transform you into asses if you are not already asses"; "strive, strive, therefore, to be asses, you who are men"). Bruno was quite aware that he was thus ranging himself alongside Erasmus and his followers while at the same time recalling Pico della Mirandola: *extrinsecus si aspexeris, feram videas, si introspexeris numen agnoscas.* Being polyvalent and ambiguous, asininity undoubtedly allowed him to grasp *coincidentia oppositorum;* but at the same time the symbol of the ass gave him the opportunity to exercise his virtuosity as a writer freed from conventions. In contrast to Pico della Mirandola, it is not by means of a rhetorical discourse on the "divinity" of man that Bruno reveals his greatness and his wisdom, but by constantly reminding us of the other side of our earthly condition: the painful but fruitful fatigue of the lowliest physical labor, the desperate but terrifying cry that scatters even the giants.

Nuccio Ordine emphasizes precisely these points and, far from considering a paradoxical theme in isolation, happy to illustrate it with earlier literary examples and to draw parallels with related themes, he analyzes its theoretical implications, then shows how this theme operates in the texts, even where it appears only in a minor role. By locating its every appearance, Ordine shows that this theme becomes the main thread running through Bruno's entire work. Without ever fragmenting the unity of this indissociably artistic and speculative body of work, he gets the best out of the study of a learned and sometimes paradoxical vocabulary.

With great sophistication, Ordine cites the beginning of *De minimo,* whose tone is almost Cartesian: if one wishes to begin to philosophize by doubting everything (*qui philosophari concupiscit de omnibus principio dubitans*), one must not come to any decision before having heard and compared the arguments from all sides, since any conclusions must be reached purely on the basis of rigorous reasoning (*de rationis lumine veritate inspicua iudicet et definiat*). At the end of the *Asino cillenico*, written a few years earlier, Mercury concludes the dialogue by proclaiming the ass to be an "academician and authority in all doctrines." Addressing the ass, he adds: "Speak among those willing to listen; consider and contemplate among mathematicians; discuss, inquire, instruct, affirm, and determine among physicists; mingle with everyone, speak with everyone, fraternize, become one and identify yourself with everyone, prevail over everyone, be everything."

The present work shows, with great precision, how Bruno ties together his various arguments; but it is also a felicitous introduction to the inimitable style of Bruno's reflection.

PREFACE

I would like to thank a few friends and colleagues who have repeatedly offered good suggestions and guidance on my manuscript. Among them are Remo Bodei, Lina Bolzoni, Giuseppe Del Vecchio, Costanzo Di Girolamo, Carlo Muscetta, Giancarlo Mazzacurati, Amneris Roselli, and Hayden White. Giulio Ferroni, my teacher and friend, merits special thanks for having proposed this fascinating topic of the ass during my university studies.

The publication of the first edition of this book in 1987 allowed me to develop friendships and collaborative relationships with eminent Bruno scholars, such as Giovanni Aquilecchia, Nicola Badaloni, Michele Ciliberto, and Biagio De Giovanni. It is difficult to convey how much their research has influenced my work. Eugenio Garin's generosity and teachings have been invaluable to me: my enthusiasm has not waned, thanks, above all, to his encouragement.

I would like to express my deep admiration for Gerardo Marotta and his cultural politics. As president of the Istituto Italiano per gli Studi Filosofici, Gerardo Marotta, through his numerous European projects, has provided a strong impetus for the promotion of Bruno studies.

My gratitude also goes to Michèle Gendreau Massaloux, commissioner of education, Universités de Paris, for involving me in numerous research activities and cultural exchanges that the Sorbonne, thanks to Massaloux's energy and initiative, conducts throughout the world.

It will be most difficult to repay Yves Hersant for his generous friendship. Alain Segonds, editor in chief of Les Belles Lettres, has created a bridge for me between Calabria and Paris.

I would like to recall a number of friends and colleagues with whom I spent time in the United States over the past few years: Leonard Barkan, Louise Clubb, Anthony Grafton, Daniel Javitch, Victoria Khan, David Quint, Thomas Roche, and Heinrich von Staden. Thanks also go to Carlo Chiarenza, director of the Fulbright program, for facilitating my first stay in America.

I owe my gratitude to Paul Oskar Kristeller for invaluable observations offered during our unforgettable meetings.

At Yale I was able to continue the heated debates on rhetoric with Paolo Valesio that we had begun in Cosenza. Dante Della Terza not only initiated me into the "secrets" of Harvard University's libraries, but, more importantly, supported my entry into Italian academic life in the States. Without Nicola Merola's affectionate friendship in these past few decisive years, I might not have had the chance to teach at the Università della Calabria.

Being a visiting professor in the Italian department of New York University gave me the opportunity to strengthen my bonds of admiration and friendship with Professor John Freccero, master of Dante studies.

Giuseppe Mazzotta helped me find at Yale, amid the snows of a ferocious winter, the warmth of our native Calabria. I am indebted to him for his inexhaustible enthusiasm and for the idea to translate this book into English. And finally, to the translators, Henryk Barański and Arielle Saiber, I express all my thanks.

BAV	Biblioteca Apostolica Vaticana
BCC	Biblioteca Civica di Cosenza
Cabala	*Cabala del cavallo pegaseo.* In *Dialoghi italiani*, edited by Giovanni Gentile, Third edition reviewed by Giovanni Aquilecchia (Florence: Sansoni, 1985).
Causa	*De la causa, principio e uno.* In *Dialoghi italiani.*
Cena	*La cena de le ceneri.* In *Dialoghi italiani.*
De l'infinito	*De l'infinito, universo e mondi.* In *Dialoghi italiani.*
D.S.	*Dictionnaire des Antiquités grecques et romaines*, edited by Ch. Daremberg and Edm. Saglio (Graz: Akademische Druck. u. Verlagsanstalt, 1969).
Eroici	*De gli eroici furori.* In *Dialoghi italiani.*
Opp. lat.	*Opera latine conscripta.* Edited by F. Fiorentino, F. Tocco, H. Vitelli, V. Imbriani, C. M. Tallarigo (Florence: Le Monnier, 1879–91). 3 volumes in 8 parts.
P.W.	*Paulys Realencyclopädie der classischen Alterumswissenschaft*, unter Mitwirkung Zahlreicher Fachgenossen herausgegeben von Georg Wissowa (Stuttgart, 1893).
Spaccio	*Spaccio de la bestia trionfante.* In *Dialoghi italiani.*

A critical edition of Bruno's complete works is being published by Les Belles Lettres under the direction of Yves Hersant and Nuccio Ordine: *Oeuvres italiennes*, ed. Giovanni Aquilecchia, and *Oeuvres latines*, ed. Rita Sturlese.

CHAPTER 1

Bruno and the Ass:
A Long-Deferred Question

In the *Cantus circaeus*, published in Paris in 1582, after the
initial exchanges between Circe and Moeris, where the sorceress
explains the secret correspondences between certain qualities of animals and those of men, the flow of questions and answers all of a
sudden dries up. Having heard Circe's explanations regarding the
nature of "pigs" and "dogs" in human form, Moeris, instead of
raising another question, allows herself a brief digression, where
she expresses the need to leave aside an examination of the symbol
of the "ass":

Moeris. For the moment, I shall remain silent about asses until I may
consider them more seriously and accordingly. (*Opp. lat.*, II,
I, p. 198)

After her request to defer to the future a more in-depth analysis,
Moeris continues with a question that restarts the flow of the dialogue. She asks for a description of the characteristics of mules, the
offspring of asses; Circe, demanding no further explanation,
launches into her answer, implicitly accepting her interlocutor's
decision:

Moeris. For the moment, I shall remain silent about asses until I may
consider them more seriously and accordingly. Those born of
asses—that is to say, mules—how might they be distinguished?

Circe. They are those who want to pass for philosophers and men of eloquence, when they are neither philosophical nor eloquent. They are those who boast of being poets and orators, but are neither. They are those who would call themselves legists and scholars of rhetoric, when they would not be deemed as such. They are those who would be grammarians and arbiters, when they would be wanting in both pursuits. They are those who would be merchants and nobles, while secretly incurring the reproach of ignoble birth. They are those who would wear togas and bear arms, when they would be as inept in war as they are in letters. They are the courtly and the pious, who would appear as animals of uncertain species. They are the beautiful and the terrible, manifestly neither woman nor man. Even though they have a mare as mother and an ass as father, [mules] are neither horse nor ass, and neighs may be heard through their braying. (*Opp. lat.*, II, I, p. 198)

Moeris's choice, which Circe upholds, cannot therefore be considered as purely circumstantial and meaningless.[1] Why else would Bruno have felt the need to introduce an element into the dialogue, one that does not belong to the symbolic structure of the work in which it appears, if not to highlight, by its very absence, his great interest in this theme? No other animal, among the many illustrious ones absent from the *Cantus circaeus*, receives such treatment. In other words, this treatment also places the ass in a position of centrality with respect to all the other animals that appear in the work's vast "bestiary." The deferral might signal the existence of an as yet unformed project for a work, still not fully matured, in which the ass would play the principal role.

But before we focus our attention upon the works that followed the *Cantus circaeus*, a brief digression will prove useful. In the same year, 1582, the ass is also mentioned in the first mnemotechnical text, the *De umbris idearum*, which Bruno published in Paris. In this instance, it involves an allusion to a lost work entitled *L'Arca di Noè*, which the author will later claim as his own, in which it is precisely the ass that plays the principal role. Once again the reference is inserted into a dialogue. There are three interlocutors: Mercury, Logifer, and Philothimus. The last two are discussing whether it is advisable to spread abroad works that only a few people can understand and that are scorned by the ignorant masses. While Logifer already illustrates the possible objections to the art of memory which will be raised by the ignorant of ill-will, Philothimus pays him back in his own coin by upholding the necessity of spreading ideas to those few readers capable of understanding them, thereby disregarding asses and pedants:

Logifer. How would you answer Master Anthoc, who considers those capable of accomplishing extraordinary feats of memory as magicians or madmen or people of this kind? See how much time he has devoted to letters.

Philothimus. I have no doubt that he is descended from that ass which was loaded onto Noah's Ark to save the species. (*Opp. lat.*, II, I, p. 10)

Two years later in 1584, in a passage from *La cena de le ceneri*, it will be precisely Theophilus who once again recalls *L'Arca di Noè:*

Filoteo. . . . But of whom must you complain, unhappy one? Do you think it ignoble to be a hard-hitting animal? Have you forgotten, Nolan, what you wrote in your book entitled *Noah's Ark?* While the animals had to arrange themselves in good order, and arguments over precedence had to be brought to an end, in what danger did the ass find itself of losing the prime position, seated astern, because it is an animal more inclined to kick than to strike blows? (*Cena*, pp. 78–80)[2]

But only the reference in the *Epistola dedicatoria* of the *Cabala del cavallo pegaseo*, published in 1585, offers us the possibility of hypothesizing when *L'Arca di Noè* was presumably published. Addressing Don Sapatino (to whom the work is dedicated) in an ironic context, Bruno invites him to accept his "ass," citing the ass of the *Arca* as an illustrious antecedent: "But if you are as wise as I believe you to be, and if you make considered judgments, you will keep it [the ass of the *Cabala*] for yourself, knowing that I have offered you something no less worthy than what I was able to offer Pope Pius V, to whom I dedicated *Noah's Ark*" (*Cabala*, pp. 841–42). Quite apart from the problem of its precise dating, which, however, can be placed during the reign of Pius V (1566–71), this lost short work has been the source of much labor among Bruno's biographers. Suggestions range from Berti's conviction that, despite being cited a number of times, *L'Arca di Noè* was never published,[3] to Predari's maintaining that the text was published in Rome in 1581,[4] though there is no documentary evidence to support this claim, and from Mondolfo's hypothesis that Bruno presented it to Pius V during his journey to Rome in 1568,[5] to Spampanato locating it among the occasional pieces written to mark the victory over the Turks by the League supported by Pius V (1571).[6]

Whatever the case may be as regards these suggestions, beyond considering the fact whether or not *L'Arca di Noè* was actually written and published, I do not intend, in this study, to dwell upon questions that could lead me to stray considerably from my principal concerns. I wanted merely to highlight that Bruno had been interested in the symbol of the ass for well over a decade. I now return to my analysis where I had left off. Which other of Bruno's works could have found room for the ass following the deferral decreed by Moeris in the *Cantus circaeus?* One has to wait another two years to discover in the *Spaccio de la bestia trionfante* (1584) a further "deferral" that, at first sight, seems to have no connection

with the ass. The celestial reform proposed by Jupiter revolution-
izes the symbolism of astronomical myth. The granting of moral
values to the heavens necessarily involves replacing negative symbols with positive ones. The assembly of the gods thus decrees all
the changes, leaving empty only the most important space, which
may be contemplated from every corner of the earth, that of the
river Eridanus and of Ursa Major:

> Let us come to the river Eridanus, said Jupiter [the gods'
> dialogue is recounted to Saulino by Sophia]; I know not
> how to describe it, since it is both on earth and in the
> heavens, while the other things we are speaking of aban-
> doned the earth to make their way heavenward. But this
> one remained at once here and there, inside and outside,
> above and below, and is heavenly as well as earthly. . . .
> Let the Eridanus, therefore, be in the heavens, but only
> as far as belief and imagination are concerned. This does
> not mean that in truth the same place may not hold some
> other thing that we will deal with shortly, because this
> seat must be considered in the same way as that of Ursa
> Major. (*Spaccio*, pp. 808–9)

Here is a new "deferral" that leaves the reader in the dark.
This time Jupiter's decision to tackle the important question later
has a direct effect upon the plot of the *Spaccio*: the conclusion, the
most significant act of the celestial reform, is left suspended. There
is no doubt that such a design conforms to a narrative strategy that
focuses attention on the moment of resolution. A year later, in 1585,
the circle seems to close in the *Cabala del cavallo pegaseo* and in
the *Asino cillenico*, which is appended to it. It is in the *Cabala* (and
in the *Asino cillenico*, which has the framework of a dialogue within
a dialogue) that the ass indisputably becomes the protagonist. Here
the reader is presented with the conclusion to the *Spaccio*. And why

could Moeris's desire for a more in-depth discussion of the symbolism of the ass also not be satisfied here? Indeed, it will fall upon the character of Saulino, who bears the family name of Bruno's mother,[7] to link the *Spaccio* to the *Cabala*. In the first dialogue he listens to Sofia's account of the celestial reform; in the second one, he reveals to his interlocutors the decision left suspended in the *Spaccio:*

Sebasto. To tell the truth, I remain in such suspense from the desire to know what the great father of the gods brought about in those two seats, the one Boreal and the other Austral, that a thousand years seemed to pass before I could see the end of your thread, regardless of how interesting, useful, and worthy it was, because my desire to be able to understand this design burns all the more for your having delayed the moment of its revelation. . . .

Saulino. Good. So that you may no longer torment yourselves in waiting for the resolution, know that the seat in the immediate proximity of the one where Ursa Minor used to be, and where you know that Truth is exalted, Ursa Major, having been expelled in the manner recounted to you [see *Spaccio*, p. 809, cited above], was replaced by abstract Asininity according to the decision of the aforementioned council. And there where you can still imagine the river Eridanus to be, it pleased these same gods that concrete Asininity be found, so that from each of the three celestial regions we may be able to contemplate Asininity, which, formed from two small lights, was as if obscured in the course of the planets, where Cancer's shell is found. (*Cabala*, pp. 862–63)

It is in the *Cabala* that the symbol of "asininity" is accorded a preeminent role. It is here that space is made for the reflections and the scattered notes that Bruno had accumulated over the years with the precise aim of using them within a context that would facilitate their integration. The metaphor of the potter, which opens the *Cabala*'s *Epistola dedicatoria,* apparently confirms this hypothesis:

> And it so happens that a potter cannot carry on with his work (not because of fading light but because of the deficiency and lack of materials) and, holding in his hand a little piece of glass, or wood, or wax, or something else not sufficient to make a vase, he spends time deliberating what he might do with it, not wanting to throw it away and desperate to see it put to good use. At long last he is able to show that it was made to be a third handle, a rim, a top of a flask, a piece for support or for plastering, or a plug to strengthen, fill, or cover over a gap, a hole, or a crack. Something similar happened to me when, after having dispatched not every one of my thoughts but only what was contained in a certain bundle of writings, and not having anything else to send, more by chance than by intention, my eyes turned toward a pile of papers that I had scorned at other times and had used as a cover for those other writings, I found that it contained part of what I am about to present to you. (*Cabala,* pp. 835–36)

The "pile of papers," scorned and "used as a cover for those other writings," finds in the *Cabala* its own autonomous space, thereby undoubtedly giving voice to some of those thoughts that Bruno had been unable to dispatch in the earlier "bundle of writings." The reflections that had found no place in the other works or that, to continue with the metaphor, were simply "leftovers," which nevertheless left traces in the contaminated texts, are gathered together in a dialogue where "asinine" matters dominate absolutely. Yet, once again, we will have to resort to another metaphor in which the "potter" continues to be the protagonist, so as to understand better

Bruno's apparent disdain for his "pile of papers." Again in the *Cabala*, Sebasto replies thus to Onorio (or the "Pegasean ass"):

Sebasto. It seems to me that this opinion is not far removed from nor violently opposed to the prophetic dogma that holds that everything rests in the hands of the universal efficient, just as clay rests in the hands of the potter. Gripped in the incessant swirl of the stars, it is made and unmade according to the vicissitudes of the generation and corruption of things, like a vase, now admired, now disdained, but yet molded from the same matter. (*Cabala*, p. 890)

The vicissitudes of texts are not far removed from those that govern matter; the same matter that, in the hands of the same potter, can be at times a vase "admired" and at other times a vase "disdained."[8]

Without this pointer, and without those I will discuss later, it would be impossible to explain Bruno's interest in "asinine" matter, which so far I have attempted to reconstruct by means of hints scattered in works preceding the *Cabala*. Within the *Cabala* itself, even where a single, indisputable direction seems assured, meaning almost always fluctuates in a space marked by ambiguity. By passively following Bruno's pointers, one would fall prey to a required path and its many traps and diversions. One would not grasp the vertiginous play of reversals that structures the asinine dialogue.

CHAPTER 2

Myths, Fables, Tales:
The "Asinine" Materials

Before I concentrate on the *Cabala*, a further digression will prove useful. This chapter reconstructs the symbolic space of the ass by taking a broad census of the myths, anecdotes, and collections of classical literature. This journey into the past provides points of reference for understanding the diachronic development of *topoi* that we will find sedimented in Renaissance culture. A comparison of the different materials reveals how the symbolic image of the ass manages to contain large areas of ambiguity, which in some ways makes it a perfect symbol of *coincidentia oppositorum*. For ease of presentation, I have assembled the different elements of my research under three main antithetical pairings: *benefic/demonic, powerful/humble, wise/ignorant.*

Benefic/demonic. The symbol of the ass appears in rites of fecundity and of regeneration, just as much as in the realms of death, where it is associated with infernal deities. In its positive role as guarantor of "life," the ass is seen as one of the spirits of the waters: "Like them [the waters]," writes Waldemar Deonna, "and in contrast to the sterile mule, it is an agent of fertility and fecundity of both plant and human life. It is this quality that unites it with the gods of vegetation and fecundity—Dionysus, Silenus, Midas, Priapus, Pan, Hera, Demeter, Cybele, Isis, Vesta, Epona—many of whom, like the ass, are associated with life-giving waters. The ass is well known for its lasciviousness, lubricity, and phallic character, which accord with this regenerative function and which explain the animal's association with deities of a similar nature, such as Dionysus, Silenus, Priapus, and other phallic beings. Hence its beneficent role as regards everything that has to do with propagation and maintaining life."[1] Priapus, the phallic god of fecundity, was originally an anthropomorphic ass,[2] and it was to him that asses were sacrificed in the town of Lampsacus.[3] Dionysus, in some sources considered to be the father of Priapus,[4] is also closely associated with the ass, upon which he rides.[5]

Indeed, Silenus,[6] Marsyas,[7] and Midas[8]—three asinine spirits whose adventures are associated with water-purification rites[9]—join the ass in the cycle of Dionysian myths. The ass of Hindu myth, apart from being a great seducer,[10] is the guardian of the waters and of riches.[11] The ass's relation to fecundity is legitimated also by fables and myths that associate it with feminine deities; it is sacred to Vesta, mother and nurse;[12] to the Phrygian goddess Cybele;[13] and to the powerful Isis.[14] In this regard, apart from asses having sexual relations with women,[15] there is no shortage of references to cosmetic[16] and pharmacological[17] uses for certain of the ass's organs as aids to many of the functions involved in childbirth and breastfeeding.

The reverse of the coin also reveals many examples in which the ass appears linked to death and the demonic. In his tale of Psyche's descent into Hades, Apuleius only mentions the presence of an ass with its driver.[18] Aelianus recounts that the ass is the only animal able to resist the dissolving action of the waters of the Styx.[19] Indeed, tradition has it that the devil is powerless against those who take an ass with them to Hell.[20] In classical Greece a part of Hades bears the animal's name.[21] Its image is represented on tombs in connection with infernal myths.[22] In Egypt it is the animal of Set, the god with the head of an ass[23] and considered a symbol of evil for having murdered his brother, Osiris.²⁴ The Greeks assimilated Set and Typhon, another dispenser of evil.²⁵ In India the cave and Hell are sometimes represented by an ass's skin or by an ass.²⁶ In the cabala, the malefic star Remfam, the emblem of Lucifer, hides in its five points the stylized image of an ass's head.²⁷ Many demons, including Lamia and Empousa, are depicted as having the legs of an ass.²⁸

Powerful/humble. The ass of the Bible is the preferred mount of patriarchs, kings, princes, the rich and the powerful. Moses sets out for Egypt on the back of an ass.²⁹ The song of Deborah is addressed to the powerful who ride on "white asses."³⁰ Abraham saddles his ass before going to sacrifice his son, Isaac.³¹ Abdon, judge of Israel, had forty sons and thirty nephews who rode on seventy ass colts.³² Abigail, the wife of Nabal, rides on an ass.³³ Ziba, the servant of the house of Saul, presents David with a couple of asses, which are, she says, the mounts of kings.³⁴ In Hindu mythology, the Asvin brothers, who are remarkably similar to the Dioscuri, Castor and Pollux, ride flying asses,³⁵ as does Indra, king of the Vedic gods.³⁶ Many peoples have used the ass in war: certain Iranian tribes,³⁷ the Carmanians of the Persian Gulf,³⁸ King Darius against the Scythians.³⁹ But the ass's boldest exploit was in defense of the Olympian gods besieged by the giants in revolt, when defeat was averted by the braying of the asses ridden by Satyrs and Sileni, which routed the enemy and left them terrified.⁴⁰ In India, too, the winged ass triumphs over more than a thousand adversaries in the Kingdom of Yama.⁴¹ A fresco in Pompeii depicts an ithyphallic ass attacking a lion,⁴² and in one of Fedro's fables, it menaces a wild boar by showing its genitalia.⁴³ A series of exploits has endowed the ass with an image of strength and courage: Homer compares Ajax to a powerful ass;⁴⁴ Jacob declares that his son, Isaac, is like a robust ass;⁴⁵ and it is no accident that Samson killed a thousand adversaries with an ass's jawbone.⁴⁶

However, along with such images of glory we also find those of humility, often accompanied by a marked contempt. This is the ass's most familiar role—that associated with the hard toil of daily life. It is no longer, therefore, a dignified mount, but a beast to be used for heavy work: for carrying goods, turning mill wheels, and, sometimes, bearing poor peasants. A condition of slavery, also in relation to the horse, its closest relative, which Apuleius recounts in the misadventures of Lucius the ass.[47] The close links between the ass and the servant[48] appear to be emphasized several times in the Bible, where in many episodes the ass is almost always mentioned last and, in general, precedes the word servant. Thanks to his wife, Sarah, Abraham receives gifts from Pharaoh:

> And it came to pass that, when Abraham came to Egypt, the Egyptians beheld that his wife was very fair. When the princes of Pharaoh saw her, they commended her before Pharaoh: and the woman was taken into Pharaoh's house.
>
> He entreated Abraham well for her sake: and he had sheep, and oxen, and he-asses, and menservants, and maidservants, and she-asses.[49]

The chiastic construction—*he-asses* and *menservants* and *maidservants* and *she-asses*—highlights a strict symbolic relationship that is confirmed by its repetition in other passages. Job possessed "seven thousand sheep, and three thousand camels, and five hundred yoke of oxen, and five hundred *she-asses*, and a very great *household*."[50] The Shunammite "called unto her husband and said, 'Send me, I pray thee, one of the *young men*, and one of the *asses*, that I may run to the man of God, and come again.' . . . Then she saddled an *ass*, and said to her *servant* . . ."[51]

Similarly, in his prophecy Zachariah, speaking of the Messiah's lowliness, adds that he rides an ass, in direct contrast to the horse, which is a tool of war:

Rejoice greatly, O daughter of Zion;
shout, O daughter of Jerusalem:
behold, thy King cometh unto thee:
he is just, and having salvation;
lowly, and riding upon an ass,
and upon a colt the foal of an ass.
And I will cut off the chariot from Ephraim,
and the horse from Jerusalem,
and the battle bow shall be cut off:
and he shall speak peace unto the heathen.[52]

Wise/ignorant. I have deliberately left until last the antithetical pairing that is of greatest interest for my study of the *Cabala*.[53] Contrary to popular tradition, the ass, by virtue of certain of its qualities, is also considered to be a symbol of knowledge. Its large ears do indeed endow it with the ability to hear over long distances; and this capacity to hear clearly can be transferred from the physical plane to the spiritual one, since without hearing, there is no true knowledge. Large ears or multiple ears are the attributes of deities and superior beings, precisely because they are a sign of their perfection.[54] The Vedic god Indra is depicted as having long ears that resemble those of an ass,[55] and "according to Hindu doctrine the ear is the seat of Brahma (*Ait. Br.* II, 40), namely, of the greatest source of strength, and it reveals the nature of the invisible world, while the eye is appointed to understanding the visible."[56] Lucius, the protagonist of the *The Golden Ass*, greatly appreciates the ass's enormous genitalia[57] and its powers of hearing. In the episode in which the miller's wife betrays her husband, Lucius the ass does not miss the opportunity to eulogize his ears, which lead him to discover the villainous intrigues: "But I, that was greatly offended, with the negligence of Fotis, who made me an ass instead of a bird, did yet comfort myself for the miserable deformity of my shape by this only means in that I had long ears, whereby I might hear all things that were done even far off.''[58] Again it is Lucius who, having been sent to the mysteries of Isis, relates *hearing* to *learning* in an aside on the reader's *curiosity:* ''Thou would'st peradventure demand, thou studious reader, what was said and done there: verily, I would tell thee if it were lawful for me to tell, thou would'st know if it were convenient for thee to hear.''[59] The image of a man with the head of an ass can also represent human wisdom and the sciences, which, being the fruit of human endeavor, were regarded, especially in the Middle Ages, as vain, precisely because of their ties to the purely terrestrial.[60] Other positive qualities include the ass's humility and its predisposition to hard work, elements that lead cabalists—we shall see what importance this concept has in Bruno's *Cabala*—to regard it as a symbol of wisdom:

> For the Jews, principally among the cabalists, the ass is the symbol of wisdom; they fashion its idea with the aid of a Sephiroth, citing as a reason that those who want to devote themselves to wisdom must content themselves with a very meager diet of the roughest kind, and everybody knows that the ass has been endowed with such parsimony. What is more, it endures penury, toil, blows, and hunger with the utmost patience, nor does it become enraged at any affront, whatever its source. It is small of spirit, poor and simple, since it is unable to distinguish thistles from lettuce. Its heart is in no way cunning, nor is it in any way touched by desire. It is so unmoved to anger that it has made everlasting peace with every species of animal. There is no task that it refuses, that it does not undertake obsequiously, and, if need be, it takes the

place of the ox in plowing the land, pulling the cart, but, most particularly, it works ceaselessly on the most useful machine of all, the mill. It carries wood, apples, vegetables, and fruit of every kind. It is thus the assiduous and indefatigable servant of all human benefits, since, as they say, it is compelled to carry mysteries.[61]

The ass as the symbol of ignorance has become proverbial. Cicero's celebrated phrase comes to mind: "So, you ass, do I now have to teach you letters? That would require not words but a beating."[62] The theme of stupidity inspired numerous caricatures in which a person wearing a toga, clogs, and ass's ears was displaying a book.[63] The ass also appears in the role of a schoolteacher instructing pupils who each appear to have a monkey's head,[64] in which the image underlines the presumption of ignorant people who, without knowing anything, arrogate to themselves the right to teach.[65] The stupidity of the ass reappears insistently in many fables, most notably in Aesop's well-known tale of the ass dressed in a lion's skin: "An ass put on a lion's skin and went around sowing terror among all the animals. He saw a fox and wanted to scare him as well. But this one, who by chance had heard its voice once before, told him: 'Rest assured that had I never heard you braying you would have scared me as well.' "[66] The same *topos* may be found in the *Pancatantra* of Hindu literature, in which, apart from the story of the ass dressed in a tiger's skin, are other tales of our protagonist being the object of humiliating derision and trickery.[67]

In light of the elements I have gathered together, one may join Waldemar Deonna, to whose work I have often had recourse, in concluding that the ass is "therefore sometimes divine, venerable, and benefic, sometimes demonic, evil, and malefic. This ambivalence of function appears frequently and, for that matter, throughout the ancient world; it exists from the time of Vedic India, in

Egypt, in Greece, in Rome, and persists into the Christian Middle Ages."[68] In the complex universe of animal symbolism, such ambivalence is not reserved for the ass alone; other animals are caught up in the play of the complementarity of symbols, which corresponds to different demands in different traditions.[69]

This brief analysis, which in no way claims to be systematic, has allowed us to define the specific space occupied by the ambiguous symbol of the ass, and to verify its persistence and its vicissitudes in the symbolic framework of the Renaissance.

CHAPTER 3

The Ass and Mercury:
A Key to *Coincidentia Oppositorum*

A first valuable pointer to follow might be the title of the brief dialogue annexed to the *Cabala*, the *Asino cillenico*. It is precisely its being a dialogue within a dialogue that suggests its centrality within the macrostructure represented by the work as a whole. So why the Cyllenic ass? On what basis does Bruno construct the relationship between the ass and Mercury, whose birthplace was Mount Cyllene?[1] Bruno himself will furnish a partial answer, six years after the publication of the *Cabala*, in the second book of the *De imaginum compositione*, the last of the mnemonic texts, published in Frankfurt in 1591. Within a complex mechanism, wherein he describes the process involved in the formation of images and ideas in order to facilitate their invention, disposition, and memorization, Bruno situates, in the symbolic space asssigned to Mercury, a passage he entitles *Asinus cyllenicus*. Here, in the opening lines, after having referred to the "asinine" dialogue that "found no favor among the public and was disliked by scholars because of its singular ideas," the relationship between the ass and Mercury is explained:

> There would have been no such deity as Mercury, if he
> had had no animal to ride on. . . . Its [the ass's] qualities
> are the opposite of Mercury's, but since opposites cannot
> subsist without their opposites, and opposites are known

by their opposites, nourishing each other and being members of the same group, it will not be wholly improper nor
too inconvenient for it [the ass] to appear in the same
court as if on a platform, thereby providing, at least for
the opposite reason, certain of Mercury's qualities that
are not mentioned and that, perhaps, are unmentionable.
(*Opp. lat.*, II, III, pp. 237–38)

Bruno's interest becomes focused explicitly on these two symbolic
images, which appear to lend themselves very well to the play of
coincidentia oppositorum. And in this same passage Bruno does not
miss the opportunity to point again to the ambiguity of the space
occupied by this pair. First of all, he describes the ass's "positive"
symbolic qualities:

The remarkable things about it are . . . a jawbone that
is long, extended, and strong, with which Samson was able
to kill a thousand Philistines (what could he have done, I
ask myself, with a complete, living ass?), and from which
there gushed forth the waters that revived the errant peoples, and many other things besides, which we spoke of
elsewhere in a particular book. . . . A powerful voice that
terrified, scattered, and defeated the giants, that is to say,
the powerful and the wise men of this world (who had
rebelled against the gods); it is not without reason that
astronomers can examine Crèche with the asses in the
constellation of Cancer, so that we recognize that the
gods, delivered thanks to this help, did not really show
themselves to be ungrateful. In proximity to the Ass,
therefore, there stand Victory, Triumph, Honor, Glory,
Majesty, and many other things (or perhaps even prac-
tically everything) from the court of Jupiter. (*Opp. lat.*,
II, III, p. 238)

Then he lists the ass's "negative" qualities together with the attributes that characterize them:

> Vacuity, Humility, and Abjection because of the obsequiousness it shows toward men and, certainly because of its domestic philanthropy for us, a Lowliness, but a Lowliness that triumphs over all forms of lowliness, and Ignorance. . . . It possesses therefore (to speak but briefly) an insipid Dullness, the Heaviness of a stone, a leaden Obtuseness, a gloomy Obscurity, a dark Deliberation, a shadowy Conception, a pitch-black Squalor, a Frigidity worthy of the Getae, a Stupidity worthy of the Syrians, a stupid Laziness, an uncouth Dilatoriness, a listless Sloth, an inert Torpor, a languid Inactivity, a slothful Acedia, an indolent Despondency. (*Opp. lat.*, II, III, pp. 238–39)

The image of Mercury, which, in the concluding part of the *Asinus cyllenicus*, is described as the polarizing symbol of the "negative" and "positive" aspects of eloquence, is subjected to the same logic:

> There is also the Germanic Mercury, who can be recognized by his clothes; his chariot (upon which are sculpted the two signs attributed to him) is drawn by two hawks; in his right hand he holds a winged scepter on which two serpents are entwined; in his left, a strip of papyrus. His helmet bears the image of a winged dragon (in my opinion) because of his shrewd vigilance. This does not mean that the Suevi are any less ingenious than any other German nation, but that, thanks to Mercury's left hand, they are more talkative, loquacious, garrulous, and sophistic than all the others. From the right hand come a lively readiness

of speech, a polite eloquence, an elegant persuasion, and
a fluent literature worthy of the highest praise. (*Opp. lat.*,
II, III, pp. 239–40)

Bruno's valuable pointers open up an area of research that can
furnish other elements useful to understanding the symbolic
space of the relationship between the ass and Mercury. We find
the image of Mercury once again linked to eloquence in Valeriano's *Hieroglyphica*, which played a fundamental role in the literature of the image in the sixteenth century,[2] and which Bruno
himself—as we shall see—used as an indirect source for a passage in the *Cabala*. This time, however, the symbolic trait that
indicates the "negative" and the "positive" elements is of a phallic nature:

> The Ancients, if they wanted to display the efficacy of
> speech and its powers of persuasion, [would display] a
> statue of Mercury at quite an advanced age, bearded and
> with his body almost wasted away, but with his sex ob-
> scenely aroused, and they granted him strength only in
> this part; there was, according to Pausanias, a statue of
> this kind at Cyllene, and I myself saw in Rome, at the
> house of Fabius Calvus of Ravenna, a bronze seal bearing
> this effigy. In this image, moreover, his clothes were well
> filled out, and there were apples hidden in his lap, clearly
> a sign of pregnancy, quite simply because speech (of
> which Mercury is the absolute symbol) at an advanced or
> very advanced age has such power of engendering and of
> action, it can deliberate, persuade, and even prove con-
> clusively the subject under discussion. Artemidorus, au-
> thor of the *Onirocritica*, writes that at Cyllene he, too,
> saw a statue of Mercury the appearance of which was
> nothing other than the image of a male member, and for

this reason the interpreters of dreams discuss the question
of what sorts of things the image of this part can signify
in a dream.[3]

On the other hand, when they want to show that a speech
is weak, they again display Mercury, but looking youthful
and definitely prepubescent, and his genital parts are
shown contracted or at rest, because [the Ancients] had
noticed that in those who had not yet come out of adoles-
cence, discourse was barren and imperfect, the reason
being that this age was not made for prudence. I saw a
statue of this kind in Naples, in the magnificent palace of
the Mattaleo family.[4]

But apart from the phallic nature of these two symbols,[5] another
common element reinforces the relationship between the ass and
Mercury: the lyre. Many images of both halves of the pairing are
associated with this instrument. As regards Mercury, the first examples appear in the Homeric epic: in the *Hymn to Hermes*, the
messenger of the gods, barely in swaddling clothes, invents the lyre
by using a tortoise shell.[6] As regards the ass, linking *asinus ad lyram*
has become proverbial.[7]

I refer once again to Valeriano's *Hieroglyphica* in order that
we understand the symbolic space of the lyre:

But those who have said that human life may be represented by means of the lyre have—it seems to me—not
just considered what we said above about the senses, the
soul, and the customs of mortals, but they have also
weighed up the matter according to the very condition of
our nature. In fact, after having discovered that, as regards the lyre, seven different notes may be distinguished,
they have noticed that the course of human life is contin-

ually driven by the same variety [that is, by seven-year cycles].[8]

In his *Contra gentes*, Athanasius compared reason to the lyre, when he speaks of the soul, of reason, and of the senses. Indeed, he claims, reason is not at all different from the lyre, as long as it is correctly tuned, or from the musician who plays it, as long as he is experienced. In fact, each of the lyre's strings emits its own sound; deep, sharp, medium, or clear, each has its own particular sound. But harmony can be neither discerned nor recognized unless one adds the art of playing the lyre. The modulation and the sweetness of the various sounds are revealed when he who holds the lyre makes each string resonate and skillfully passes over each string. In the same way, as long as the senses in the body are arranged like a lyre, if a wise intellect rules over them, then the spirit discerns what is dissonant and what is consonant, and which temperament ought to be applied to each thing, so that from then on [the spirit] does nothing or ponders nothing that cannot respond to modes and tones, which are the source of hearing a harmonious concert.[9]

The art of the musician,[10] his capacity of knowing how to use reason harmoniously, is a fundamental prerequisite for finding one's bearings in human life, which is continually stirred by variety. It will be Fortune herself who, in one of the famous pages of the *Spaccio*, underlines the role of the musician, because "the beauty of music and the excellence of harmony must no longer principally be attributed to the lyre and instrument, but to the skill of the artist who handles it" (*Spaccio*, p. 684). The musician's art constitutes the only possibility for "navigating" amid the multiplicity; a multiplicity that Bruno sees as being perfectly incarnated in the symbol of the ass. It is precisely thanks to the ass's ambiguous "positive" and "negative" values that one is able to perceive the reflections of a philosophy of knowledge. It is no accident that in the final exchange, which closes the micro-dialogue of the *Asino cillenico* and consequently the macro-dialogue of the *Cabala*, Mercury and the ass each describe the qualities of the other, recognizing that they are both "everything in everyone":

Ass. . . . But in truth here is my Cyllenean; I recognize him by his staff and his wings.—Welcome, graceful winged creature, messenger of Jupiter, faithful interpreter of the will of all the gods, generous giver of the sciences, inspirer of the arts, constant oracle to mathematicians, admirable computist, elegant orator, beautiful of face and lovely of appearance, eloquent figure and graceful personage, a man among men, a woman among women, a wretch among the wretched, blessed among the blessed, everything among everyone; you rejoice with those who rejoice, you weep with those who weep; thus you can go and stop everywhere, since you are well considered and accepted. What good things do you bring?

Mercury. Ass, since you would call yourself and claim to be an academician, I, who have granted you other gifts and graces, now with full authority order, constitute, and confirm you to be an academician and authority in all doctrines, so that you may enter and reside everywhere, and that no one may bar you from their doorway or insult you or impede you in any way, *quibuscumque in oppositum non obstantibus.* Enter, therefore, where you will and where it pleases you. . . . Speak among those willing to listen; consider and contemplate among mathematicians; discuss, inquire, instruct, affirm, and determine among physicists; mingle with everyone, speak with everyone, fraternize, become one and identify yourself with everyone, prevail over everyone, be everything. (*Asino cillenico*, pp. 922–23)[11]

CHAPTER 4

The Ambiguous Space of Asininity

The theme of *varietas*, of incessant vicissitude, forms an important element of reflection in Bruno's philosophy. The entire universe, in all its different material aspects, must conform to the laws of change. The most obvious result of this state of affairs is the continual generation and decay of atomic particles, because "it is not in the natural scheme of things for anything to be eternal, apart from material substance that, according to this same scheme of things, must be continually changing" (*Cena*, p. 156). Everything that exists, in heaven and on earth, above and below, is a mark of the range of the multiple:

Nothing stays still, but evolves and turns,
Whatever in heaven and beneath heaven is espied.
All things move, now upward, now downward,
Be it a long or a short movement,
Or a heavy or a light one;
And perhaps all things move at the same pace
And toward the same point.
For all things run their course.
For across water there moves a swirl,
Of which the same part flows
Now up and down, now down and up;
And the same swirl
To everyone imparts the same destiny.

(De l'infinito, pp. 434–35)

The laws of *varietas* are necessary because, as Sophia underlines in the *Spaccio*, "if in bodies, matter and being there were no change, variety and vicissitude, there would be nothing useful, nothing good, nothing pleasurable" (*Spaccio*, p. 571). But even man's very existential condition, his pursuit of pleasure, appears to be subject to the continual crossing of opposites:

Sophia. We maintain that every pleasure consists in nothing other than in a certain transition, passage, and movement. It is certain that the condition of hunger is painful and sad; unpleasant and heavy is the condition of satiety; yet pleasure is found in moving from one to the other. The state of ardent love torments, the state of fulfilled desire causes grief; but satisfaction comes in the transition from one state to the other. No pleasure is found in any present condition, unless one has suffered in the past. (*Spaccio*, pp. 571–72)

Sophia. . . . Whoever has been sitting or lying down, enjoys and appreciates walking; and whoever has exercised his feet, finds comfort in sitting. Whoever has remained too long indoors finds pleasure in the countryside; whoever has had his fill of meadows, longs for a room. Eating too much of the same food, however delicious, in the end causes nausea. So that the shift from one opposite to the other becomes a source of satisfaction for those participating in the process, similarly the shift from one opposite to the other satisfies the intermediary; and, finally, we see so much familiarity between one opposite and another that they appear to be more suited to each other than the similar to its similar. (*Spaccio*, p. 572)[1]

In Bruno's view of things, *varietas* and *coincidentia oppositorum* converge in a common space where "the beginning, the middle, and the end, the birth, the growth, and the perfection of everything we see is accomplished from opposites, by means of opposites, within opposites, toward opposites. Where there is opposition, there is action and reaction, there is movement, diversity, multiplicity, order, degrees, succession, and vicissitude" (*Spaccio*, p. 573).

But not only matter and men are subject to the laws of change. The gods, too, whom everyone considers to be above all things, suffer their effects. Jupiter himself, the highest authority of Olympus, reveals their particular implications:

> You see, my body withers and my brain becomes damp; pimples sprout on me and my teeth fall out; my skin yellows and my hair turns silver; my eyelids become stretched and my sight diminishes; my breathing becomes weaker and my cough stronger; my buttocks are stiffening and my step is becoming unsure; my wrist trembles and my ribs are fusing together; my articulations are growing thin and my joints are swelling up; finally (and this torments me most of all), since my heels are hardening and my poise is becoming lax, the bag on my pipe is lengthening and my staff is becoming shorter. (*Spaccio*, pp. 589–90)

> Venus, O Venus, he [Jupiter] said to her; is it possible that you cannot consider even once the condition we are in, especially your own? Do you think what men imagine of us to be true, that the old are always old, the young are always young, children are always children, and that we remain thus eternally, like on the day we left the earth and ascended to Heaven; and that, just as down there paintings and portraits show us to be exactly the same, in the same measure up here our vital constitution never ceases to change and change again? (*Spaccio*, p. 587)

It is Jupiter's tragic confession that triggers the celestial reform.
On the very same day that the anniversary of the gods' triumph
over the giants is commemorated, a victory in which the ass played
a decisive role,[2] the king of Olympus decides to expel "vice" and
replace it with "virtue." Time is now running short: the signs of
change reveal that dissolution is imminent, and that the moment is
approaching when one will have to account for one's actions to Fate.
Therefore Jupiter decides to transform the celebration into a great
council of the gods, into a celestial plebiscite ready to grant moral
values to the zodiac:

> Would you like to know why I have dedicated a feast day
> to this, especially one like today's? Does it seem to you,
> then, that this is worthy of feast day? And do you not
> believe that this ought to be the most tragic day of the
> entire year? Who among you, after due consideration,
> will not judge it a most shameful thing to celebrate the
> commemoration of our victory over the giants, at a time
> when we are scorned and vilified by the earth's mice?
> (*Spaccio*, pp. 597–98)

> Alas, gods, what are we doing? What are we thinking?
> Why are we dawdling? We have prevaricated, we have
> persisted in error, and we see pain joining with and per-
> sisting in error. Let us see, therefore, let us see to our own
> affairs; because, just as fate has refused us the capacity
> not to fall, so too have we been accorded the power to rise
> up. Thus, just as we have been all too ready to fall, so we
> are also equipped once again to get up on our feet. (*Spac-
> cio*, p. 610)

At the heart of this great celestial reform, announced precisely
on the anniversary of a victory in which asses played a decisive

role, Jupiter recognizes the value of "asininity," covertly antici-
pating, by means of the technique of deferral, the resolution that,
left suspended in the *Spaccio*, will be revealed in the *Cabala*:[3]

> As regards the pure majesty of those two asses that shine
> in Cancer's space, I dare not say anything, because the
> kingdom of the heavens entirely belongs to them by right
> and by reason; I will demonstrate many good reasons for
> this another time, since I dare not speak about such an
> important subject only in passing. Yet I am pained by and
> lament only this one thing: that these divine animals have
> been accorded such scant regard. They have not been
> granted their own house, but the abode of that retrograde
> aquatic animal, and they have been provided with but two
> miserable stars, one bequeathed to the first and the other
> to the second—and, in their size, they are not even major
> stars, but fourth-grade ones. (*Spaccio*, pp. 602–3)

Saulino (the character who appears in a learning role in the *Spaccio*
and in a revelatory one in the *Cabala*) is accorded the difficult task
of speaking on "such an important subject" not "in passing," but
at length. Jupiter's decision was therefore not unjustified, since,
already in the initial exchanges, Saulino's interlocutors in the *Cabala* turn against this triumph of asininity:

Saulino. Good. So that you may no longer torment yourselves in waiting for the resolution, know that the seat in the immediate
proximity of the one where Ursa Minor used to be, and where
you know that Truth is exalted, Ursa Major, having been expelled in the manner recounted to you [see *Spaccio*, p. 809],
was replaced by abstract Asininity according to the decision of
the aforementioned council. And there where you can still
imagine the river Eridanus to be, it pleased these same gods

that concrete Asininity be found, so that from each of the three
celestial regions we may be able to contemplate Asininity,
which, formed from two small lights, was as if obscured in the
course of the planets, where Cancer's shell is found.

Coribante. *Procul, o procul este profani!* [Begone far away, profane
ones; *Aeneid*, VI.258]. This is sacrilege, profanity, to make us
believe (although it cannot be thus in reality) that, beside the
honorable and eminent seat of Truth, there be the idea of such
a foul and shameful species, which the wise Egyptians in their
hieroglyphics considered to be the embodiment of ignorance,
as Horapollon testifies numerous times. Similarly, the priests
of Babylon used an ass's head upon the torso and nape of a
man to indicate a person who is inexperienced and averse to
any discipline.

Sebasto. It is not necessary to go back to the time and the land of
Egypt, since there is not and there has never been a people
whose common parlance does not confirm what Coribante
says.

Saulino. This is the reason why I have deferred a discussion of these
two seats until last, for, given the habits of speech and belief,
you would have believed me to be speaking in parables. You
would have continued listening to my description of the reform
of the other celestial seats with less conviction and attention,
if I had not first made you fit for that truth with a prolix litany
of reflections; since these two seats by themselves merit at least
as much consideration as the value that you see in the subject
in question. (*Cabala*, pp. 862–64)

The space of asininity cannot, therefore, be read in a single manner.
The symbol cannot be resolved in terms of a negative connotation,
exclusively justified by "the habits of speech and belief." Saulino's
difficult endeavor moves in another direction: that of providing el-

ements dispersed here and there within the text, in such a way as to make possible the construction of the puzzle by recovering its pieces. We shall therefore have to collect more "signs" so as to orient ourselves better as regards asininity's movements between "positive" and "negative" poles.

In the *Cabala*'s *Epistola dedicatoria*, Bruno does not miss the opportunity of alluding to the difficulties posed by "asinine" matter. Within an ambiguous context and repeating a formula already used for different ends in the *Candelaio*,[4] he reveals the not insignificant problem of choosing the work's dedicatee, since "every treatise and consideration must be expounded, offered and presented to one who belongs to the profession in question or has attained the required level in it" (*Cabala*, p. 837). Indeed, the "contents" of the work will trigger the difficult search for a worthy dedicatee: "At first I thought of presenting this [the *Cabala*] to a knight, who, having gazed upon it, said that he had not studied enough to be able to understand its mysteries, and that therefore it could not interest him. I offered it next to one of these *ministri verbi Dei*; he claimed that he was a friend in the literal sense, and that he took no delight in such expositions as properly belonged to Origen, and which are accepted by scholastics and other enemies of their profession" (*Cabala*, p. 836). The *Cabala* has thus little chance of being a success among the "friends in the literal sense" and those who cannot "understand its mysteries." Reading the *Cabala* requires quite other talents, which Bruno ironically attributes to the "most reverend Signor Don Sapatino," bishop of Casamárciano. Bruno may perhaps be referring to a humble cleric from the parish of Santa Prima, which lies in the region where he was born.[5] However, beyond the actual existence of this historical character (Bruno often recalls in his works relatives and fellow citizens), what is most striking is the list of ideal encyclopedic requirements of the dedicatee:

> Fixing my gaze upon the question of encyclopedic matter, I remembered your encyclopedic mind, which appears to embrace everything, thanks less to its fecundity and richness than to its singular wandering excellence that seems to grant it everything and even more than everything. Certainly nobody could understand everything more expressly than you, since you remain outside of everything. You can enter into anything, because nothing can enclose you; you can have everything, because you possess nothing. (I know not whether I will express myself better by describing your ineffable intellect). I know not whether you would call yourself a theologian or a philosopher or a Cabalist, but I do know that you are all of these, if not in essence, then by your participation; if not in fact, then potentially; if not closely, then from a distance. (*Cabala*, p. 837)

In these lines, which hover between the serious and the comic, Bruno throws down a "challenge" to the reader: there is no easy way, but from the outset everything becomes complicated.

In light of these indications, it will prove useful to stop and consider the manner in which certain key words that frequently recur in the *Cabala* are used interchangeably. These are the terms "asininity," "madness," and "ignorance," which Bruno often employs as synonyms:

Saulino. So that you may not be afraid when you hear the name of the ass, asininity, bestiality, ignorance, madness . . . (p. 864)

Saulino. Because wisdom created without ignorance or madness, is, consequently, devoid of the asininity she signifies. (p. 873)

Sebasto. Now show me the truth of your assumptions, because I want
to concede every inference; because I find nothing inappro-
priate in stating that whoever is ignorant, by virtue of being
ignorant, is stupid; and whoever is stupid, by virtue of being
stupid, is an ass: therefore, all ignorance is asininity. (p. 874)

Saulino. . . . Now if wisdom mistakes truth for ignorance, it will consequently mistake it for stupidity, and consequently for asininity. Whoever has such knowledge, has something of the ass
in him, and participates in that idea. (p. 874)

Saulino. . . . O holy ignorance, O divine madness, O superhuman asininity! (p. 879)

Once the semantic common ground of the triad ("asininity," "madness," "ignorance") has been identified, we can identify the opposing triad that reflects it:

Saulino. Have you never heard that madness, ignorance, and asininity
in this world are wisdom, learning, and divinity in the other?
(*Cabala*, p. 864)

Another said that he saw the heavens opened, and many, many
other matters held by those beloved of God, to whom is revealed what is hidden from human wisdom, which is an ex-
quisite asininity in the eyes of rational discourse: since these
madness, asininities, and bestialities are wisdoms, heroic actions, and intelligences before our God. (*Cabala*, p. 857)

Asininity, therefore, moves through an ambiguous space, where its
negative or positive value can be deciphered in each instance, by
means of the clues that Bruno scatters in the text. An initial indi-
cation emerges from the dichotomous structure based on the ver-

ticality of the opposition between above and below, to which, as we shall see, correspond other antithetical pairings, such as bestial/ divine or human bestiality/divine bestiality. Within these continual reversals, the interpretative key cannot be separated from a specific analysis of each individual element in relation to a particular context.[6]

In the *Spaccio* and in the *Cabala*, although asininity is the triumphant beast that needs to be banished and that predominates among men (below), it finds, on the contrary, a positive space among the stars (above). But apart from Jupiter, the Jewish cabala, too, accords asininity the seat of Wisdom, in the divine universe of the Sephiroth:[7] "Consider now that, according to the cabalistic revelation Hochma—to which correspond the forms or wheels known as the Cherubim, who exert their influence in the eighth sphere, where lies the virtue of Raziel's intelligence—the ass or asininity is the symbol of wisdom" (*Cabala*, p. 866).

CHAPTER 5

Man and the Ass, between
"Bestiality" and "Divinity"

The symbol of the ass therefore lends itself easily to Bruno's method, which projects onto human beings the same symbolic qualities as those of asininity: to the divine and bestial nature of the ass corresponds the image of man as the mediator between bestiality and divinity. The particular experience of Onorio, whose name might suggest the evil ass, reveals how the human soul is no different to that of asses or of other living beings. At the basis of every living organism lies the same "corporal matter" and the same "spiritual matter." The testimony of Onorio (who, having died on earth in the guise of an ass, transmigrates into human bodies, each time returning to Heaven as the Pegasean ass) describes the generative process with great clarity:

Onorio. . . . As I grazed on a steep and stony ravine, taken with the desire of getting my teeth into a cardoon, which had grown some way down toward the precipice, [I thought that] I could stretch out my neck without peril, and, scorning any qualms of conscience and the instinct of natural reason, I leaned out so far that I could no longer cling on; and I fell from the high cliff; then my master realized that he had bought me for the crows. Freed from the prison of my body, I became a wandering spirit devoid of limbs; and I came to consider that, as far as spiritual substance was concerned, I was no different in kind

or type from all the other spirits that, following the dissolution
of other animals and compound bodies, were in the process of
transmigrating. And I saw how Fate not only removes all difference, as regards the nature of corporal matter, between the
human body and that of the ass, and between the animal body
and the body of those things considered to be soulless; but also,
as regards the nature of spiritual matter, how it removes all
difference between the asinine soul and the human soul, and
between the soul that constitutes the said animals and that
which is found in all things. . . . So, fleeing from the fortunate
fields, without sipping from the waters of the rapid Lethe,
among that multitude whose principal guide was Mercury, I
feigned to drink from that humor [the waters of the Lethe]
along with the others; but I did nothing more than approach
it and touch it with my lips, in order to deceive those watching
from above, for whom it was enough to see that my mouth and
chin were wet. Through the Cornean door I took the path toward the purest air, and, leaving the depths behind me and
beneath my feet, I came to find myself upon Mount Parnassus,
which—and this is no legend—on account of its Hippocrene
spring is consecrated by father Apollo to his daughters, the
Muses. There, by the power and order of fate, I returned to
being an ass, but without losing those intelligible faculties of
which the animal spirit was not widowed and deprived, and by
the strength of whose [the animal spirit's] virtue there emerged
on both my flanks the form and substance of two wings more
than sufficient to bear the weight of my body right up to the
stars. My appearance was no longer simply that of an ass, and
I was called flying ass, or Pegasean horse. Thus I was made
the executor of many orders given by provident Jupiter, I
served Bellerophon, I lived through many celebrated and most
honorable adventures, and, finally, I was assumed into Heaven

around the edges of Andromeda and Cygnus, on one side, and
Pisces and Aquarius on the other. (*Cabala*, pp. 882–84)

Onorio's tale reveals the concept of Bruno's naturalism. There
is no difference between men and other living things as regards
the composition of their bodies. Man's ontological status appears
on the same plane of natural equality with every possible form of
life:

Sebasto. So, you would claim that invariably there is no substantial
   difference between the soul of man and that of animals? and
   that they differ only in appearance?

Onorio. Man's soul is the same in its specific and generic essence as
   that of flies, marine oysters, and plants, and anything whatsoever that is animated or may have a soul; since there is no
   body that, with more or less vivacity and perfection, may show
   no sign of a spirit within itself. (*Cabala*, p. 885)

However, even though the same matter forms the basis of every
living being, the particular "physical constitution" of each species
determines its relationship with nature. It is solely the use that the
body can make of itself which creates different forms of behavior
among living beings: in order to maintain life, every species selects
the forms best suited to the operations of its own corporality. And,
unlike animals, only man, by virtue of his particular physical constitution, can attain divinity:

Onorio. . . . Now, this spirit [common to all living beings], according
   to fate or providence, order or fortune, comes to enter the
   body now of one species, now of another, and, according to
   the diversity of constitutions and limbs, it comes to possess
   different degrees and perfections of mental ingenuity and operation. Hence, that spirit or soul that dwelt in the spider and
   was possessed of that industry and those claws and limbs of a

certain number, quantity, and form, once it enters into the human cycle of procreation, acquires a different intelligence, other instruments, attitudes, and activities. In addition, if it were possible, or occurred in reality, that the head of a snake were to form and shape itself into the figure of a human head, and its torso were to grow as much as the limits of this species would allow, if its tongue were to widen, its shoulders to broaden, if it were to sprout arms and hands, and in place of its tail there were to appear a pair of legs, then it would comprehend, appear, breathe, talk, function, and walk no less than a man; because it would be nothing other than human. Just as, conversely, a man would be nothing other than a snake, if his arms and legs were to contract as if into a trunk, and his bones were to knit together to form a spine, if he were to coil and take on all the physical aspects, habits, and constitutions of a snake. Then his intelligence would be more or less lively; instead of talking, he would hiss; instead of walking, he would slither; instead of building a house, he would dig out a nest; and instead of a room, he would prefer a hole. And just as before he depended on those limbs, now he depends on these limbs, these instruments, powers, and actions, just as one and the same artisan, armed with different instruments and excited in different ways by the limits of the matter at his disposal, conceives of different schemes and executes different pieces of work. Therefore, you can understand that it is possible for many animals to have greater mental ingenuity and a much more enlightened intellect than man (thus Moses was not speaking lightheartedly when he declared the snake to be the wisest animal on earth); but a lack of instruments renders him inferior, just as a wealth and abundance of these grants him a great superiority. (*Cabala*, pp. 885–87)

Man's superiority over other animals is not decreed by abstract hierarchies, but has a concrete basis in nature, in the capacity of the organs of his body to perform operations denied other
species. The possibility of attaining the most ambitious objectives
resides wholly in the instruments of the body. Thus, the hand of
man, the "organ of organs," is the instrument thanks to which he
may dominate every other species:

Onorio. . . . Examine a little more closely the truth of what I am saying; ask yourself what would happen if man had twice the mental ingenuity that he does, and if his agent intellect shone even
more brightly than it does, but, in addition to all this, his hands
were transformed into two feet, with everything else remaining
in its normal dimension; tell me, where would "civilized
conversation" remain *impune?* . . . And, as a consequence,
where would one find the basic principles of doctrines, the
invention of disciplines, the congregations of citizens, the
structure of buildings, and all the other things that testify to
human greatness and excellence, and that make man the truly
invincible victor over other species? All this, if you look at it
carefully, refers principally not to the dictates of mental ingenuity but rather to those of the hand, organ of organs. (*Cabala*, p. 887)[1]

Man can become "god of the earth" by exercising one of his natural
qualities. The process of his "becoming divine" depends on his
ability to know how to use in harmony his intelligence and physical
potential:

Sophia. . . . And [Jupiter] added that the gods had granted man both
an intellect and hands, and they had made them in their image,
giving him power over the other animals; which consists in
being able to function not only according to nature and what

is common but, in addition, also outside its laws. Consequently, by shaping or by being able to shape other natures,
other courses, other orders, thanks to his mental ingenuity and
that freedom, without which he would not share a similarity
with the gods, he came to consider himself god of the earth. It
is certainly true that once this divine attribute becomes idle,
it becomes frustrating and vain, just as the eye that cannot see
and the hand that cannot hold are useless. For this reason,
providence has decided that man be occupied in activity
thanks to his hands, and in contemplation thanks to his intellect, in such a way that he never contemplates without acting,
and never acts without contemplating. . . . In this way, the
more and more humanity distances itself from the condition of
animals thanks to their urgent and pressing activities, the
closer they come to the divine being. (*Spaccio*, pp. 732–33)

Humanity overcomes its bestial state in the transition from nature to culture. This course has led it to dominate the natural
cycles, thereby shaping them to its own needs. Fulvio Papi
states, "There exists, therefore, a continuity between nature and
civilization; not in the sense that man is naturally civilized, but
in the sense that his physical constitution permits him to behave
in ways that give rise to phenomena that had not been envisaged
by the natural cycle."[2]

Bruno develops in an original way the theme of eulogizing
the "hands." Other sixteenth-century writers had already dealt
with the same *topos*. As Papi has shown, Ronsard's position appears to be very close to Bruno's; in his poetic work, *Paradoxe*
(1571), dedicated to King Charles IX, Ronsard clearly states that
"les Mains font l'homme et le font de la beste/Estre veincueur,
non les pieds, ny la teste" (Hands, not the head nor the feet,
make conquerors of the man and the beast).[3] In the *Zodiacus vi-*

tae, albeit from a different perspective, Marcellus Palingenius
Stellatus also maintains that if asses had hands and the power of
speech they would be wiser than men, precisely in order to underline the fact that without these physical gifts, man would become the most miserable of animals.[4]

But this same theme is developed along entirely opposite lines
by other writers. If Sansovino uses it to bring together Aristotelian
finalist anatomy and Christian providence ("And it was fitting that,
being made of divine substance, man should have an instrument by
means of which he could put into effect those things that proceed
from his intellect"), in Du Bartas the hand becomes an instrument
of humiliation to expiate guilt by means of hard labor, according to
Calvinist laws of redemption.[5] In Bruno there is nothing of all this.
Aristotle's finalist conception, which sustains his eulogy of the hand,
is overturned: "the hand is not a teleological attribute of man's
essence; however, physical concretion becomes what is culturally
called man, because it is endowed with this organ."[6] Lucretius's
criticism of the finalist conception of the bodily organs[7] allows
Bruno to return the theme of the hand to "its original Anaxagorean
meaning, and finally to transpose it into the context of a Lucretian
vision of the process of civilization."[8]

It is thus, within this view of things, that the oscillation between
"negative" and "positive" asininity takes place. On the one hand,
we have a vision of the world based on action (both intellectual and
material), wherein work and toil represent the only possibilities for
the development of knowledge and civilization. On the other, we
have the gangrene of negative asininity, wherein Aristotelians and
Skeptics, evangelical reformers and upholders of the myth of the
golden age act as brakes upon the development of knowledge and
of "civilized conversation." It is precisely in this space that the
wheel of metamorphosis takes shape: in it "where the man sits at
the top and a beast at the bottom, a half-man, half-beast descends

from the left, and a half-beast, half-man ascends from the right"
(*Eroici*, p. 1003). Corresponding to the arrogance and ignorance of
negative asses are the humility and willingness to work hard of positive asses. It is in relation to positions such as these that Bruno
utilizes the symbolic power of the ass.

CHAPTER 6

Positive Asininity: Toil, Humility, Tolerance

In this chapter we shall look at positive asininity and the role
of Toil in the acquisition of knowledge and in the building of civilization. It is precisely Saulino who, in the *Cabala*, underlines the
symbolic relationship between the ass and toil:

Saulino. Some Talmudists advance the moral reason for such an influence, tree, ladder, or dependence, saying that nevertheless
the ass is the symbol of wisdom in the divine Sephiroths, because whosoever wishes to penetrate its secrets and hidden re-
cesses, must habitually be sober and patient, with the snout,
head, and back of an ass; he must possess a humble, re-
strained, and modest soul, and senses that do not distinguish
between thistles and lettuce. (*Cabala*, p. 867)

The same arguments can also be found in the works of Agrippa of
Nettesheim and Pierio Valeriano, two authors who certainly exerted
an influence on Bruno. In the concluding chapter of *De incertitudine et vanitate scientiarum*, entitled *Ad encomium asini digressio*,
Agrippa dwells on the positive qualities of asininity:

In fact, the teachers of the Jews explain that this one [the
ass] is the symbol of exceptional courage and strength, of
patience and clemency, and that his influx comes from a
Sephiroth named Hochma—that is to say, wisdom. Indeed, the conditions of the life of the ass are absolutely
necessary to those wishing to study wisdom: living on a

meager diet, content with anything at all, quite able to endure penury, famine, toil, blows, negligence; suffering all persecution with great patience; very simple and very poor in spirit, so that it is unable to distinguish between lettuce and thistles; with a heart that is innocent and pure, free of any bitterness; it lives in peace with all living things, patiently offering its back to every load.[1]

Similarly, the chapter on the ass in Valeriano's *Hieroglyphica* includes a paragraph with the title *Labor indefessus*, in which, alongside the cabalists' theory, there appears an anecdote that confirms the link between the ass and toil:

But I do not wish to conceal what this opinion upholds, knowing what was done as a joke by Ptolemy when he cheerfully mocked one of Heraclitus of Lycia's compositions eulogizing toil. Indeed, when Heraclitus met the king, who asked him what he had in his hand, he offered him a book that he had entitled *ponou encomion*; the king took the book and erased the first "p" of the title, and so, instead of a eulogy of toil, he showed him that it now was a eulogy of the ass, since it read *onou encomion*. . . . For the Jews, principally among the Cabalists, the ass is the symbol of wisdom; they fashion its idea with the aid of a Sephiroth, citing as a reason that those who want to devote themselves to wisdom must content themselves with a very meager diet of the roughest kind, and everybody knows that the ass has been endowed with such parsimony. What is more, it endures penury, toil, blows, and hunger with the utmost patience, nor does it become enraged at any affront, whatever its source. It is small of spirit, poor and simple, since it is unable to distinguish thistles from lettuce. Its heart is in no way cunning, nor

is it in any way touched by desire. It is so unmoved to
anger that it has made everlasting peace with every species of animal. There is no task that it refuses . . . since,
as they say, it is compelled to carry mysteries.[2]

Humility, tolerance, a predisposition to hard work: these are the
symbolic qualities that Bruno celebrates in positive asininity. They
are vital to the process of constructing civilization, just as without
them it would be impossible to find one's way through the labyrinth
of knowledge. Without this premise, it would be impossible to understand the determining role that Jupiter and all the gods accord
Toil in the celestial reform:

> Scale, overcome, and cross with your spirit, if that is pos-
> sible, every stony and rough mountain. Feel such fervor
> that not only do you endure and surpass yourself, but,
> what is more, you may also have no sense of the difficulty
> facing you, no sense of its being toil; for toil thus ceases
> to be toil, just as a heavy body does not find itself heavy.
> But you will not be worthy of the name of toil, if you
> cannot so surpass yourself that you cannot recognize what
> you are: toil. . . . But you, Toil, delight in noble enter-
> prises and not in toil for yourself; become—I say—one
> and the same thing with the toil that, outside of such
> virtuous enterprises and acts, is not a pleasure in itself
> but an intolerable hardship. Take courage, then, if you
> are a virtue, do not concern yourself with base things,
> with frivolous things, with vain things. If you wish to be
> there where the sublime pole of Truth lies vertically above
> you, cross this Apennine, scale these Alps, sail across this
> rock-strewn Ocean, overcome these severe Riff moun-
> tains, cross this barren and frozen Caucasus, penetrate
> inaccessible heights, and enter into that happy circle,

where there is perpetual light and neither darkness nor
cold is ever seen, but the climate is one of constant
temperate warmth and it is eternally dawn or daylight.
(*Spaccio*, pp. 712–13)

The sublime pole of truth, which in the *Cabala*, as we know, Jupiter
assigned to asininity, can be attained through Toil. But, as we have
seen, the path is far from easy: it is necessary to scale mountains,
to sail across rock-strewn oceans, to penetrate "inaccessible
heights," to overcome limitless peaks. Numerous impediments ob-
struct the roads leading out of the darkness. The only chance of
reaching the light, the eternal light of day, seems to lie in the positive
qualities of Toil: without committed perseverance in constant research and without a predisposition to sacrifice, all efforts will be
in vain. Thus, in the program that Toil presents to the gods, we find
once again a celebration of industriousness:

See how I, Toil, get into step, get ready, roll up my
sleeves. Begone all torpor, all idleness, all negligence, all
desirous acedia, get out all slackness! You, my dear Industry, propose for consideration your advantage and
your end. Render salutary the many calumnies of others,
the many fruits of maliciousness and envy, and that well-
justified fear of yours that chased you from your native
abode, alienated you from your friends, sent you far away
from your homeland, and banished you to unfriendly
climes. Make glorious with me, my dear Industry, that
exile and those trials; let calmness reign, and in that land
let there be tranquillity, freedom, and peace. Come on,
Diligence, what are you doing? why do we laze about and
sleep so much in life, when we will have to laze about and
sleep so much in death? Even if we expect another life or
another kind of existence for ourselves, it will not be the

same as the one we have now; so this one, having no hope
of ever returning, passes by eternally. You, Hope, what
are you doing? why do you not spur me on? why do you
not urge me on? Come on, let me expect a salutary success
from difficult things, as long as I do not begin before the
right moment and do not stop in time; and do not let me
promise myself things for living, but only for living well.
You, Zeal, help me always, so that I do not tempt unworthy things from spirits of good, and so that I do not stretch
my hands into affairs that give rise to greater affairs. . . .
Wisdom, do not let me retreat from uncertain and doubt-
ful things, nor turn my back on them, but gradually remove myself from them to safety. . . . Animosity, when
difficulties weigh me down, insult me, and resist me, do
not fail, with the voice of your lively fervor, to keep repeating in my ear this maxim: *Tu ne cede malis, sed contra audentior ito* [Do not give in to wickedness, but, on
the contrary, go forth with greater boldness; *Aeneid*,
VI.95]. . . . You, Patience, reassure me, restrain me,
and give me your noble Idleness, whose sister is not In-
dolence, but whose brother is Tolerance. . . . Come to
me, O generous and heroic and solicitous Fear; let your
spur prevent me from losing my place among the illustrious before I lose it among the living. Make sure that before torpor and death relieve me of my hands, I may find
myself sufficiently well provided that the glory of my work
cannot be taken away from me. (*Spaccio*, pp. 715–18)

The process of man's "becoming divine" is made concrete in
Toil's design. She presents herself as the positive model for divine
men who, armed with Industry, Hope, Tolerance, Animosity, and
Wisdom, strive to attain the "glory of their work" before death

"relieves them of their hands." In these important pages of the *Spaccio,* charged as they are with heroic tension, a flash of auto-biography clearly shines through. It is precisely the hard road of exile that symbolizes the difficulties that divine man must compete against in order to continue on the adventure of knowledge. The reply of the Cumaean Sibyl (*Tu ne cede malis, sed contra audentior ito / Quam tua te fortuna sinet*) sounds like a warning for humanity as a whole, or, rather, for those who fight desperately to attain the highest point on the wheel of metamorphosis. The first hemistich of Virgil's next verse (*Quam tua te fortuna sinet*), which Bruno omit-ted from the quotation, sanctions the challenge to fortune. One must not succumb to evil things, but face them in a manner that is bolder than that permitted by fortune.[3] Once again the role of Toil is stressed, since only Toil is granted the possibility of grabbing "Fortune by the hair": "Pass then, you, goddess Solicitude or Toil; and I want (said Jupiter) difficulty to run ahead of you and to flee from you. Drive away Misadventure, grab Fortune by the hair; hasten the turn of its wheel when you deem the moment most opportune; and when things appear just right, drive a nail through it, to halt its progress" (*Spaccio,* p. 713).[4] Jupiter's invitation, which echoes a page of Machiavelli's *The Prince,*[5] further strengthens faith in the possibility of controlling events by means of one's own labors. Within this vision of civilization, where all spiritual teleology is ab-sent, man's destiny can only lie—to continue the metaphor—in his own hands. Man alone is responsible for the paths he takes: it is his responsibility to know how to live with dignity, to know how fully to exploit his natural potential.

But the process of man's "becoming divine" is hampered by other men who live in the darkness of bestiality and look for "ordinary and easy things" in an idle existence stripped of any heroic impulse. One must steer clear of precisely these negative asses. This is why Toil wishes her work to be at the same time "hidden" and "out in the open":

> You yourself [Wisdom] (to avoid my being discovered by my enemies [it is Toil who is speaking] and thereby having them vent their fury on me) cover my tracks by following me. . . . Let my work be hidden and out in the open: out in the open, so that not everyone will go in search of it and inquire after it; hidden, so that not all, but very few will find it. You well know that hidden things are always sought out, while things that are locked away attract the covetousness of thieves. Furthermore, what is on view is deemed contemptible, while the open ark is not searched for diligently, and little value is placed on what cannot be seen to be carefully guarded. (*Spaccio*, p. 716)

By means of an act of concealment it is possible to create further levels of selection. Only divine men will be able to overcome the difficulties of the journey; they are the only ones motivated to experience to the full the adventure of knowledge: "The difficulty lies in holding back sluggards. Ordinary and easy things are for vulgar and common people; rare, heroic, and divine men take this path of difficulty, so that the palm of immortality must of necessity be granted to them" (*Cena*, p. 63). Modes of behavior and intense industriousness are the elements that determine *dignitas hominis;* they are the elements thanks to which humanity distinguishes itself on the many paths of individual experience.

CHAPTER 7

Negative Asininity:
Idleness, Arrogance, Unidimensionality

In contrast to the qualities of positive asininity embodied in the image of Toil, Bruno personifies the qualities of negative asininity in the ideology of idleness and in the resurrection of the myth of the golden age. If positive asses live in the light of knowledge, negative asses vegetate in the darkness of ignorance. It is against the latter that Bruno shoots his arrows: at upholders of idleness; at Aristotelians and Skeptics who curb the processes of knowledge; at Christ and the evangelical reformers who encourage inaction and ignorance so as to attain immortality in another world. Bruno thus concentrates his scathing criticism on these three blights that are capable of destroying the processes of knowledge and the progress of civilization.

a) *The Myth of the Golden Age.* The discovery of the New World plunged European ethnocentrism into crisis. The model of life of primitive peoples, as described in numerous travel writings, lent itself very well to the resurrection of the literary *topos* of the golden age.[1] "The symbol of a civilization where men lived in close harmony with nature, far from the rigid and ineluctable constraints of a world composed of conflicting bodies of laws, institutions, and doctrines, entered into contact with the malaise of European culture, by then disturbed in its humanist sense of balance and in its celebration of new technical developments brought about by the material and intellectual ferocity of the wars of religion. Such were the conditions that encouraged the metamorphosis of the classic dream of a lost paradise into the affirmation of a condition that is natural, original, and positive in its candor, where virtue flourishes as naturally as a growing shoot."[2] In just this spontaneous vision of civilization, however, Bruno glimpsed the germ of an ideology of idleness that opposed any intervention on humanity's part in the construction of its own existence: "There is nobody who does not glorify the golden age, when men were asses, when they did not know how to work the land, or how to dominate one another, or to understand more than another; their shelter was dens and caves, they leapt on each other like animals, there was little concealment, or jealousy, or spice in their lust and gluttony; everything was communal, meals consisted of apples, chestnuts, and acorns eaten raw as mother nature had made them" (*Cabala*, p. 855). Indeed, as a counter to the industriousness of Toil, Idleness is given the task of defending the myth of the golden age before the council of the gods:

O gods, who is the one to have cherished this much lauded golden age? who has instituted it, who has maintained it, if not the law of Idleness, the law of nature? Who has swept it away? who has driven it almost irrevocably from the world, if not ambitious Solicitude, curious Toil? Is she not the one to have disturbed the centuries, caused discord in the world and led it to an age of iron, mud, and clay, having put nations to the wheel and hurled them toward a certain turmoil and perdition, after having uplifted them with pride and love of things new, and with desire for individual honor and glory? . . . Everybody extols the beautiful golden age, when I rendered souls calm and tranquil, and they owed nothing to this virtuous goddess of yours; their bodies needed but the seasoning of hunger to make sweeter and more worthy of praise meals of acorns, apples, chestnuts, peaches, and roots, which benevolent nature proffered; by nourishing men better, she cherished them more and allowed them to live longer, which cannot be said of today's many artificial condiments discovered by Industry and Study, the ministers of Toil. . . . Everybody exalts the golden age, while they esteem and declare to be a virtue that villain which extinguished it by inventing mine and yours: this Toil that divided and apportioned between this one and that one not just the earth (which belongs to all its living inhabitants), but also the sea, and perhaps even the air as well. . . . I ask you, will this Toil be more favored, which, being so rebellious and deaf to all advice, so averse to and contrary about nature's gifts, devotes her thoughts and hands to artificial endeavors and machinations that corrupt the world and pervert the law of our mother? Do you not hear in these times how the world, having realized too late the ills that it causes, mourns that age when, under my government, the human species was kept happy and contented, and with screams and wails spurns the present age, in which Solicitude and industrious Toil cause turmoil by holding everything in check with the spur of ambitious Honor? (*Spaccio*, pp. 726–29)[3]

In Idleness's defense address, Bruno includes a series of *topoi* that propose a vision of the world essentially based on inaction. Within this apotheosis of stasis, men live in an undignified condition of equality, whose common denominator is idleness. Indeed, differences cannot exist where there is no possibility for change and where everything is always the same as itself. We should not be surprised, therefore, if Toil's vicissitudes shatter the mythical tranquillity of the golden age, by triggering dynamic mechanisms of differentiation. Inherent in action and change is also the possibility of creating inequality and injustice. In his reply to Idleness, Jupiter himself underlines this contradiction: "You must not be surprised to see injustices and wrongs growing alongside industry; because, if cattle and apes were as virtuous and intelligent as men, they would have the same concerns, the same desires, and the same vices" (*Spaccio*, p. 733). But, as we shall see later, Bruno firmly believes that man, through the progress of civilization, can contain and, in some cases, neutralize the effects of "injustices and wrongs." It is important now to define this ideology of idleness as advocated by negative asses. Neither civilization nor knowledge could ever exist in the world extolled by Idleness. It assumes the form of an earthly paradise whose inhabitants vegetate in a state wherein they are wholly incapable of knowing how to ask questions of themselves and of nature. It is not by chance that "the first father of men, when he was a good man" and "the first mother of women, when she was a good woman" could boast that Idleness was their sole companion (*Spaccio*, p. 731):

> Remember, O faithful ones, that our first parents at that
> time pleased God and lived in His grace, under His pro-
> tection, happy in the earthly paradise, where they were
> asses, namely, simple and ignorant of good and evil; when
> they could not be titillated by the desire to know good and
> evil, and consequently could not have any knowledge of
> them; when they could believe a lie told them by the ser-
> pent; when they could be made to believe even this: that
> although God had told them that they would die, the con-
> trary might be the case. In this condition they were

> happy, they were grateful, free of all pain, care, and trou-
> ble. (*Cabala*, p. 855)

The peace of paradise can be broken. Plucking the fruit from the
tree of knowledge means unleashing processes of change; and the
punishment inflicted is indeed eloquent: pain and toil will mark
the life of men (*Spaccio*, p. 731).

  b) *Skeptics and Aristotelians.* Negative asininity also distinguishes itself in the "contemplative life." False philosophers and
pedants (as regards the latter, Giovanni Bernardo's invective in the
Candelaio comes to mind)[4] spend their life discussing stupidities and
polluting whatever argument ends up on their lips. So they, too,
are clearly worthy of living in the house of Idleness:

> And in order to show you, O Jupiter, and you other gods,
> that in the house of Idleness, in addition to the active ones
> we have already mentioned, there is no shortage of edu-
> cated and cultured people who are busy with their stud-
> ies: do you really think that in the house of Idleness a life
> of contemplation means being idle; in the place where
> there is no shortage of grammarians arguing whether the
> noun or the verb came first? Or why adjectives sometimes
> come before and sometimes after the noun?. . . . Where
> there is no shortage of dialecticians examining whether
> Chrysoloras, a disciple of Porphyry, was said to have
> a mouth of gold because it was a natural attribute, or
> as a result of his reputation, or simply by virtue of his
> name; whether the *Peri hermeneias* should precede or
> follow or, indeed, *ad libitum*, precede and follow the *Cat-*
> *egories*. . . . Where metaphysicians rack their brains
> over the principle of individuation; over the living being
> as being; . . . and over a host of such subjects, which
> cause so many hoods to shake and which drain the sap

from the brains of so many protosophists. (*Spaccio*, pp. 741–44)

Following on from the asininity of the authors of these "sheeplike treatises," in one of the best comic passages of his Italian dialogues, Bruno describes the stupidity of those readers who wear themselves out trying to figure what the treatises mean:

> And what merits compassion and ridicule, is that reading these little books and sheeplike treatises caused Salvio to become dumbfounded and Ortensio to become melancholic, Serafino to lose weight, Cammaroto to turn pale, Ambruogio to age, Gregorio to go mad, Reginaldo to become lost in abstraction, Bonifacio to swell up, and the most reverend Don Cocchiarone, full of infinite and noble wonder, to pace up and down his room, well away from the rude and ignoble populace; adjusting the hem of his literary toga here and there, shifting one foot, then the other, thrusting out his chest now to the right side, now to the left, with the commented text under his armpit, and seemingly wanting to throw to the ground the flea that he holds between his fingers, with his pensive brow all furrowed, with raised eyebrows and eyes wide, like a man utterly astonished, he will bring to the ears of those present, concluding with a deep and emphatic sigh, this sentence: *Huc usque alii philosophi non pervenerunt* [Other philosophers have never gone so far]. If he finds himself teaching a book written by some energumen or someone otherwise inspired, which expresses and draws out no more sentiment than may be found in the soul of a horse, then, to show he has hit the nail on the head, he will exclaim: *O magnum mysterium!* (*Cabala*, pp. 897–99)

But Bruno's generalized invective becomes specific when he concentrates on demolishing two schools of philosophy, skepticism and Aristotelianism. Bruno sees in both a rigid standpoint that cannot engender a positive relationship with knowledge:

> Others turn to it [the contemplation of truth] and try to find it by means of ignorance. And of these, some are afflicted by that ignorance said to be born of simple negation, neither knowing, nor claiming to know; others by that ignorance said to be born of a perverse disposition, whereby the less they know and the more false information they soak up, the more they think they know; thus, in order to learn the truth, they have to work twice as hard in order to cast off the disposition contrary [to knowledge] in order to learn its opposite. (*Cabala*, pp. 874–75)

The "we know nothing" of the Skeptics and the "we know everything" of the Aristotelians[5] come together in a homogeneous *Weltanschauung* that lacks all information and wherein tautology reigns supreme. The negation of sense and the totality of possible senses is placed on a common epistemological plane marked, as result of absence in the one case and excess in the other, by non-sense. The road of negative asininity is yet another version of the ideology of stasis, which is characterized by theoretical positions devoid of all cultural dynamism. There can be no knowledge within universes that are closed, uniform, inactive, and far removed from the vicissitudes of the search for knowledge.

Sebasto is charged with demolishing the Skeptics' position while illustrating, not without irony, its fundamental theoretical principles:

Sebasto. These idlers, to avoid the effort of explaining things, and so as not to blame their inertia and envy of the industry of others, in wanting to appear superior and not satisfied with concealing their own faintheartedness, unable to overtake them or to keep up with them, or to find the means of doing something for themselves, lest they prejudice their vain presumption by revealing their imbecilic minds, their crude sense, and their limited intellect; and to make the rest appear unfit to judge their blindness, they put the blame on nature, on things that are difficult to understand, and not principally on the misunderstanding of dogmatists. Because by doing so, they would have been forced to open to comparison their sound understanding, which would have given rise to greater conviction, having generated a clearer idea in the minds of those who delight in contemplating natural things. And so, wanting to appear wiser than the rest with the least effort and intellect and no risk of losing face, these sensationalists said that nothing can be determined, because nothing is known; and that consequently those who claim to understand and speak assertively are more delirious than those who do not understand and do not speak. The others, known as Pyrrhonians, to appear highly knowledgeable, said that even what the sensationalists say cannot be understood, since nothing can be determined or known. Thus, while the sensationalists claimed that those who believed they understood did not understand, the Pyrrhonians now claimed that the sensationalists could not understand whether the others, who believed they understood, actually understood or not. . . . And so, we can easily extend this noble ladder of philosophy to the point of proving demonstratively that the highest form of philosophy and perfect contemplation belongs to those who not only do not affirm or deny that they know or do not know but who also cannot even affirm or deny; with the result

> that asses are the most divine of animals and that asininity,
> her sister, is the companion and secretary of truth. (*Cabala*,
> pp. 904–6)

The terms of the opposition between the two kinds of asininity are
clearly set out here—the Skeptics' limit being marked by "avoiding
the effort of explaining things." Faced with the complexities presented by knowledge, the simplest way out is to negate its existence.
Such logic lends itself very well to the need to renounce "industry,"
so as to exalt a situation wherein one wishes to "appear wiser than
the rest" with "the least effort and intellect." In this instance, the
relationship between truth and asininity leans toward the side of
the beast: by negating knowledge, ignorance becomes the only truth
to which negative asses aspire.[6]

Situated on the opposite but complementary side of the same
front are Aristotle and Aristotelians. Here Bruno's narrative strategy reaches levels of considerable comedy, and the invective turns
into a biting confession. It is Onorio who recounts the events of his
transmigration into the body of Aristotle. By the laws of metempsychosis, it fell to him to leave the celestial region, which, as we have
seen, he inhabited in the guise of the Pegasean ass[7] (high-positive),
and incarnated on earth as Aristotle (low-negative):

Onorio. Now, as I have said, since I found myself in the celestial region
in the guise of the Pegasean horse, fate ordained that, following
my conversion to inferior things (due to the degree of affection
I was thence acquiring, as Plotinus the Platonist describes so
well), as if drunk on nectar, I was proclaimed variously as a
philosopher, a poet, a pedant, and left my image in heaven,
where I returned between transmigrations to deposit the memory of the personae I had acquired in my bodily abode. . . .
Of these memorable personae the most recent have been those
I began to take on during the lifetime of Philip of Macedonia,

following, as is believed, my conception by the seed of Nicom-
achus. Here, after having been the disciple of Aristarchus,
Plato, and others, thanks to my father, one of Philip's advi-
sors, I was promoted to the rank of tutor to Alexander the
Great. Under his reign, although well-versed in the humanistic
sciences, in which I was more eminent than all my predeces-
sors, I presumed to be a natural philosopher, since it is normal
for pedants always to be rash and presumptious. And thus,
since all knowledge of philosophy was lost, with Socrates dead,
Plato banished, and others variously dispersed, I remained
alone, one-eyed among the blind; and I easily acquired a reputation not just as a rhetorician, politician, and logician, but
also as a philosopher. By giving improper and foolish versions
of the opinions of the Ancients, and in so inept a manner that
not even children or senile old women would speak and understand in the way I led those fine gentlemen to speak and
understand, I came to present myself as the reformer of that
discipline about which I knew absolutely nothing. I declared
myself the prince of peripatetics; I taught in Athens beneath
the porticos of the Lyceum, where, guided by the light, or
rather by the darkness that reigned within me, I understood
and taught the nature of principles and substance of things in
a corrupt way, I raved more than delirium itself about the
essence of the soul, quite unable to have a clear understanding
of the nature of motion and of the universe. In short, it was I
who dragged natural and divine science to the base of the
wheel, just as it had been exalted at the time of the Chaldeans
and Pythagoreans. (*Cabala*, pp. 892–94)

Onorio/Aristotle's self-critique is based essentially on his claim of
"being a natural philosopher," and it is precisely on this theme
that Bruno unleashes his corrosive irony:

Onorio. [My ignorance] comes as no surprise, dear brother; since in
   no way can it be possible for them [the Aristotelians] to understand my understanding of those things that I did not understand; or that they would wish to find a structure or an
   argument in what I want to tell you, when I myself did not
   know what I wanted to say. . . . Fearing others would notice
   this, and that as a result I would lose my reputation as a pro-
   tosophist, I tried to make sure that whoever studied my natural
   philosophy (in which I was and indeed felt completely ignorant)
   would think and believe, unless they had some spark of intelligence, that all its defects and confusion that they noticed did
   not represent my deepest intent, but rather what they, according to their capacities, could superficially understand of
   what I was saying. So I arranged for that *Letter to Alexander*
   to be published, in which I professed that my books on physics
   were both clear and obscure. (*Cabala*, pp. 895–96)

The polemic against Aristotle's physics, which Bruno attacked elsewhere with assured authority,[8] encapsulates the rejection of a
closed, static view of the world sanctioned by the separation between heaven and earth. For Aristotle, science cannot exist where
the laws of change stir up matter, since, by definition, it must deal
with what is stable and eternal. "The subject of science must be
eternal, immutable, true, constant, simple, one, always the same,
everywhere the same" (*Opp. lat.*, I, I, p. 84). This summary of
Aristotle's viewpoint, as proposed by Bruno in his *Acrostimus camoeracensis*, embodies the tautology of knowledge. The eternal nature of the laws of trajectories reflects the existence of a world that
has been completed and always remains the same as itself. Such a
world is completely alien to Bruno's open vision of a universe where
infinite worlds mark infinite paths for the atoms of matter to aggre-
gate. On this plane, Skeptics and Aristotelians find themselves in a

common epistemological position that engenders stasis and inaction. In both cases, knowledge coincides with tautology, with the negation of all tension toward the boundless adventure of knowledge.

c) *Christ and Evangelical Reformers.* The third dimension of negative asininity is embodied in certain principles of Christianity. "Holy ignorance" becomes the only path to salvation, and only the renunciation of knowledge can guarantee rewards in the next world. The sonnet "In lode de l'asino" (Eulogy of the ass), which appears in the *Cabala* between the *Epistola dedicatoria* and the *Declamazione allo studioso, divoto e pio lettore*, clearly sets out the principles of "holy asininity":

O holy asininity, holy ignorance,
Holy foolishness and pious devotion,
You alone can make souls so good,
Which human intelligence and study cannot;
You do not pay wearisome attention
To any art whatever, nor to any invention,
Nor to the philosophic contemplation
Of heaven where you build your abode.
Curious minds, what good is it to study,
To want to know the workings of nature,
Whether the stars are made of earth, fire or sea?
Holy asininity does not care about this;
But wants to remain with hands joined and kneeling,
Waiting for God to proclaim her destiny.
Nothing lasts,
But the fruit of eternal rest,
Which God accords after our funerals.[9]

Again we find the terms of a radical opposition between two standpoints. On one side, there is "holy asininity," which, disregarding "study" and "the workings of nature," invites men to wait "with

hands joined and kneeling" for God's reward of "eternal rest."
On the other, there is "human intelligence," "study," "wearisome
attention / To any art whatever," "invention," "philosophic contemplation." The inaction of "holy ignorance" is counterbalanced
by the alternative model of "human intelligence," which asks questions about "the workings of nature." In the space inhabited by
negative asininity, there is no room for Toil and for "divine men";
evangelical "true knowledge" holds that "nothing causes a surer
fall into the center and abyss of Tartarus than philosophical and
rational contemplations, which are born of the senses, grow in the
faculty of speech, and mature in the human intellect" (*Cabala*, p.
857).

In the celestial reform of the *Spaccio*, the image of "presumptious Orion" (*Spaccio*, p. 774) polarizes all the negative elements
of Christianity and, paradoxically, embodies the figure and ideology
of Christ:

> Then Neptune asked:—O gods, what will you do with my
> favorite, my lovely minion, Orion, who (as the etymolo-
> gists say) makes the heavens urinate with fright?—Here,
> replied Momus:—Allow me to make a proposition, O
> gods. The macaroni has dropped into the cheese, as they
> say in Naples, because he can work wonders. As Neptune
> knows, he can walk over the waters of the sea without
> sinking or getting his feet wet, and as a result of this he
> will be able to do many other fine tricks. Let us send him
> among men and fool them with whatever we fancy and
> pleases us, making them believe that white is black, that
> human intellect, by which they think to see clearly, is but
> a blindness; and that what reason renders excellent, good,
> and perfect is vile, wicked, and absolutely evil; that na-
> ture is a filthy whore, that the law of nature is villainous;

that nature and divinity cannot come together for the
same good end, and that the justice of one is not subordinate to the justice of the other, but that they are opposites, like darkness and light. . . . Because these are
gifts of nature and scorned by the gods, and are left to
those who are incapable of greater privileges, in other
words, the supernatural ones granted by the divinity, like
those of leaping above water, making crabs dance, making the lame turn somersaults, letting moles see without
spectacles, and innumerable other fine tricks. With this
he will persuade them that philosophy, all contemplation
and all magic that would make them similar to us, is pure
folly; that every heroic deed is mere cowardice; and that
ignorance is the finest science in the world, because it is
acquired effortlessly and does not afflict the soul with melancholy. (*Spaccio,* pp. 803–5)

The identification of Christ with Orion is rather suspect, however,
since the only element that justifies their symbolic relationship is
that they both walked on water.[10] But an answer can perhaps be
found in the *Cabala,* in the fact that Orion is virtually an anagram
of Onorio. In this case, two aspects of negative asininity may reciprocally allude to each other: the negative image of Onorio/Aristotle,
presumptuous guardian of universal truths, corresponds to the image of presumptuous Orion, prophet of "holy ignorance" and in-
activity. The miracles and tricks of Orion/Christ are transformed
into the fraud organized by Onorio/Aristotle: natural philosophy,
disparaged by the first, is irrevocably sentenced to death by the
second.

The analogies paradoxically appear to be backed up by their
proselytes' proximity, when Aristotelian asses are flanked by asses
for whom the kingdom of heaven awaits:

Here you can see those who have been redeemed, those
who have been called, those who have been predestined,
those who have been saved: the she-ass, the ass foal, the
simple, the poor in mind, little children, those who
speak with a child's voice. Yes, these are the ones who
enter the kingdom of heaven; scorning the world and its
pomp, they trample their clothes, they have banished
from themselves every bodily care, they have trampled
underfoot the flesh that surrounds their soul and hurled
it to the ground, so that the she-ass and her dear foal
may pass with greater glory and triumph. (*Cabala*, p.
854)[11]

But the dissolution of knowledge is also accelerated by the absurd
pretensions of evangelical reformers who, with their pedantic lu-
cubrations, have destroyed civilized conversation and peace among
peoples:

May it [sound judgment] deem whether, while calling
themselves ministers of one who raises the dead and heals
the sick, it is not they who, more than anyone whom the
earth nourishes, cripple the healthy and kill the living,
not so much by fire and steel, but by their pernicious
tongues. May it consider what kind of peace and harmony
they propose to wretched peoples, if perhaps they want
and hope that the whole world would agree and consent
to their malicious and most presumptuous ignorance, and
approve their evil conscience, while they refuse to agree
or to consent to any law, justice, or doctrine. Nowhere in
the world and at no other time do such discord and dis-
sonance appear as are found among them. (*Spaccio*, p.
661)

These promoters of the "loafing sect of pedants" do not live off their own work but, being lazy, "they live off the labor of those who have worked for people other than them, and have built temples, chapels, hospices, hospitals, colleges, and universities; thus they rob openly and seize the hereditary wealth of others" (*Spaccio*, p. 623). Their punishment, as proposed by Saturn ("moreover, it seems fair to me that, once they have left their body, they should transmigrate from body to body over many centuries, in different guises and many times, and that they should live as pigs, the laziest animals in the world, or as marine oysters stuck to the rocks") is rejected by the gods; however, that put forward by Mercury is successful, because these asses will have to endure the toils of their fellows:[12] "Justice, said Mercury, demands the contrary. It seems fair to me that the punishment for idleness ought to be toil. But it would be better if they were to live as asses, thereby remaining ignorant and eliminating idleness; and in such a case, let them be at the mercy of unceasing labor, with little hay and straw for food, and plenty of beatings as reward" (*Spaccio*, p. 626). The picture of negative asininity seems to be complete: the negation of civilization and the exaltation of the myth of the golden age, the negation of earthly life and the exaltation of a life after death. Inaction, holy ignorance, arrogance, presumption, idleness, renunciation, waiting—these are the negative connotations that Bruno situates at the basis of human bestiality.

Within such a *Weltanschauung*, there is no possibility of change, and the human beast is forced to vegetate for all eternity, the prisoner of a fixed, unidimensional condition. For them there can be no metamorphosis; they will remain asses for all eternity:

> What did they do? What stance did they take? They
> halted their steps, folded or lowered their arms, closed
> their eyes, banished all personal care and study, re-

proached every human thought, negated all natural feel-
ing, and finally saw themselves as asses. And those who
were not already asses transformed themselves into this
animal; they lifted, stretched, pointed, enlarged, and
magnified their ears. They concentrated and united all the
power of their soul into the faculty of hearing, and believed only what they heard, like he of whom it is said: *In
auditu auris obedivit mihi* [He is all ears and obeys me;
Psalm 17.45]. There they concentrated and captured
their vegetative, sensitive, and intellectual faculties, and
they wrapped their five fingers into a single hoof, so that
they could not pick the forbidden fruit of the tree of
knowledge as Adam did, and thus they were deprived of
the fruits of the tree of life. (*Cabala*, p. 878)

Once they "wrapped their five fingers into a single hoof," the wheel
of metamorphosis veered wholly toward the side of the beast. Without hands, they were no longer able to "pick the forbidden fruit of
the tree of knowledge." Only positive asininity can embark upon
the adventure of knowledge, with humility, tolerance, toil, and industry becoming the only means by which man can find release from
his natural condition of savagery. The transition from *feritas* to
humanitas is marked by the process of "becoming divine" undergone by positive asses. Metamorphosis and change characterize this
universe, which is pluridimensional, open, unstable and which certainly does not negate vicissitude. In the face of universal knowledge, only the humble recognition of one's own asininity provides
the key to the laborious search for the truths that escape us.

CHAPTER 8

The Oration of Fortune

In light of these considerations, it will be easier to grasp the full significance of Fortune's oration. In these marvelous passages of the *Spaccio*, Bruno presents yet another image of man as master of his fate. Fortune is ascribed a fundamental role whereby, apart from making authoritative use of "Reason, Truth, Sophia, Justice, and other deities" (*Spaccio*, p. 685), she has access to "those places that are closed even to Jupiter himself." Hence, in the celestial reform, the father of the gods grants her the universe as a whole:

> However (let Momus say what he likes), since I consider your reasons, O Goddess [Fortune], to be all too valid, I conclude that, if no further allegations are made against your cause which prove to be more valid than those already put forward, I dare not assign you a space as if I already wanted to tie you to it and relegate you there. But I grant you—indeed, I bequeath to you—the power you have shown throughout heaven, since the authority you have by yourself is so great that you can enter those places that are closed even to Jupiter himself, as well as to all the other gods. And I do not wish to speak any further on this matter because we are all most deeply indebted to you. By unlocking every door and opening every path, and by having every space at your disposal, you make yours all that belongs to others; and so the seats of others also become yours. Hence, all that is subject to the fate

of change, without exception passes through the urn, through the revolution, and through the hand of your greatness. (*Spaccio*, pp. 695–96)

The image of Fortune, on a level higher even than that occupied by Jupiter, appears to encompass the dialectic between necessity and chance. Nobody can escape the urn of change, but only a few are favored by the hand of the blindfolded goddess. It is precisely her lack of eyesight, which does not imply a lack of knowledge ("But, even though I may be bereft of sight, I am not bereft of hearing and intelligence"),[1] that guarantees total equality for all in the face of destiny:

I see neither miters, nor togas, nor crowns, nor skills, nor talents; I discern neither merits nor demerits; since, even if they exist, they are not on account of some having such a nature and of others having another, but most certainly are of the circumstances and the opportunities that present themselves, or of the chances that befall this person or that one. . . . I put everyone into the same urn and in that huge belly they are mixed, blended, and shaken up. Then the die is cast, and good luck to whoever scores well and hard luck to whoever scores badly! In this way, inside the urn of Fortune no distinction is made between the greatest and the smallest; indeed, in there, all are equally great and equally small, since it is others, not I, who draw distinctions between them, that is to say, before they go into the urn and after they come out. Whilse inside, all are shaken up in the same way, by the same hand and in the same vessel. . . . I, therefore, who treat the whole world in the same way and consider all to be one mass, no part of which I deem more or less worthy than another, lest the vessel be filled with shame; I, who throw everyone

into the same urn of change and motion, treat everyone
in equal measure and stir everyone equally, without paying more attention to one over another, I come to be the
most just, even though it seems to all of you that the opposite is true. (*Spaccio*, pp. 690–92)

Within this natural mechanism, there can be no injustices. The common root of all human beings is respected, and within the urn each
person's "token is the same as that of everyone else" (*Spaccio*, p.
691). But if Fortune extracts a host of incapable and inept people,
it is not her fault. She cannot be held liable for a responsibility that
belongs to Virtue. How can virtuous men be extracted if the urn is
infested by beasts?

Because of you, it comes about that, when my hand draws
the lots, more often than not—for bad, as well as for
good, by misfortune, as well as good fortune—it finds the
wicked rather than the good, the ignorant rather than the
wise, the deceitful rather than the truthful. Why is this?
why? Prudence comes along and throws no more than two
or three names into the urn; Wisdom comes and puts in
no more than four or five; Truth comes and leaves no
more than one, or less, if that were possible. And then,
out of the hundreds of thousands that are poured into the
urn, you expect my hand to draw one of these eight or
nine, rather than one of the eight or nine hundred thousand. Now, it is up to you to change your ways! Virtue,
you let the virtuous outnumber the vicious; Knowledge,
you let the number of wise men be greater than that of
the foolish; Truth, you make sure that you are known
and visible to the greatest number—and there is no doubt
that in such circumstances a greater number of your people than of their opposites would be drawn regularly and

rewarded. Ensure that everyone be just, truthful, wise, and good, and there is no doubt that in such circumstances no rank or honor that I dispense could fall upon liars, the iniquitous, or the mad. (*Spaccio*, pp. 692–93)

Fortune recognizes man's capacity to determine events. If necessity imposes irreversible laws, man's freedom, his capacity potentially to carry out any operation whatsoever, can change the course of things. The possibility follows, from the necessity that the number of those in power be small, that this choice is made in a positive way:

> So, it is hardly my fault but that of your iniquity, if an idler or a rogue becomes a prince or a rich man, because, being cruel with your enlightenment and splendor, you did not remove his roguery or his idleness beforehand, nor do you do it now; and even afterward you do not purge him of his roguish idleness so that such a man may not hold the throne. The mistake is not in there being a prince, but that a rogue becomes a prince. Since princedom and roguery are two separate things, the fault certainly does not lie in the princedom I grant, but in the roguery you allow to continue. . . . Now, it is not possible for a princedom to be granted to everyone; it is not possible for everyone to have the luck of the draw, but it is possible for everyone to be given an equal chance. From this possibility arises the necessity for one of the crowd to be successful, and this does not entail injustice or evil, since it is not possible for there to be more than one. The mistake lies, however, in the fact that he is craven, that he is a rogue, that he is not virtuous; and this wrong is not caused by Fortune, who makes him a prince or a rich

man, but by the goddess Virtue, who does not or did not
make him virtuous. (*Spaccio*, pp. 693–95)

The example of the princedom, apart from dispelling Momus's naive
doubts ("But when everyone would be identical, equal, and similar,
you would be no less iniquitous, because although everyone would
be equally worthy of princedom, you would not make them all
princes, but only one among them"; *Spaccio*, p. 694), clearly marks
the boundary between what *must* be and what *can* be, showing that
man may intervene only in those spaces not ruled by necessity. The
relationship between the necessity of there being only one prince
and the possibility that he might be a rogue or virtuous cannot be
considered in its specific terms, since it translates paradigmatically
the general dialectic between necessity and chance/freedom, which,
from physics to ethics, dominates the entire universe. A complex
universe, where, as Fortune underlines, one must never forget the
governing principle of relativity: "Besides the fact that nothing is
absolutely bad—because the viper is not deadly and venomous to
the viper; nor is the dragon, the lion, the bear to the bear, to the
lion, to the dragon—everything is bad with respect to something
else. Like you, virtuous gods, are considered bad by the corrupt
ones, while the gods of the day and of light are considered bad by
those of the night and darkness; and you consider each other as
good, just as they consider each other as good" (*Spaccio*, p. 686).

The capacity to find a positive way through this labyrinth of
differences once again highlights the dual connotation of asininity,
where the unproductive unidimensionality of negative asses is counterbalanced by the dynamic pluridimensionality of positive asses.
And only the latter are granted the possibility of grabbing "Fortune
by the hair." The apology in defense of toil, as pronounced by
Jupiter, is transformed into an apology in defense of "divine men":
"Pass then, you, goddess Solicitude or Toil; and I want (said Ju-

piter) difficulty to run ahead of you and to flee from you. Drive away Misadventure, grab Fortune by the hair; hasten the turn of its wheel when you deem the moment most opportune; and when things appear just right, drive a nail through it, to halt its progress" (*Spaccio*, p. 713). "Nature," writes Nicola Badaloni, "offers everyone the chance of good fortune. Working in order to seize it is what allows Bruno's 'humanism' to cease being an exaltation of man in purely general terms, and to become rather that of man devoted to a specific task and subject to the changes imposed by fortune. The objective situation is conditioned precisely by this fortune which demands hard work in order for it to be seized and maintained."[2] The turn of the wheel, which had so terrorized medieval man, can therefore be affected by work. The possibility of driving a nail through it neutralizes the image of man as passive in the face of the powers that fight over him, dragging him first upward and then downward. In this instance, too, Bruno originally elaborates a common Renaissance theme. As Cassirer notes,[3] the iconography of the time, in contrast precisely to that of the Middle Ages, replaces the *wheel* with the *sail*, but here man stands beside it and has the helm.

The image of the *asinus ad lyram*, of which I spoke earlier,[4] again reveals its ambiguity. It is Fortune herself who recognizes that "the beauty of music and the excellence of harmony must no longer principally be attributed to the lyre and instrument, but to the skill of the artist who handles it" (*Spaccio*, p. 684).

Hence, which *asinus ad lyram* are we talking about? Certainly not negative asses. Their closed, unidimensional state cannot put to good use an instrument that, by virtue of its different "voices," embodies the variety that continually drives the "course of human life."[5] These ignorant musicians have no possibility of recognizing the harmony of multiplicity. Positive asses, however, are able to obtain quite different results. The lyre does not present them with any problems; indeed, they know how to pluck the strings with assured skill and seek out a sweet sound. As Valeriano states in the *Hieroglyphica*,[6] only those who know how to use reason to find their way through multiplicity may be regarded as perfect musicians.

The harmony of sound depends on reason's ability to recognize harmony in diversity. So it is no accident that, in place of the nine strings of the lyre, Jupiter raises to heaven the nine Muses of knowledge:

> And my wish (if other council members agree) is that, in place of this nine-stringed lyre of his [Mercury's], there should come the venerable mother, Mnemosyne, and her daughters, the nine Muses.—At this all the gods nodded in approbation, and the uplifted goddess gave them thanks, together with her daughters. Arithmetic, the eldest, said she thanked them more times than all the numbers she could think of, and for more thousands of millennia than the intellect could ever imagine through her additions. Geometry thanked them more than all the forms and figures that could be drawn, and all the atoms that could be found in the fantastic resolutions of continuous magnitudes. Music thanked them more than all the harmonies and symphonies that could ever be imagined. Logic thanked them more than all the absurdities of her grammarians, all the false persuasions of her rhetoricians, and all the sophisms and false demonstrations of the dialecticians. Poetry thanked them more than all the feet her bards have used and will come to use in creating the flow of their many verses. Astrology thanked them more than all the stars contained in the immense space of the ethereal region, if one can say more. Physics gave them as many thanks as there can be primary and sec-

ondary principles and elements in the bosom of nature. Metaphysics gave them more thanks than all forms of ideas and types of outcomes and efficient causes upon natural effects, both as regards the reality of things and as regards the concepts that represent them. Ethics gave them as many thanks as there can be customs, habits, laws, forms of justice and crimes in this and every other world of the universe. (*Spaccio*, pp. 701–2)

The harmony of knowledge is attained by the balanced use of all the instruments of knowing. Arithmetic, Geometry, Music, Logic, Poetry, Astrology, Physics, Metaphysics, and Ethics, more than just representing the specific nature of every field of inquiry, are often the only means of finding a way through the complex universe of knowledge. In the hands of negative asses the lyre can only become "the instrument of charlatans"; and this is why, in the celestial reform, the father of the gods wanted metaphorically to substitute its strings:

'Now, what decision will be taken regarding my lyre?' said Mercury. To which Momus replied, 'You keep it for your own amusement, to pass the time when you are on a boat or staying at an inn. Or if you choose to make a present of it, by giving it to someone who deserves it most of all, and you do not wish to go too far to find him, then get to Naples, to the Piazza de l'Olmo, or to Venice, to Saint Mark's Square, around eventide, since the coryphaei of those who go on stage come to these two places, and there you will be able find the one who *iure meriti* [deserves it most].' Mercury asked, 'Why one of these rather than anyone else?' Momus replied, 'Because these days the lyre has principally become the instrument of charlatans, used to capture and keep hold of an audience, the better to sell

their pills and potions, just as the small rebec has become
the instrument of blind beggars.' (*Spaccio*, pp. 700–701)

The metaphor of substitution expresses the hope for change. Together with the lyre of the "charlatans," "Ignorance, Inertia, and
Bestiality" are cast down; the nine Muses are raised up to replace
strings no longer in use: "Where the nine-stringed lyre is to be seen,
the Muse-mother ascends with her nine daughters . . . ; Ignorance,
Inertia, and Bestiality fall as a consequence" (*Spaccio*, p. 563).
Bruno again unequivocally sets out the qualities of negative asses,
still keeping within a particular set of connotations: "Ignorance,
Inertia, and Bestiality" are the common thread that runs through
this ideology of unproductive stasis.

A brief digression will prove useful in highlighting yet another element that forges the link between the ass and fortune:
the necessity of change, the perennial vicissitude of everything.
In Sebastian Brant's *Narrenschiff* (1494), we find a xylograph,
possibly by Dürer,[8] that shows a wheel being turned, with the
aid of a stick, by an outstretched hand in the top left-hand corner. There are three figures at three of the wheel's cardinal
points: in the west, there is an ass's head with a man's legs; in
the south, a whole ass; and in the east, a man's head, looking
downward and wearing a fool's cap, with the hind legs of an
ass.[9] The wheel turns from west to east. The engraving appears
at least twice in the poem: the first, in connection with the theme
of fortune (*De fortunae mutabilitate*), and the second, linked to
the theme of the precariousness of kingdoms (*De secularis poten-
tiae exitu*).[10] In both cases, every principle of eternal stability is
rejected; rather, the only possible form of stability is constant
change. The destiny of human events and the destiny of kingdoms seem to be linked to the perennial cycles of nature: generation and corruption (but also, *climax* and *anticlimax*,

ascensus and *descensus, augmentum* and *declinatio*) are posited as the general model for change in everything.[11]

The ass, the wheel, and fortune appear once again in another xylograph to be found in the German translation of Petrarch's *De remediis utriusque Fortunae* (1532).[12] This time, it is fortune herself, in her usual guise of a blindfolded woman, who directly turns the handle that moves the wheel. Once more we find three figures at three of the wheel's cardinal points: in the east, there is the torso and head of a man, looking upward, with the hind legs of an ass; in the south, is the head of an ass wearing a crown and its front legs holding a scepter, with the torso and legs of a man; and in the west, a whole ass looks downward. The wheel turns from east to west in contrast to the wheel depicted in the *Narrenschiff*. The xylograph is linked to Dialogue XC of Book One, significantly entitled *De tranquillo statu*. Here, Pleasure and Reason discuss the theme of toil and death. Although the first interlocutor, having worked so much, thinks it is right to bring an end to toil, the second invites him to renounce the dangerous condition of stasis, which is poorly reconciled with the perpetual movement of fortune and nature:

Pleasure. Since things are suitably arranged, I am tranquil.

Reason. Obviously, because like your ship upon the ocean waves, your spirit, upon the worries of life, reaches the port of toil and terror. But it is not so; it is now that you have most to fear. You fail to see that the things of men are never at rest, that whoever sits at the top of the moving wheel, is on the verge of ruin.

Pleasure. Everything moves as I wish it to.

Reason. You have spoken well; everything moves, because nothing stays at rest.[13]

Apart from the numerous possible meanings inherent in the xylographs under discussion—including those stemming from the content of the texts to which they are tied—what is clearly evident is the strict symbolic relationship between the change brought about by the wheel and the metamorphosis represented by the asinine figures. As we have seen, this is a theme that recurs frequently in Bruno's dialogues. However, he does not concentrate on the negative aspects of the wheel (since the turn of the wheel can, of course, be determined by Toil), but is drawn, rather, to the necessity of change. The vicissitude of metamorphosis is a perfect example of the vicissitude of all that exists: "Now this change and vicissitude are represented by the wheel of metamorphosis, where the man sits at the top and a beast at the bottom, a half-man, half-beast descends from the left, and a half-beast, half-man ascends from the right" (*Eroici*, p. 1003). The turn of the wheel serves to illustrate a dynamic relationship with reality, where only by rejecting stasis will it be possible to seize the "opportunity"[14] at the right moment and be ready to "grab Fortune by the hair."

CHAPTER 9

In the Labyrinth of Truth

The opposition between negative and positive asses may also be found in the context of the search for truth. Bruno grants positive asses the possibility of embarking on the adventure of knowledge through the use of reason: "Others move themselves to the contemplation of truth by way of doctrine and rational cognition, through the strength of the agent intellect which penetrates the mind and excites its inner light. But these are rare, as the poet says: *Pauci quos ardens evexit ad aethera virtus* [Few are those whose ardent virtue elevates them to the ether; Virgil, *Aeneid* VI. 129–30]" (*Cabala*, p. 874). The pattern does not change in the *Eroici furori*, wherein Bruno presents exactly the same dichotomy in his specific analysis of different types of "frenzy":

> Several types of frenzy are supposed to and do exist, all of which fall into one of two categories. Some express nothing more than blindness, stupidity, and irrational impulse, leading to untamed savagery. . . . Others, used to or adept at contemplation, and naturally possessed of a lucid and intellectual mind, spurred on by an internal stimulus and spontaneous fervor induced by love of the divine, of justice, of truth, of glory, and by a burning desire and strength of purpose, are able to sharpen their senses; and, inspired by their cogitative faculties, they kindle the light of reason, which allows them to see more than is usual. Such people, in the end, come to

speak and act not as receptacles and instruments, but as principal authors and efficient causes. (*Eroici*, pp. 986–87)

Bruno also recognizes the possibility that some people, being "the repository of gods and divine spirits, say and do admirable things, without them or others knowing the reason why" (*Eroici*, p. 986). Such people, lacking any "reason and sense of their own," are favored by grace, so that "the world may be sure that since they clearly do not speak from their own knowledge and experience, it must follow that their words and actions are guided by a superior intelligence" (*Eroici*, p. 986). But, of these two positions, one divinely inspired and the other laboriously sought by one's own reason, Bruno does not hesitate to consider the second as the only dignified way man has of attaining divinity: "The first have more dignity, power, and efficacy within themselves, because they have been granted divinity; the second are more worthy, more powerful, and effective, and are divine. The first are worthy, like the ass that bears the sacraments; the second, like a thing that is sacred. In the first, one considers and sees divinity itself, and this is admired, adored, and obeyed; in the second, one considers and sees the excellence of one's own humanity" (*Eroici*, p. 987). Bruno does not accord to assess who bear mysteries the same depth as he does to positive asses, in whom "one considers and sees the excellence of one's own humanity." Indeed, while the first bear "the sacraments," "the second are more worthy, more powerful, and effective, and are divine"; to all intents and purposes they are "like a thing that is sacred." The image of the *asinus portans mysteria*, which has its roots in the ancient custom of using the ass as the vehicle for divinities associated with mysteries (Dionysus, Isis, and Cybele),[1] finds an echo also in anticlerical satire. In *The Faerie Queene*,

Spenser makes fun of priests who claimed to be "the sacred" and not merely "bearers of the sacred."[2]

Bruno, therefore, concentrates his attention on those who, in seeking knowledge, manifest "the excellence of their own humanity." Simply by reversing Saulino's statement, we can see where the path to truth lies: "Given that the human intellect has some sort of access to the truth, such access, if not granted by science and cognition, must necessarily be granted by ignorance and asininity" (*Cabala*, p. 901). Indeed, it is Saulino himself who reminds us that "nothing stands closer to truth than science" (*Cabala*, p. 872). But we also find, together with science, Sophia:

> 'So be it,' added the gods; 'but let his [Cepheus's] place be taken by Sophia, because the poor thing must also enjoy the fruits and fortunes of Truth, her inseparable companion, with whom she has always shared her worries, calamities, pains, and toils. Besides, if she does not administer them with her, I know not how she will ever be welcomed and honored.' 'Most willingly,' said Jupiter, 'it is granted and I give my consent, O Gods. Order and reason demand it; and, most of all, it would have been a mistake if I had allocated her a place by herself without the other, where she could not have been happy, far from her much-loved sister and dear companion.' (*Spaccio*, pp. 620–21)

Reason, science, and Sophia are the only means for traveling the hard road of knowledge. One must not forget, however, that truth "loves the company of a few and wise men, she hates the multitude, she does not show herself to those who do not seek her for her own sake, and she does not want to be revealed to those who do not open up to her with humility" (*Spaccio*, pp. 647–48), and that the search for her costs "time, debate, study, and toil" (*Eroici*, p. 1157).

Again, the qualities of positive asininity take center stage, as humility and toil become indispensable assets for obtaining good results. The quest for truth requires perseverance, because truth does not reside in easily accessible places:

> It is necessary, therefore, for the human soul to be endowed with light, ingenuity and the right instruments with which to catch her. Here contemplation comes to the rescue, and logic—a most suitable organ for the tracking down of truth—comes into play in order to distinguish, find, and judge. So the forest is scoured for the things of nature, where many objects are under shadow and cloak; and in the thickness, denseness, and desert of her solitude, truth finds shelter in caves and caverns bristling with thorns, covered over by coarse, wooded, and thick-leaved bushes, where, for the worthiest and most excellent of reasons, she takes the greatest care to hide, cover, and immerse herself—just as we wish to conceal our greatest treasures with the utmost care and attention—so that she may not be discovered by her many and varied pursuers (some of whom have greater talent and expertise, others less) without great difficulty. (*Eroici*, pp. 1121–22)

In Bruno's mind, the twisting paths of truth are equated with his own tortuous existential experience, wherein pain, toil, and exile were the price he had to pay on the journey toward the "domus sapientiae":

> I have come, among others, spurred on by the desire to see the seat of wisdom [*domus sapientiae*], burning with the desire to contemplate this Palace. To do this, I am not ashamed to say that I experienced poverty, envy, and

hatred, the execrations and ingratitude of those whom I wanted to help and actually did so, the sign of extreme barbarism and an absolutely sordid avarice. From these people, who owed me love, service, and honor, I received only reproach, calumny, injury, and even infamy. I am not ashamed of having been subjected to derision and scorn by ignoble and stupid people, the type of people who, while really being animals, are full of pride as a result of a reckless arrogance, are adorned and blessed with the image and appearance of men, and to do this, I am not ashamed of having suffered toil, pain, and exile, because my toil has allowed me to progress, my pain has afforded me experience, and my exile has allowed me to learn; because in brief toil I felt prolonged repose, in mild pain immense joy, and in short exile a boundless homeland. (*Opp. lat.*, I, I, pp. 21–22)

This important passage in the *Oratio valedictoria* clearly underlines Bruno's position: "to do this, I am not ashamed of having suffered toil, pain, and exile." Not everyone is capable of embarking upon the search for truth. It can only be done by those positive assess who, like Bruno, can bear the *burden* of difficulties this search imposes: "because this burden [the acquisition of truth] is not made for the shoulders of just anyone, but for those able to bear it, like the Nolan" (*Cena*, p. 36). But it must be remembered that thanks to the technique of concealment, insults from negative asses can be avoided; therefore the holders of truth must not "communicate it to all sorts of people if, as they say, they do not want to wash the ass's head, see what swine do with pearls, or allow the fruit of their study and toil to produce rash and foolish ignorance, along with presumption and barbarity, its perpetual and faithful companions" (*Cena*, pp. 36–37).

The necessary talents and the trials to be overcome are many, the most important thing being not so much "winning the prize," but not dying as "a coward and a loafer":

Common and easy things are for the vulgar and common people; exceptional, heroic, and divine men take the path of difficulty so that necessity has no choice but to grant them the palm of immortality. What is more, even if it is ultimately not possible to win the prize, keep on running and concentrate your efforts on something of such importance, and keep going until your final breath. Not only winners are praised, but also those who do not die as a coward and a loafer, since they blame fate for their defeat and death, and they show the world that it was not any fault of theirs, but that of fortune that they have met such an end. Not only he who deserved the prize is worthy of honor, but also everyone who has run well, who is also judged worthy and sufficient to have deserved it, despite not having won it. And shame on those who, halfway through their career, stop in desperation and, even though they are last, do not go to the end with that breath and vigor of which they are still capable. Make room, therefore, for perseverance, because if toil is great, the reward shall not be negligible. (*Cena*, pp. 63–64)

Along with Humility, Toil, and Perseverance, Tolerance makes up the final element in the list of qualities that characterize positive asses. Bruno's carefully constructed position would collapse in its entirety if truth could not be sought along different trajectories. The complexities of the universe cannot be investigated from the point of view of a single philosophical system. Many paths can lead to "the cognition of natural things":

However, it does not appear to me that any philosophy is worthy of rejection, especially when, irrespective of its basic principles or the type of construction it proposes, it involves the perfection of speculative science and the cognition of natural things, a perspective actually achieved by many of the most ancient philosophers. Since it is the stuff of ambition, of a presumptuous, vain, and envious mind, to want to persuade others that there is but one way to investigate and attain the cognition of nature; and it is the stuff of madness and of a man without argument to believe this oneself. Although the most constant and solid way, the most contemplative and distinct way, and the highest form of considering things must always be most preferred, honored, and attained, one must not condemn another way that itself produces no shortage of good fruits, albeit from another tree. (*Causa*, p. 275)

But is there any limit to the search for truth? Does it ever come to an end? In the *De immenso*, Bruno does not hesitate in giving an answer to these questions:

In fact, every time we judge that there is still some truth to be known, as long as we judge that there is still some good to be gained, we always look for a new [truth], we always desire another [good thing]. So, there will never be an end to our quest and to our desire for an ultimate truth or for the limits of good things. Each and every one of us has an inborn appetite for all things: man desires that everything that exists for a time should exist forever, that what is seen somewhere be seen everywhere, that what one owns be possessed by all, that what is partially used be used entirely; as if it were possible for him to dominate everything, he still seeks what nevertheless

dominates him; he is not happy with what he has obtained
as long as there is still something left to acquire. Similarly,
particle matter, whether corporeal or incorporeal, is
never satisfied, and although it has received particular
forms throughout eternity, it nevertheless eternally desires to receive others, because it is never satisfied. (*Opp.
lat.*, I, I, pp. 203–4)

For Bruno, truth appears to coincide with the search itself for
truth. The constant human tension toward totality is what triggers
the mechanism of the quest: "there will never be an end to our
quest and to our desire for an ultimate truth or for the limits of
good things." The image of man who "desires that everything that
exists for a time should exist forever, that what is seen somewhere
be seen everywhere, that what one owns be possessed by all" unequivocally expresses his existential vicissitude in a universe where
there is always some new knowledge to be gained ("as long as there
is still something left to acquire"). Humanity's destiny appears to
be very close to that of matter, which "is never satisfied, and although it has received particular forms throughout eternity, it nevertheless eternally desires to receive others, because it is never
satisfied." Matter's unsatisfied search for new forms is equivalent
to humanity's unsatisfied search for truth. Physics, ethics, and
knowledge move within a reality ruled by a continual dynamism.
Dissatisfaction, in its positive sense of inexhaustible activity, is contrasted to satiety and the closed world of stasis:

So it is that nobody is satisfied with his condition, apart
from lunatics or fools, who feel all the more satisfied when
they find themselves at the peak of the dark phase of their
madness, where they have little or no awareness of their
negative state; they enjoy the present without fearing for
the future, they rejoice in what they are in the condition

> they are in, and have no regrets or cares for what they
> are or could be; in short, they have no sense of contra-
> riety, which is represented by the tree of science of good
> and evil. (*Eroici*, p. 975)

The condition of satiety recalls the ideology of negative asses:
"From this we can see that ignorance is the mother of sensual
happiness and contentment, which is also the garden of the paradise of animals, as is made clear in the *Cabala del cavallo pegaseo*" (*Eroici*, p. 975). For these people knowledge means
common belief ("vulgata fides"), and so they use any means to
attack nature, reason, and the senses ("Naturae indicto, rationi
ac sensibus, acri"):

> So they have decided to remain enclosed within them-
> > selves
> And not to run and touch any doubtful limits,
> Or an uncertain goal, even if this is the best thing to do.
> None among them has decided to use their powers as
> > much
> As possible and to push themselves over their limits;
> As if they have no judgment and reason.
> Whoever lacks judgment must live with the multitude
> > since
> He is judged unworthy of living with the few.
> Take a shepherd, marked by fortune,
> Safely follow the sheep-tracks of your own kind.
> May the empty fox's den not please you, my friend,
> Do not slip into the hidden lairs of deer,
> Do not dare to sleep in the den of the mild lion,
> Unhappy me, because you are not of higher birth,
> Because you are ignorant, made defenseless by your jaws,
> > your fingers, and your mouth; . . .

Be content, therefore, with little, as if this were everything;
Because you are rich enough, since you are unaware of
your poverty;
And in good health, since you are unaware of your sick-
ness.

(Opp. lat., I, II, pp. 242–43)

Becoming enclosed within oneself means being happy with very little, since one believes that this is everything. Such unidimensionality removes any possibility of raising oneself above the condition of negative bestiality. The process of becoming divine can only be undergone by positive asses, who are ready to pursue the difficult search: "It is enough that everyone join the race, that everyone do what they can; because the heroic intelligence would rather fall or fail with dignity and in the pursuit of high goals, which reveals the dignity of his intelligence, than to attain perfection in less noble and low things" (*Eroici,* p. 999). For humanity, the search for truth involves living in perfect harmony with the laws of becoming, since its existential course encapsulates the course of the entire universe. "Mental experience," states Badaloni in this regard, "runs parallel to that of the changing reality of things. It is far from unimportant that up to the *De monade,* the *De minimo* and the *De immenso,* Bruno's thought concentrated on discovering the unity of the atom by intellectual means, thereby confirming the materialistic nature of intellectual contemplation itself."[3] The multiplicity of forms and their continual decomposition into atoms prove that the eternal does not exist and offers a model of knowledge wherein truth becomes the fruit of the inexhaustible process of knowing. The only eternal truth lies in the constancy of everything, in the eternal nature of matter, which, beyond its infinite aggregations and decompositions, is preserved in the indestructible unity of the atom.

Without a rational awareness of this dialectical process, which involves the infinite mutability and constancy of everything, it is not possible to contemplate the bare bones of nature. The experience of Actaeon is a positive *exemplum* of the search for truth: "Thus Actaeon, with these thoughts, these dogs that sought goodness, wisdom, beauty, the sylvan wild beast outside themselves, and in that way he caught up with it, enraptured by such great beauty, he himself became the prey, seeing himself turn into what he was chasing; and he noticed that in the eyes of his dogs, in his thoughts, he became the coveted prey, for, having already assumed divinity within himself, there was no need to look for it on the outside" (*Eroici*, p. 1008). Actaeon discovers the presence of divinity within himself, and precisely when he comes to contemplate it he becomes divine; when, after so much difficult searching, he manages to harmonize with it:

> And so we see Actaeon, pursued by his own dogs, persecuted by his own thoughts, running and forging a new path. His strength is renewed to proceed divinely and with lighter steps (that is, with greater ease and a more effective vigor) into denser thickets, into deserts, into the region of incomprehensibility. From the vulgar and common man that he was, he becomes exceptional and heroic, with fine manners and thoughts, and he leads an extraordinary life. Here his many big dogs put him to death; here ends his life in the eyes of the mad and sensual world of blindness and illusion, and he begins to live on the plane of the intellect; he lives the life of gods, feeds on ambrosia and becomes drunk on nectar. (*Eroici*, pp. 1008–9)

Actaeon's adventure, on which many Bruno scholars have dwelt,[4] is given substance by his entry "into denser thickets, into deserts, into the region of incomprehensibility" and concludes in his contemplation of nature. Diana appears to Actaeon in her objective form; and in her particular guise of infinite mutability,[5] she reveals herself to be what is constant in everything. Through the use of reason, divine man can attain the intellectual life and understand the dialectical relationship between the one and the many. Understanding nature, being in harmony with it, renders men divine, and thus the process of acquiring knowledge is identified with that of becoming divine. "Taking possession of the cognitive object has transformed the subject seeking to know it, since knowing is not a seeing without desire, and once the object of the amorous enterprise is attained, one can never be the same again. Truth has entered us and we we are inside truth. This possession of truth by 'contracting' it into ourselves means that divinity, which, as natural beings, is always within us, has been rendered explicit and manifest precisely by the pursuit of the object of knowledge."[6] Divinity manifests itself throughout the natural universe, where ideas and matter become different natural modalities of being. Unlike Cusanus,[7] Bruno closes the gap between divinity and the world, since God comes to be identified with matter that produces everything and with nature that gives life to all things.[8]

It is easy, within this context, to understand the special regard Bruno has for the particular, for what is local, for every single atomic particle, which has its own history and course. Positive asses, who live in harmony with the laws of nature, will have no difficulty in recognizing this diffuse natural divinity, even in "the smallest trifles." It is appropriate at this point to take a look at some of the greatest passages in the *Spaccio*, where, by order of Jupiter, Mercury descends to earth to look after all "that must be provided for on earth":

He [Jupiter] decreed that today at midday two of the
many melons in Franzino's field should ripen; but that
they should not be picked for another three days, by
which time they will no longer be regarded as fit to eat.
He wishes that at the same time on the jujube tree, which
lies at the foot of Mount Cicala, in the house of Gioan
Bruno, thirty jujubes be perfectly ripe, seventeen be
shaken off and fall to the ground, and fifteen be worm-
eaten. That Vasta, the wife of Albenzio, while wanting to
frizz the hair around her temples, should overheat the
iron causing fifty-seven of them to be burned; but that she
should not burn her head and, just this once, not blas-
pheme when the smell hits her and that with a little patience it should pass. . . . When Laurenza is combing her
hair, let seventeen hairs fall out, thirteen break, and of
these, let ten grow back within three days and the other
seven not at all. Let Antonio Savolino's bitch conceive five
puppies, of which three will live when the time comes and
two will be thrown away; and of the three, let the first
look like its mother, the second be mottled, and the third
look partly like its father and partly like Polidoro's
dog. . . . Let the skirt that Master Danese is cutting on
his table be torn in two. Let twelve bedbugs emerge from
the boards of Constantino's bed and let them make their
way to the bolster: seven of the biggest, four of the smallest, and one in between; and what shall become of them
will be discussed this evening by candlelight. At fifteen
minutes past the same hour, due to movement of the
tongue, which she has rolled around her palate four
times, let Fiurulo's old woman lose the third molar in her
lower right jaw; let this happen without bleeding or pain,
since the said molar has served its time, having lasted

through exactly seventeen annual revolutions of the moon. With the hundred and twelfth thrust, let Ambruoggio release and finish doing the business with his wife; may he not make her pregnant this time, but the next, with the seed that is being formed from the boiled leek he is eating now with gravy and millet bread. Let the hairs of puberty begin to grow on the chest of Martinello's son, and, at the same time, let his voice begin to break. (*Spaccio*, pp. 633–36)[9]

This comic description of everyday life, wherein Bruno recalls the places and people of his youth, underlines the need to dwell on "the smallest trifles," on things that might appear wholly superfluous. Bruno insists on the need to use a microscope when watching human life as it flows through the particular preoccupations of each protagonist. Shifting one's attention to the various characters (be they human, plant, or animal) necessarily involves a change of perspective, as one immerses oneself in the specific universe of each micro-history. In short, Mercury's intervention gives Bruno the opportunity to show how each thing, be it large or small, forms part of the whole. Bruno destroys every hierarchy and false value-judgment that threaten to annul difference and overlook the life pulsating even in beings invisible to the human eye. Mercury, in fact, replies thus to Sophia's perplexity:

But you are kidding yourself, Sophia, if you think that the least things are not taken care of just as much as the principal ones, for the greatest and most principal of things are worthless without the least and most abject ones. Everything, therefore, however small, is under the wing of infinitely great providence; the smallest trifle, however insignificant, is of the greatest importance in the order of the whole and of the universe; for large things are made up of small ones, and small ones of smaller ones, and these are made up of individual and minimal ones. This is how I am able to understand the great substances, as well as the great efficacies and effects. (*Spaccio*, p. 643)

Isis, too, in defending the religion of the Egyptians, who worshiped divinity in nature (animals, plants, rocks), responds by describing the natural common structure of existence:

And they [the defamers of the Egyptian religion] do not consider that divinity reveals itself in all things; though for universal and superior purposes it reveals itself in great things and general principles; and for purposes that are close at hand, useful, and necessary to the various actions of human life, it is found and seen in the most abject of things, yet, for the reasons given, divinity is concealed in everything; for divinity makes itself clear and communicates right down to the least and, among these, according to their capacity; without its presence nothing would have being, for it is the essence of being of the first to the very last. (*Spaccio*, pp. 786–87)

Franzino's melons, Antonio Savolino's bitch, the bugs from Constantino's bed, the molar of Fiurulo's old woman, "the hairs of puberty" of Martinello's son are different forms of the *explicatio* of the world of nature. The destiny of all that exists is ruled by the same necessity, which, in every species, makes itself clear at different times and in different ways:

In all things, the most general and most appropriate image is the development of human life, because all things have a feeble beginning, a period of growth, a point of balance, a decline, and death. But among these things some are made in such a way that they die and dissipate at birth or while growing. On the other hand, others live through every stage of life; some, like certain species, live through every stage of life in just a few years, while others take longer; thus, dogs age quicker than horses, horses quicker than humans, and humans quicker than deer. (*Opp. lat.*, II, III, pp. 107–8)

As we have seen in Fortune's discourse, Bruno's idea of necessity does not annul contingency and variability. "The vicissitudinal order of the universe," Papi observes, "is therefore regulated by an internal necessity; however, this order refers to natural events, to the birth and the death of all living things, to the perpetual appearance and disappearance of living forms within the framework of nature identifying with itself, in which the multiplicity reverts to its basic form. At its highest level, philosophy is the understanding of this essential unity."[10] Within this multiplicity of different times and different ways that control the birth and the death of every cluster of atoms, even magic can be used to foresee the outcome of things, to recognize relationships of sympathy and antipathy, to explain the recurrence of certain events; in short, to return the different forms of individual behavior to a natural order. Badaloni believes that "magic, basically, is the possibility we can acquire of foreseeing and governing the passages that occur from one species to another in the process of becoming entities. For this reason it presents itself as a knowledge of the general behavior of things, and thus, given a particular case, this can be reconsidered in light of the normal behavior of nature."[11]

The only possibility of finding one's position in this storm-racked ocean is by recognizing the dialectical relationship between singularity and multiplicity, between necessity and liberty. Perhaps this is the only eternal truth, a truth that Bruno situates in the place of Ursa Major, as a sure guide for those "who go erring about this tempestuous sea of errors":

> Let her [Ursa Major] go where she will, as long as she is free and vacates that place where, since it is the most eminent seat, I want Truth to reside; because there the claws of slander do not reach, the malice of envy does not poison, the darkness of error does not deepen. There she will stay fixed and firm; there she will not be buffetted by swells and storms; there she will be the sure guide of those who go erring about this sea of errors; and there she will show herself to be a lucid and clear mirror of contemplation. (*Spaccio*, p. 618)

Science and philosophy are defined according to their statute of stability. Amid the swirling waters, in the fluidity of a constantly restless universe, knowledge is the only beacon that can show us a path to safety.

Erring, in the sense both of "moving hither and thither without a precise goal" and of "far from the truth," finds its fixed point in the knowledge of the laws of nature. Bruno's drowning man recalls Lucretius's ("It is sweet, when upon the great sea the winds stir up the waves, / to watch from dry land the great efforts of another"): for both authors, dry land represents those places fortified by science ("But nothing is sweeter than to occupy the high places fortified by the clear science of the wise").[12] Those who grope blindly in the darkness of ignorance, dragged by the vortex of the waves, are counterbalanced by those who are divine and able to find in knowledge the sure guide that saves them from the turbulence of the multiplicity. Badaloni notes that "the only way left for the individual to affirm his freedom remains the Epicurean one, which is based on intellectual elevation and on the ethical integrity of the wise man."[13] All this involves a paradox. The condition of negative asses, foundering in "the sea of errors," corresponds to the vision of a finite universe and of a closed science; the stable condition of positive asses, who are guided by the knowledge of the laws of nature, corresponds to the vision of an infinite universe and of an open science. If the dynamic search for knowledge can lead us safely to shore, then unproductive inaction condemns us to being swallowed up by the storm.

CHAPTER 10

From Orion to Chiron:
Opposing Images of the Religious Cult

There remains one aspect that needs clarifying and that merits particular attention. In the closing pages of the *Spaccio*, Jupiter assigns "a celestial seat" to the centaur Chiron, thereby reaffirming the importance of religion:

> Having myself pronounced all kinds of things against Chiron, I now take them all back; and I declare that Chiron the centaur—a most just man who at one time lived on Mount Pelion, where he taught medicine to Asclepius, astrology to Hercules, and the cithara to Achilles, curing the sick, and explaining how to reach the stars, how to attach resonant strings to wood and how to pluck them— does not seem to me unworthy of heaven. Indeed, I deem him most worthy of it, because in this celestial temple, by this altar he serves, there is no other priest but him; and you can see him holding that sacrificial animal, and carrying on his belt a flask for libations. And since the altar, the fanon, and the oratory are indispensable, and all this would be useless without the officiant, therefore may he live, remain, and stay there forever, unless fate determines otherwise. (*Spaccio*, p. 825)

Despite not having expressed a positive judgment on Chiron at the beginning of the council,[1] in the end the father of the gods recognizes the necessary importance of the "fanon," the "altar," and the "oratory." Momus's irony clearly highlights the close relationship between Chiron and Christ, both of whom possess a dual nature:

> Now, what shall we do with this man enclosed within an animal, or with this animal imprisoned within a man, where one person is composed of two natures, and two substances come together in a hypostatic union? Here two things unite to make a third entity; and of this there is no doubt at all. But here lies the difficulty: whether this third entity is a better thing than the one or the other, or than one of the two parts, or whether it is worse. What I mean to say is: does the union of a human being and a horse produce a deity worthy of a celestial seat or an animal worthy only of the herd and the stable? In the end (whatever Isis, Jupiter, and the others may have said about the excellence of being an animal, and that, to become divine, man should possess animal qualities, and, in wanting to show himself to be highly divine, he should reckon to reveal the animal in equal measure), I shall never be able to believe that a being which is neither a complete and perfect man nor a perfect and complete animal, but part animal and part man, could be any better than if a piece of trouser were stitched to a piece of coat, since there is no better garment than a coat or a pair of trousers, nor anything as good as this one or that one. (*Spaccio*, pp. 823–24)

Bruno highlights a clear opposition. The positive image of Christ-Chiron (a symbol of the pluridimensionality of religion) is followed by the negative image of Christ-Orion (a symbol of the unidimensionality of religion). In the culture of the centaur, religion regains its natural dimension of elasticity. If Momus's invective attacks the mystery of Christ's dual nature, it does not neutralize, however, the positive value of Chiron's particular physical makeup. Jupiter's disagreement with Momus's position (" 'Momus, Momus,' replied Jupiter, 'the mystery of this thing is secret and great, and you cannot understand it; but, since it is something superior and great, you must simply believe it' "; *Spaccio*, p. 824) is not an end in itself, but the necessary consequence of a choice based on the ideology of change. The mystery of the centaur embodies the possibility of metamorphosis, since it is no longer a condition of strict uniformity, but a dual nature that points to the positive path of transformation.

If humanity, moving from its bestial nature, has to elevate itself to divinity, by the same token the gods, too, moving from their divine state, must know that "whoever is unable to become an animal cannot remain superior": "I can say nothing about Capricorn [states Jupiter], since he seems to me most worthy of gaining heaven by having been of great benefit to it in teaching us the means with which to defeat the Python; because it was necessary for the gods to transform themselves into animals, if they wished to have glory in that war. And he also taught us that whoever is unable to become an animal cannot remain superior" (*Spaccio*, p. 602). Metamorphosis is the only guarantee of victory. Those unable to traverse the boundaries between opposites cannot understand the transformations of reality and so adapt to them. Religion cannot enclose itself within an abstract world, but must test itself against change and keep in step with the times. Bruno attacks the degenerate aspects of cults,[2] but recognizes the importance of religion as a form of education.[3] To all intents and purposes, it must be at the service of the state and of "civil conversation"; in other words, it must subject itself to political power, so that a balanced and just society can be achieved:

[Judgment] should allow statues to be erected not to
idlers, to the enemies of the state of republicans who,
scorning morals and human life, offer us words and
dreams, but to those who build temples to the gods, who
exalt the cult and the zeal for such a law and religion that
ignite the magnanimity and ardor of that glory which
comes from serving one's country and being of use to humanity; whence are instituted universities dedicated to
the teaching of morals, letters, and arms. Refrain from
promising love, honor, and the reward of eternal life and
immortality to those who sanction pedants and speakers
of parables; but promise them to those who please the
gods by striving toward perfecting their intellect and that
of others, toward serving the community, and toward res-
olutely observing magnanimity, justice, and compassion
in their every deed. (*Spaccio*, p. 659)

Bruno regards the experience of the "Roman people" as a positive
exemplum of such a state of affairs, wherein the laws of the state
and those of religion merge in order to encourage the progress of
civilization:

Who [the gods] for this reason praised the Roman people
above all others, since by their magnificent gestures, more
than any other nation, they knew how to conform and
resemble them, forgiving the humble, subduing the
proud, remitting wrongs, not forgetting favors, helping
the needy, defending the afflicted, freeing the oppressed,
restraining the violent, encouraging the worthy, humbling
the wrongdoers, striking terror into the latter and exter-
minating them to the last with scourges and hatchets while
the former are accorded honor and glory with statues and
colossi. Consequently, this people appeared the most re-

strained and the least tempted by the vices of the unciv-
ilized and the barbarous, and the most refined and given
to generous undertakings than has ever been seen in others. And while their law and religion was such, such were
their customs and manners, such was their honor and
their happiness. (*Spaccio*, pp. 659–60)

Papi notes that "for Bruno 'civilization' has a single course, running from Egypt to Greece to Rome, through to the possibilities of
reform that he senses in his own time. The historical course of barbarism runs from Aristotle in philosophy, to 'paradoxical' Christianity in religion, with Protestantism being the darkness and
'neo-barbarism' of his own time.'"[4] Within this context, Bruno sees
Henry III of Valois as a possible continuator of the ancient civilization. Immediately after Chiron's celestial seat is assigned, there
follows the eulogy of the king of France:

> Then Apollo asked: 'What shall become of that Tiara?
> what is in store for that Crown? what shall we do with it?'
> 'This one, this crown,' replied Jupiter, 'is the one which,
> not without fate's great provision, not without the instinct
> of divine spirit, and not without the highest merit, awaits
> the most indomitable Henry the Third, king of magnani-
> mous, powerful, and combative France. He who after this
> one and that of Poland, looks forward, as he proved at
> the beginning of his reign, when he ordered that most
> celebrated enterprise to which, by integrating the two
> lower crowns into another more eminent and beautiful
> one, there would be added, as its heart, the motto: *Tertia
> coelo manet.*' (*Spaccio*, p. 826)

The dual nature of Bruno's centaur expresses a new concept of the
Church, where political power and the religious system come to-

gether in the scheme of a catholicizing monarchy, sustained by Henry III of Valois. The motto *Tertia coelo manet*,[5] apart from responding to the calls for peace in a Europe torn apart by religious wars, supports humanity's mission to correct society's imbalances. "Civil conversation" can be maintained only through the rehabilitation of the religious system and the issuing of prudent laws:

> Since the gods are removed from all passion, their anger and pleasure are purely active, and not passive; and for this reason they do not threaten punishment or promise reward for their own wrongs or good deeds, but for what is committed among peoples and in civil conversation, to whose aid they have come with their divine laws, finding human laws and statutes insufficient. Consequently, it is wrong, foolish, profane, and blameworthy to think that the gods demand humanity's reverence, fear, love, worship, and respect for any other reason or benefit than that of humanity itself; seeing that they are most glorious in themselves, and that no further glory could be given to them from elsewhere, they have made laws not to obtain glory, but to pass on glory to humanity. (*Spaccio*, pp. 656–57)

In Bruno's view, the efficacy of religion is measured purely in terms of achieving objectives; the Egyptian, Roman, or Catholic religions in themselves do not possess any element that makes one better than the other, but their superiority is gauged by their contribution to the preservation of the political community. In the great variety of nations and cultures that populate the world, the different religious traditions must be respected and judged purely in light of their moral objectives. Badaloni writes, "The fact that Bruno should have become a Calvinist in Switzerland, 'politically' pro-Catholic in France, and a Lutheran in Germany basically shows his profound disinterest in the single solutions of dogmatic religion. Bruno accepts as a matter of fact the existence of particular creeds within certain countries, and submits to them without hesitation.''[6] Bruno's religious tolerance is the expression of his deeply held conviction that no religion is philosophically true.[7] Religious peace permits political power (in its various forms: monarchy in France and England, republic in Venice) to deal with the problems that unsettle society, but, above all, it permits philosophers, who are far removed from the dogma of faith, to live in a climate of freedom of thought.

Bruno is aware of the profound transformations sweeping the nations of Europe; and he knows full well that the passage from nature to civilization involves certain contradictions. The path of positive asininity, necessary to lift oneself out of the state of bestiality, also involves negative elements, which, in her oration against Toil, Idleness carefully points out: it has created "mine and yours," it has divided not just the earth "but, what is more, the sea and perhaps even the air," it has given free rein to colonial conquest, the "strongest" stripping the "most worthy" (*Spaccio*, p. 728). But Jupiter's reply to Idleness opens new areas of thought: "You must not be surprised at the injustices and wrongs that come with industry" (*Spaccio*, p. 733). Divine man, through the use of reason, has to recognize the significant aspects of reality, and must not be surprised if the dialectic of forms expressed in nature is reflected also in society. We find the laws of change and the vicissitudes of opposites also within the social community:

> There have to be artisans, laborers, farmers, servants, footmen, the lowborn, the humble, the poor, the pedantic, and others of the same ilk; because otherwise there could be no philosophers, thinkers, cultivators of the mind, masters, captains, noble, eminent, rich, wise people and others who would be as heroic as the gods. So why

should we strive to corrupt the state of nature, which has divided the universe into things major and minor, superior and inferior, clear and obscure, worthy and unworthy, not just around us, but also, and yet more, within us, within our very substance, right down to that part of our substance that is immaterial? (*Eroici*, pp. 1113–14)

The condition of "neutrality and bestial equality" among humanity does not express the multiplicity of reality, which finds its natural expression in the dialectic of rank. Fractures and differences can never be eliminated, since they are part of the universal design of the dialectic of opposites. Yet, just as in the hierarchy of matter the "smallest trifles" have the same importance as large atomic amalgams, since every element has its own precise function, so in the social order the diversity among ranks does not diminish their dialectical importance.[8] Although differences remain, fractures can be minimized, however, by the use of laws that aim for a degree of balance:

Sophia is succeeded by law, her daughter; the former wants to act through the latter, the latter to be used by the former; it is through the law that princes reign, and kingdoms and republics are maintained. She, by adapting herself to the character and customs of nations and peoples, represses audacity with fear, and ensures goodness among the wicked. . . . Then, he [Jupiter] ordered and charged her with dealing above all and being rigorous with those things that were accorded her from the beginning and were of first and principal concern: that is, all that pertains to the communion of humanity, to civil conversation, so that the powerful might be upheld by the humble and the weak not oppressed by the strongest; so that tyrants might be deposed and just rulers and kings

> enthroned and sworn in, republics might be favored, vi-
> olence might not influence reason, ignorance might not
> disparage doctrine, so that the poor might be helped by
> the rich, the virtues and studies useful and necessary to
> the community might be promoted, encouraged, and
> maintained; so that those who profit from them might be
> praised and rewarded, and the envious, the mean, and
> the selfish scorned and kept down. (*Spaccio*, pp. 652–53)

The law, therefore, is the daughter of Sophia, "because a law that does not have Sophia as its mother and rational intellect as its father, is not a true or a good one" (*Spaccio*, p. 622). Sophia and reason, once again, represent the sole possibility of understanding the vicissitudes of the social, since only by recognizing the dialectic of rank can laws be decreed that in harmony with it minimize imbalance and discord. Within this context, where even rank fluctuates according to the universal law of vicissitude, nature appears in the guise of fortune: all of humanity finds itself in the same condition of equality. Only a few will manage to free themselves from the multitude; and these will be the heroic ones. Indeed, Bruno's firm hope is that "cures are not dispensed according to the rank of one's blood, one's nobility, one's title, or one's wealth; but according to the virtues that put forth the fruits of activity; so that the just might rule, the wealthy might contribute, the learned might teach, the prudent might guide, the strong might fight, those with sound judgment might advise, and those with authority might command" (*Spaccio*, p. 772). "It is in this sense," Badaloni observes, "that in Bruno's writings the most typical ideals of the bourgeoisie in its formative phase are reflected: the spirit of activity, the aversion toward violence that attacks natural right, and the theorization of the state founded upon respect for the law. To this it should be added that Bruno sees that these ideals can only be realized if the new state's ruling classes embrace unbiased philosophical thought.'"⁹

Society, too, becomes the theater of human conquest. In the struggle to affirm oneself, many will be crushed and few will succeed in grabbing Fortune "by the hair." The qualities of positive asininity (humility, toil, tolerance, dynamism) become indispensable for reaching any goal. The myth of Prometheus, insofar as it exalts individual activity, relates to those aspirations of positive asses, which I have attempted to describe. The Titan appears twice in Bruno's Italian dialogues. In the *Cabala*, linked to the theme of fire, he becomes the hero in opposition to negative asses, who "banished all care and study, reproached every human thought," refusing "to stretch out their hands and pick the forbidden fruit from the tree of science, thus being deprived of the fruit from the tree of life, or, like Prometheus (who is a metaphor for the same thing), stretching out their hands to steal Jupiter's fire, in order to light the flame of rational power" (*Cabala*, p. 878). In the *Spaccio*, however, linked to the theme of water, he appears together with the ass, who squanders the fruits of his achievements:¹⁰

> When Prometheus had suborned my son, your brother and father Jupiter, to give him those wineskins and barrels full of eternal life, it came to pass that after he loaded an ass, putting them on that animal to take them to the realm of men, the ass (which on that part of the journey went ahead of its driver), scorched by the sun, burned by the heat, parched by its toil, feeling its lungs withering with thirst, was invited to the spring by the serpent; where (it being sunk so low, with the water two or three palms below ground level) the ass was forced to bend and stretch so much, in order to touch the surface of the liquid with

its lips, that the barrels fell off its back, the skins burst,
and eternal life spilled out. (*Spaccio*, pp. 816–17)

In both cases, Prometheus is presented as a positive symbol, indeed,
as an antinegative ass. Although in the *Spaccio* the ass spills the
"barrels of eternal life," which Prometheus had acquired, in the
Cabala the ass renounces knowledge, repudiating Prometheus, who
had stolen fire "to light the flame of rational power." With this
myth, too, Bruno once again presents the opposition between the
two asininities: on the one hand, the Titan (the positive ass) who
sharpens his mind for the conquest of knowledge and immortality;
on the other, those who claim to know everything (the Aristotelians),
those who think that nothing can be known (the Skeptics), those
who refute earthly science in the name of divine science; in short,
the negative asses enclosed in their unproductive unidimensionality.
The fact that Bruno uses Prometheus in relation to the themes of
fire and water could be considered of little importance, given that
the two episodes are at the heart of the mythology of the Titan.
However, it is suggestive that water and fire both recall the idea of
dynamism; of the four natural elements, only they represent the
flux of instability.[11] This idea reappears many times in the *De rerum
natura*. According to Michel Serres, Lucretius shows that of the
four elements earth and air are quite stable in themselves (taking
back what they give, and vice versa), while fire and water appear
in their condition of constant dynamism.[12] Epistemologically, my
suggestion is not invalid, since in Bruno's view the march of science
expresses movement and perpetual dynamism. And the myth of
Prometheus embodies this endless tension: R. Trousson observes
that "Prometheus, therefore, is here the symbol of humanity's autonomy and of its unique capacity to function rationally. The Titan
claims his right to seek scientific and philosophical truth. He embodies the fearless revolt against dogma and spiritual constraint.

Together with the author of the *Cabala*, humanity scales Olympus and forces itself on the gods, making demands instead of entreaties. Thus, Bruno affirms himself as one of the most perfect examples of the 'heroism' of the Renaissance.'"[13]

The same torture to which Prometheus is condemned could become a metaphor for the endless search for knowledge. The fact that once the eagle has fed upon the Titan's liver, it grows back again, recalls the condition of humanity, which, just as it believes that it has reached the end of the road, discovers that other paths fork into two, that other truths are waiting to be investigated. This image of the acquisition of knowledge is not far removed from that evoked by Bruno in the *De immenso* (*Opp. lat.*, I, I, pp. 203–4), wherein matter's unsatisfied search for new forms exemplifies humanity's unsatisfied search for new truths: both involve the tension of striving toward a totality that does not exist. In this context, too, Prometheus's torment does not appear as a passive acceptance of his punishment, but is the symbol of the arduous path of knowledge.

Other Renaissance writers have paid attention to the myth of the Titan, for different reasons. Trousson suggests that a distinction should be drawn between the use philosophers and poets have made of it. The former, within the limits of their particular concerns, have seen Prometheus as a symbol of the human condition, thereby definitively eliminating the Titan's divine attributes (Pomponazzi, Bovillus, Bacon). The latter have fused the myth with Christianity or have illustrated the *topos* of the pains of love by means of Prometheus's torment (Ronsard, Lorenzo de' Medici).[14] It is the philosophers, therefore, who deserve the credit for having helped reshape the nature of the Titan, who ceases to be a god and becomes a man—a human hero in revolt, perpetually searching for scientific truth, as Bruno describes him in his original interpretation of the myth.

CHAPTER 11

The Ass in the Guise of the Sileni:
Appearances Are Deceptive

Having been led this far by the guiding thread of asininity in
its dual connotation, we are now in a better position to understand
some of Bruno's statements, which on the face of it do not seem to
make sense, but, in fact, fully justify the path we have taken: "In
conclusion (lest I rack my brain and yours any further), it seems
to me that [the ass] is the very soul of the world, that it is in everything and is everything everywhere. So now you can measure the
importance and influence of the venerable subject we are discussing
and debating at present" (*Cabala*, p. 843). In short, the symbol of
the ass has allowed us to read certain portions of Bruno's work
from a particular perspective, without ignoring the major themes
of his philosophy. The scorned "pile of papers" I spoke of at the
beginning[1] has in fact proved to contain valuable reflections in
which Bruno uses a different linguistic style to tackle questions examined in some of his other works:

> Since here you have not just the living triumphant beast,
> but, and moreover, the thirty broken seals, perfect bliss,
> cleared shadows, and the conquered ark; where the ass
> (who is not envious of the existence of the wheels of time,
> of the immensity of the universe, of the happiness of in-
> telligence, of the light of the sun, of Jupiter's baldachin)
> moderates, declares, consoles, opens doors, and presides.

He is not in any way an ass of the stable, nor one of the
field, but one that can appear anywhere, go anywhere,
enter everywhere, sit everywhere, communicate, understand, advise, define, and do everything. (*Cabala*, p. 842)

The allusions to the *Spaccio de la bestia trionfante*, the *Explicatio
triginta sigillorum*,[2] the *De umbris idearum*, and *L'Arca di Noè*,
apart from highlighting the subtle link with the theme of asininity,[3]
which I attempted to reconstruct in the first chapter, are an invitation to extend one's research into the realms of Bruno's entire
philosophy. The model proposed by Bruno is very close to one of
Erasmus's most famous *Adagia*: in the *Sileni Alcibiadis*, the Rot-
terdam humanist reminds us that "the Sileni were small split stat-
uettes, made in such a way that the two parts could be separated
and opened; when closed they affected a ridiculous and monstrous
playing of the flute, but, once opened, they immediately revealed a
deity, so that a jolly deception made the sculptor's art more agree-
able."[4]

This adage may be applied to something that "in appearance
and, as they say, at first glance, seems ridiculous and worthless,
but, in fact, for those who look at it more deeply and closely, is
admirable; or to a man who, because of his dress and appearance,
is looked down upon, but in truth holds great things in his heart."[5]
However, just as divinity can hide behind comic images, so too, very
often, those who parade their wisdom are hiding a profound ignorance. The Sileni, therefore, are also endowed with a dual meaning;
and Erasmus contrasts the many negative Sileni with the few
positive ones: "Today some good Sileni still hide among us, but
unfortunately they are very few in number. Most of humanity re-
sembles a Silenus in reverse. For if one thoroughly examines the
nature of things, it will be found that nobody is further from true
wisdom than those who publicly profess their wisdom with the help

of fine titles, the sage's cap, splendid sashes, or rings without dia-
monds.''[6] The paradoxical nature of the proverb lends itself very
well to Bruno's method. The technique of reversal creates an imbalance in points of view, overturns commonplaces, and defines a
new relationship between appearance and reality. It does not come
as a surprise, therefore, that the theme of the Sileni appears several
times in Bruno's work:[7]

> So we will let the multitude laugh, joke, play pranks, and
> admire itself in the guise of the gesturing, comical, and
> histrionic Sileni, who mask their treasure of goodness and
> truth, keeping it well hidden and safe. While, on the con-
> trary, there are more than enough people who, beneath
> stern brows, meek faces, long beards, and solemn, mag-
> isterial togas, studiously, and to the detriment of all, hide
> their ignorance, which is as base as it is conceited, and
> their villainy, which is as pernicious as it is renowned.
> (*Spaccio*, pp. 550–51)

No wonder, then, that the concept of asininity merits particular attention; for when you look into the ass, if you can manage
it, you will find a priceless treasure. The superficial appearance of
the ass gives little away, but above all it is deceptive. Those who
only contemplate this aspect, having no desire to penetrate its meaning, will get no surprises—only the odd laugh and a little disdain.
Bruno is thinking of such people when, in the *De imaginum compositione*, he speaks of the lack of success of the *Cabala* and the
Asino cillenico among the general public and false scholars: "the
image and shape of this animal are well known; various authors
have written on the subject, and in a particular style we, too, have
written a piece on the subject of this animal, but since it found no
favor among the public and was disliked by scholars because of its
sinister ideas, it was suppressed" (*Opp. lat.*, II, III, p. 237). The

external image of the ass offers little to the eye observing it. The distance of the object and the immobility of the observer make any contact impossible. In order to understand, it is necessary to act; it is, to be precise, necessary to use one's hands and slowly to open the Silenus to get inside. It will then become apparent that a treasure has been found. The effort of movement is rewarded, as the initial image gives way to another and the search extends toward new horizons. Now it is easy to understand why the theme of asininity "found no favor among the public and was disliked by scholars because of its sinister ideas." The multitude and "scholars" (grammarians, Aristotelians, Skeptics, pedants, and so forth) have not used their hands, they have not ventured into the depths of the Silenus, but have blindly put their faith in their immobility. The metaphor of the hands reproduces here the dynamic process involved in acquiring knowledge, since only those who open the Silenus can go beyond appearances. The ass is one short step from the Silenus, and their symbolic affinity justifies their similarity. Alcibiades' comments on the nature of Socrates' discourses, which he makes in Plato's *Symposium*, help us to understand the close relationship between asses and Sileni:

> For there is a point I omitted when I began—how his talk most of all resembles the Sileni that are made to open. If you choose to listen to Socrates' discourses you would feel them at first to be quite ridiculous; on the outside they are clothed with such absurd words and phrases—all, of course, the hide of a mocking satyr. His talk is of pack-asses, smiths, cobblers, and tanners, and he seems always to be using the same terms for the same things; so that anyone inexpert and thoughtless might laugh his speeches to scorn. But when these are opened, and you obtain a fresh view of them by getting inside, first of all you will

discover that they are the only speeches with any sense in them; and secondly, that none are so divine, so rich in images of virtue, so largely—nay, so completely—intent on all things proper for the study of such as would attain both grace and worth.[9]

In explaining a Silenus (asinine divinity) or "explaining" the ass— the one a statuette, the other a "pile of papers"—one cannot rely in either case on their physiognomy. It is precisely the Cyllenean ass that, in order to defend itself, recalls the emblematic case of Socrates:

> In this regard, consider the example of Socrates, whom Zopyros, the physiognomist, judged to be excessive, stupid, idiotic, effeminate, desirous of young boys, and inconsistent; all of which the philosopher admitted, but not that the act corresponding to such tendencies had been consummated. For he was restrained by his continuous study of philosophy, which handed him a sturdy helm to combat the crashing waves of his natural indispositions, since there is nothing that cannot be conquered through study. (*Asino cillenico*, p. 919)

Again we find ourselves upon a stormy sea, with the hurricanes hitting us every time we decide to venture into the ocean of knowledge. But the "continuous study of philosophy" enables us to sail confidently and *hands* us "a sturdy helm" with which "to combat the crashing waves" and take us safely to shore. The precise nature of the turmoil matters little, for "there is nothing that cannot be conquered through study." Socrates' *exemplum* confirms that appearances are very often deceptive. It is necessary to break through the skin, to go beyond the surface. The text's entire destiny lies here: regardless of whether it is high or low, excellent or contempt-

ible, fertile or barren. The final outcome is played out between those
who will split open the Silenus and those who, on the contrary, will
only contemplate its exterior appearance:

> Thus . . . I present you with these dialogues, which
> certainly will be as good or as bad, as esteemed or as
> worthless, as excellent or as contemptible, as wise or as
> ignorant, as high or as low, as useful or as useless, as
> fertile or as barren, as serious or as dissolute, as sacred
> or as profane as the hands into which they may fall, some
> people being of one kind, and others quite the opposite.
> And since there are so many more fools and wicked people
> than wise and just ones, this means that if I want to attain
> glory or the other fruits produced by the multitude of
> voices, and hope that my studies and work will be a pleas-
> ant success, I should, then, expect discontent and con-
> sider silence to be much better than words. But if I
> consider the eye of eternal truth, through which things
> appear all the more precious and illustrious, not only
> when they are known, searched for, and possessed by
> very few people, but also when they are vilified, scorned,
> and persecuted, then I shall endeavor all the more to
> cleave the violent rapids, when I see their vehemence in-
> crease as a result of the swirling, deep, and rising passage.
> (*Spaccio*, p. 550)

Bruno is well aware of the difficulties in store for the "asinine
dialogues." Again it is necessary to sail against the current—the
swirling and tumultuous waters of "the violent rapids" hinder our
passage. Now the metaphor of the potter, of whom I spoke in chapter one, becomes much clearer, since the vicissitudes of matter
through which "the same clay" can be made into "a vase, now
admired, now scorned" (*Cabala*, p. 890) are no different from the

vicissitudes of texts. The same "dialogues" will be judged "excellent or contemptible," although their textual specificity remains identical. One question that is asked repeatedly is whether the ass will be "split open." In other words, the theme of the Sileni becomes a coded message, containing instructions for the reader on how to use the texts. Bruno's interest in the *adagium*, as Cantimori rightly points out, goes beyond Erasmus's ideas on religion and transforms the literary play of metaphor into a veritable ideological horizon.[10]

The closest model in this context could be Rabelais. The prologue to *Gargantua* begins with some thoughts on the theme of the Sileni: "Now Silenus, in ancient days, was a little box, of the kind we see today in apothecaries' shops, painted on the outside with such gay, comical figures. . . . But inside these boxes were kept rare drugs such as balm, ambergris, cardamom, musk, civet, mineral essences, and other precious things."[11] A few lines farther on the allusions become explicit as Rabelais directly addresses the reader in an invitation to look for the rare drugs contained within the text:

> That is the reason why you must open this book and carefully weigh up its contents. You will discover then that the drug within is far more valuable than the box promised; that is to say, that the subjects here treated are not so foolish as the title on the cover suggested.
>
> But even suppose that the literal meanings you find to be jolly enough nonsense, in perfect keeping with the title, you must still not be deterred, as by the Sirens' song, but must interpret in a more sublime sense what you may possibly have thought, at first, was uttered in mere lightheartedness.[12]

The technique of reversal, as proposed by the particular nature of the Sileni, also directly determines the concept of the comic in both

Bruno and Rabelais. The boundary between opposites, to which
Erasmus was already alluding in his *Eulogy of Madness*, by means
of universalizing the two faces of the Sileni,[13] necessarily becomes
blurred. The space of laughter and of tears no longer refers to two
separate spheres, but constitutes a point of convergence where opposing elements engender each other reciprocally. The motto of the
Candelaio (*In tristitia hilaris, in hilaritate tristis*) breaks the rigid
antinomy between laughter and tears, by presenting itself as a particular expression of the general law of *coincidentia oppositorum*.[14]
Bruno reinterprets the contiguity between *hilaritas* and *tristitia* by
the fusion of two *topoi* widespread in Renaissance culture: Heraclitus crying and Democritus laughing.[15] In the *Proprologo* of the
Candelaio, Bruno invites us to consider that laughter and tears are,
of necessity, present together: "Consider who comes and who goes,
what is done and what is said, what is meant and what could be
meant, because it is certain that if you contemplate these human
actions and pronouncements in the spirit of Heraclitus or Democritus, you will have occasion either to laugh a lot or to cry a lot"
(p. 32). Rabelais, too, formulates the possibility of the contamina-
tion between *hilaritas* and *tristitia*, by drawing on Democritus and
Heraclitus: on hearing Maistre Janotus de Bragmardo's harangue,
Ponocrates and Eudemon burst out laughing until the tears run
down their cheeks, thereby transforming themselves into the living
image of "Heraclitizing Democritus and democritizing Heraclitus."[16] Rabelais compares Ponocrates' and Eudemon's situation to
that of Crassus and Philomene as described in two anecdotes in
which (by chance?) the ass is the protagonist. On the one hand,
there is Crassus running the risk of "giving his soul to God," having
seen "a foolish ass who was eating thistles," and on the other, there
is Philomene dying "with laughter," having seen "an ass who was
eating figs."[17]

   I am not concerned here with giving a detailed analysis of the complex relationship between Bruno and Rabelais, which, anyway, has already been examined from a different perspective by Spampanato and Tetel.[18] I have limited myself to a number of textual comparisons in order to understand better the use of certain literary *topoi*. And once again, a suggestive idea springs to mind: if, in certain circumstances, the sight of an ass can encourage the breakdown of the barriers between laughter and tears, it comes as no surprise if this same ass legitimates the dissolution of the boundary between the serious and the comic. In the *Epistola esplicatoria* of the *Spaccio*, it is Bruno himself who reminds the reader that "if you see serious and lighthearted subjects, bear in mind that they are all equally worthy of being considered through no ordinary spectacles" (*Spaccio*, p. 555). The space of asininity, therefore, becomes a privileged area, where opposites explode in reciprocal interaction. Within this fluidity of roles, Bruno hopes for an unceasing shift from one position to another, from the serious to the comic, from the low to the high. He invites us to consider the poles of two extremes as entities of equal value. The theme of the Sileni confirms the need for these continual crossovers; not just in order to understand the ambiguous *double face* mechanism of asininity, but above all, as Giulio Ferroni suggests in an essay on the comic structure of the *Candelaio*, to grasp the relationships of transformation between appearance and reality, which are simulated and experienced on the stage of the "theater of the world."[19]

But within the symbolic language of texts, based also on the mechanism of reversal proposed by the Sileni, Bruno identifies a necessary distinction when he counterbalances senseless writings, which end up turning into incomprehensible "sheeplike treatises," which "caused . . . Ortensio to become melancholic, Serafino to lose weight, Cammaroto to turn pale" (*Cabala*, p. 897), and writings that, although composed around complex symbolic structures, remain firmly in touch with reality. While the former deserve the reaction of the intelligent reader who "with great charm and grace went to throw it [the book] down the toilet, saying, 'Brother, you do not want to be understood; and I do not want to understand you' " (*Cabalà*, p. 897),[20] the latter, on the contrary, reward the reader's efforts by offering useful matters for reflection and valuable pointers for research. Very often symbolic language proves to be a bag of wind, a veil that shrouds the author's ignorance. The symbology of the ass as proposed by Bruno is, however, quite another matter. We have seen the treasure hidden inside the ass/Silenus, and the manner in which Bruno has spoken to us of reality, faithfully keeping his promises:

> Here Giordano speaks in the vernacular, he names things freely, he calls by name those things that nature has brought into being; he does not call shameful what nature renders worthy; he does not hide what she leaves out in the open; he calls bread, bread; wine, wine; a head; a head; a foot, a foot; and other parts by their proper name. . . . He judges philosophers as philosophers, pedants as pedants, . . . leeches as leeches, the useless, mountebanks, charlatans, tricksters, cardsharps, playactors, parrots for what they say they are, show themselves to be, and are in reality; and he judges the industrious, the beneficent, the wise, and the heroic for what they are. (*Spaccio*, pp. 551–52)

Bruno's declaration, which brings to mind Aretino's saying that calls "bread, bread [and] a prick, a prick,"[21] is not belied by the dual connotation of asininity. Here, "the industrious, the beneficent, the wise, and the heroic" belong to the concept of positive asininity; "the useless, mountebanks, charlatans, tricksters" pack the ranks of negative asses. In this "bestiary," Bruno has not spared generous praise for the former and scathing criticism for the latter.

CHAPTER 12

The Literature of the Ass before Bruno

Bruno's interest in the symbol of the ass does not spring out of nowhere. It has its roots in a literary tradition that was widespread in Renaissance culture. One has only to think of the success of Apuleius's *Asinus aureus*, with its numerous editions, the commentary by Beroaldo, and Boiardo's and Firenzuola's Italian translations.[1] To this list could be added the *Asino*, Machiavelli's short poem in terza rima,[2] Cornelius Agrippa's *Ad encomium asini digressio*,[3] Teofilo Folengo's *Macaronea*,[4] the *Asinesca gloria* attributed to Anton Francesco Doni,[5] the *Ragionamento sovra del asino*,[6] and other works of poetry and prose.[7] Within the literature of the ass, Bruno's position may be found at the far end of the diachronic arc of the Renaissance, at a period when these texts were widely read. Bruno was aware that he had happened upon a subject that many authors before him had already tackled, albeit from different perspectives. For this reason he feels the need to carve out his own original space:

> Alas! why, with great regret in my heart, with deep sorrow in my spirit, and a great burden on my soul, do my eyes see this incapable, stupid, and profane multitude that thinks so falsely, speaks so mordantly, and writes so fearfully to create, apart from expressions of derision, contempt, and reproach, all these wicked works deemed to be of literary importance which go to the presses, to libraries, everywhere: *The Golden Ass, In Praise of the*

Ass, Eulogy of the Ass, which think only of mocking glorious asininity with ironic sentences, of laughing at it and deriding it? Now who will convince the world not to think that I am doing the same? Who will be able to stop tongues from reducing me to one who follows in the footsteps of those others who democritize this subject? Who will be able to stop them from believing, affirming, and confirming that I do not intend, in all truth and sincerity, to praise the ass and asininity, but rather that I wish to add more oil to the lamp that others have lit? (*Cabala,* pp. 846–47)

Bruno's explicit reference to "all these works deemed to be of literary importance which go to the presses, to libraries, everywhere," apart from being a *topos* of the literature of the ass,[8] reveals the subject's great popularity among contemporary readers, as well as Bruno's direct knowledge of these works. Indeed, this fact was not overlooked by Spampanato, who was the first to research the asinine matter of the sixteenth century. His work provides a wealth of bibliographical information, but almost no interpretation.[9] His noteworthy study limits itself to exposition and highlighting the thematic similarities between the different works.

The "Ragionamento" by G. B. Pino. It is useful to consider Giovan Battista Pino's *Ragionamento sovra del asino,* which Spampananto unfortunately left out of his survey. This rare work, very few copies of which are known to exist,[10] was probably published in Naples between 1551 and 1552.[11] It provides a series of very useful points that in different forms are to be found in Bruno's *Cabala.* From the outset, despite admitting the difficulty he faces in taking on the task of singing the ass's praises in a period when this "genre" was all the rage, Pino is confident in the possibility of finding something new to say:

Not that discussing it [the ass] is anything new, for I know
that, before me, Lucius Apuleius and others, and in our
time many authors, have taken on this task and have said
what seemed important to them on the subject. And if I
will do the same, it is not to compete with such talented
men, but because I have come to consider that, since the
subject of the ass is infinite, there are still a few things
left I can talk to you about that have not been discussed
before; something you will be unable to deny, once you
have heard me. And, furthermore, I am convinced that
however much is said on the subject, there will always be
a lot more to say.[12]

The author unequivocally situates his *Ragionamento* in a comic
context, within the conventions of a "low" style, which breaks down
the rigid rules codified by pedants:

Thus—hoping to talk of things in a manner as different
as I am removed from the greatness of those before me
who have written about the ass—I will ensure that, with
the lowness of my style, I will speak before you in a manner wholly appropriate to me and to the subject in question.[13]

So that, not wanting to praise the ass in the way they
[epideictic orators] praise their animals, breaking the
chains of the undisciplined rules of speech of which I had
almost become prisoner, and, jumping, unreined and un-
muzzled, from pillar to post . . . [14]

The text, therefore, does not have a homogenous narrative structure, but makes room for fables, tales, proverbs, and, on occasion,
learned philosophical quotations, which are held together by the

common denominator of asininity. The core of the introduction is based wholly on a complex play on the word "ass," which reveals that, among the many "mysteries" this word embraces, it also contains certain fundamental kinds of knowledge:

> Inasmuch as—to be absolutely clear—I weighed up the importance of this word ASINO, and drew out of it such great sweetness, as to feel beside myself with the rapture instilled in me by the discoveries it proffered, as well as with the profound mysteries contained within it. Above all, I can see it representing all the various aspects of this machine of the world; and, so that you might understand me, look at me paint on this dish with wine the word: A.SI.NO. You can see that it is formed of three syllables, of which the last two mystically reveal the whole of creation, whereby things either are and declare themselves to be so by the SI, or negate their existence, because they are not, by the NO.[15]

Pino's argument becomes more interesting when, through another play on letters, he posits the ass as the symbolic mediator between the space of *feritas* and that of *humanitas:* "But, coming back to what I started, if we consider the first and last letters of the word, we can see an A and an O which perhaps could refer to the Alpha and the Omega much lauded by the Greeks, or to that A and O about which I plan to tell you so much. It is as if it is saying that the ass, which is the king of the animals, is linked to *l'Omo* [man], Master of all."[16] The dual nature of the ass is directly linked to the dual nature of man, since "there can be no ass without man, nor man without the ass, and they seemingly correspond to one another."[17] Pino substitutes the model of the ass-centaur (half ass and half man) for Machiavelli's centaur Chiron,[18] in the conviction that only "by amalgamating the actions of these two natures" is it possible to attain "the kind of life that can make us happy:"[19]

> Machiavelli does not deny that the great men of the world ought to have these two sides to them, that of wisdom and that of folly, or, more precisely, that of man and that of the beast. And he says that it appears that the poets alluded to this when they told of Achilles being given over as a disciple to Chiron, who was half man and half beast, so that he might be taught how to govern his peoples and rule his state, using both natures at the same time; I mean that of man and that of the beast, or, rather, that of the ass, which, for the reasons mentioned already, is closer to the nature of man than is any other nature of any other animal. And I do not know how those who maintain that Chiron's beast was a horse and not an ass could possibly defend their position, given that the head is missing, without which the matter cannot be settled. Nevertheless, his lower limbs were more those of an ass than of a horse, for he had a splendid tail, of which we will speak later.[20]

The model of the ass-centaur embodies the need for change and encourages the dynamic crossing over of opposites. Wisdom involves the capacity of abandoning a unidimensional position in order to adapt oneself to the *varietas* of nature. Passing through the antithetical spheres of *humanitas* and *feritas* means entering an existential dimension driven by the pluridimensionality of experience. Again we are faced with the dual connotation of asininity: on the one hand, we have negative asses enclosed in their static universe and devoid of any intellectual urgings toward new forms of knowledge. On the other, we have positive asses, capable of recognizing that the ideology of change offers the only possibility of grasping the essential elements of a continually evolving system of knowledge. The symbol of the ass-centaur, which in the Middle Ages represented vain, material science in opposition to divine truths,[21] acquires a precise positive value. Within a wholly secular environment, it posits itself as the *exemplum* of wisdom, as the exaltation of intellectual dynamism.

Humanity as a whole is not immune to this dichotomy; there will be negative asses incapable of understanding the importance of roses; there will be positive asses who, through them, will learn how to change their own condition:

> For this reason, many believe that asses, whom nature has made with four legs and art has taught to go round on two (like the bears and the dogs of the blind who dance and perform marvels on two legs), carry a rose in their mouth when these are in bloom, as if they wanted to be transformed into humans; but their knowledge is so slight that they do not eat the rose, but just chew the stem. And just as they are about to chew the rose and become human, they spit it on the ground, thus remaining in their initial condition of asses.
>
> Other asses carry a rose in their hands, sniffing it as they walk along, and, wanting to show themselves to be sober asses, they do not chew it, nor taste it, nor swallow it. And these asses think they can become human thanks to the smell, without the authority and approval of taste, thereby remaining brutish beasts, held in low esteem by asses, together with those other small and big animals that, it has to be said, like to carry a bunch or a bundle of roses in their hands, in the belief that many roses, and not just one, make men.[22]

Although the katabasis into the ass might become necessary, as the experience of Lucius the ass in Apuleius's story teaches us,[23] one must not remain enclosed within the space of *feritas* and renounce the anabasis toward *humanitas*. One's relationship with the rose translates in symbolic terms one's relationship with knowledge and the various ways of relating with the processes of acquiring knowledge. There will be asses who "do not eat the rose, but just chew the stem," some who "carry a rose in their hands," thinking they can become human "thanks to the smell," and some who "like to carry a bunch or a bundle of roses in their hands, in the belief that many roses, and not just one, make men." But there will also be asses who, on the contrary, will eat roses and taste the petals of metamorphosis. One must get to know the rose, penetrate its hidden secrets, chew its petals, and take possession of its powers. There are no other means by which to become human again, or to cross the boundary between opposites. An attitude of sleepy contemplation is not enough; smell, touch, and sight are of little use—they do not allow for any process of metamorphosis—and so one remains an ass forever, trapped in a state of static bestiality. To this negative sphere, Pino relegates false philosophers, intransigent rulers, and pedants who, like Bembo, have "massacred this our noble tongue."[24] What is quite different is the relationship with knowledge enjoyed by those asses who know how to metamorphose and who live in harmony with the *varietas* of nature.

But the *Ragionamento*, apart from other possible textual comparisons with Bruno's *Cabala*,[25] also presents another level of reading, which can help us understand an obscure area of the *Spaccio*. The category of intransigent rulers was not included in the list of negative asses purely by chance; in fact, the work makes explicit reference to the uprisings of 1547, which broke out in Naples in protest against the attempted establishment of a tribunal of the Inquisition.[26] At that time, Pino stood out for his antigovernment stance, so much so that he was elected by the people to be their representative in the delegation that went to Florence to explain to

Charles V the causes of the revolt.[27] The text therefore contains polemical allusions to the asinine nature of Viceroy Don Pedro of Toledo. Was Bruno referring to the Naples uprisings of 1547 when, in the *Spaccio*, Mercury alludes to the insane discord that rages in the "Parthenopean Kingdom" (that is, the Neapolitan)?

Mercury: The reason for this [my being pressed] is that, as a matter
of urgency, I have been sent by Jupiter to deal with and extin-
guish the blaze that has begun to excite insane and savage Discord in this Parthenopean Kingdom.

Sophia: O Mercury, how has this pestilential Fury rushed from over
the Alps and across the sea to this noble country?

Mercury: It has been summoned by someone's foolish ambition and
insane trust; it has been invited with most generous but nonetheless uncertain promises; it has been stirred by false hopes;
it is awaited by a twofold jealousy, which manifests itself in the
people by the desire to preserve the same liberty they have
always enjoyed, and the fear of being submitted to yet harsher
servitude; and in the Prince by the worry of losing everything
for having wanted to embrace too much.

Sophia: What is the origin and the fundamental cause of this?

Mercury: The great avarice that operates under the pretext of wanting
to preserve Religion.

Sophia: To my mind, the pretext appears to be false and, correct me
if I am wrong, it is inexcusable; for there is no need of protec-
tion or caution where there is no threat of ruin or peril, where
people's souls remain the same, and where the cult of that goddess has not thrived, as it has elsewhere. (*Spaccio*, pp. 719–21)

Contrary to Fiorentino's opinion that the allusion is to the distur-
bances in Naples of 1585, which were sparked by the cornering of
the grain market, Spampanato is in no doubt that Bruno intended
to allude to the violent uprisings of 1547.[28] The textual references

themselves support the latter view, since Bruno speaks of "the great avarice that operates under the pretext of wanting to preserve Religion" precisely to underline the uselessness of a tribunal of the Inquisition in a "most religious" city. Evidently, Don Pedro of Toledo's ambitions correspond to "the Prince [getting] fatter and fatter" (*Spaccio*, p. 722). One has only to read contemporary chronicles to find further correlations with the allusions contained in the *Spaccio*.[29] The only things Spampanato is unsure about are "how" Bruno came to hear the news and "why" he would have particularly wanted to mention the uprisings of 1547. There could be many answers to these questions, but, apart from those offered by Spampanato,[30] I believe that we should not underestimate the possibility Bruno was influenced by reading the *Ragionamento*. As we have seen, many textual elements support a link between Bruno and Pino; and given Bruno's interest in the literature of the ass, it is probable that he read one of the most important texts of the "genre." So, why not recall the uprisings of 1547 almost forty years later and in a different context, but still in keeping with the theme of asininity?

Machiavelli's "Asino" and Other Examples. In this résumé of the literature of the ass, Machiavelli's *Asino* (*The Ass*), which was probably written in about 1517[31] and is the first example of its kind in the sixteenth century, merits particular attention. This short poem in tercets, which unfortunately remained unfinished, recounts the author's own experience of being metamorphosed into an ass, as a necessary "reflection" of such a "wicked and sad time" (I.97–102). The descent into *feritas*, therefore, is not seen as a degradation, as a deliberate abandonment of one's rational faculties, but, on the contrary, it assumes a positive connotation that, beyond rigid humanistic values, recognizes the validity of crossing over into a sphere that is antithetical to *humanitas*.

Machiavelli's anthropology demands movement between opposites. "Man" and "beast," "comic" and "serious" are not ir-
reconcilable extremes, but prove to be a dignified way of responding
to the "vagaries" of fortune. Giulio Ferroni states that "the neg-
ativity that the humanistic tradition attributes to the figure of the
'beast' can be turned against the tradition itself. One discovers that
true 'asses' are those who remain immobile while affirming their
own unshakably unidimensional and 'human' worth. On the other
hand, those who are willing to descend into animality, those who,
like the author, would become 'asses' when necessary, in effect establish an active relationship with external nature, thereby affirming in a rational way the autonomy of 'comic' and 'bestial' space.''[32]
After the fall of the Florentine Republic, Machiavelli's sense of isolation weighed heavily on him and *The Ass* therefore translates this
state of mind, within a precise literary project, into an attempt at
regaining his lost equilibrium. So it is not surprising that from the
outset Machiavelli claims the right to indulge in "saying negative
things" and creating a strictly contiguous relationship between the
poet's stance and the nature of the ass:

> But this wicked and sad time
> in which, without needing the eyes of Argus,
> one can see more bad than good.
>
> So if I spread a little venom,
> though I am out of the habit of speaking ill,
> it is the time which have provided ample material.
>
> And if our Ass, which has trod so many
> paths in this our world
> to see the mind of every mortal being,
>
> were to measure how far it has come,
> heaven itself could not stop it from braying.

> So, let no one approach
> this uncouth and stubborn beast,
> lest they suffer a deal of asinine jibes;
> for we all know well that it is a law of its nature
> that it excels in the game of
> two kicks and a couple of farts.[33]

The adventure in the wood, which is also found in Folengo's asinine medley,[34] presents itself as an inverted image of the descent into Hell described in *The Divine Comedy*. Here, Dante's material is reused in a "comic" and "bestial" context, assuming an autonomous and *opposite* space that avoids any desecration of the model.[35] Within this "dark, murky, and blind place,"[36] the poet encounters a young maiden in the service of Circe who is willing to answer all his questions ("do not be concerned about telling me / what you know of the course of my life"; III.74–75). And having dwelt on the necessity for the stars to be in constant motion ("See the stars and heaven, see the moon, / see the other planets wandering / high and low unceasingly"; III.88–90), the maiden invites her interlocutor to "change skin" in order to adapt to the vagaries of fortune:

> But before these stars show themselves
> to be on your side, it would as well for you
> to roam the world wearing another skin;
> for that providence which preserves
> the human species, decrees that you suffer
> this hardship for your greater good.
> So you must rid yourself completely
> of all semblance of humanity, and in a different guise
> come with me and graze among the other animals.
> (III.115–23)

The poem includes reflections of a political and anthropological nature that echo Machiavelli's other work. The poet, in fact, making use of a moment of solitude, cannot resist the temptation of abandoning himself to the suggestions of thought:

> And because one thought is answered with another,
> my mind pursued those things passed
> which time does not yet from me conceal;
>
> and here and there my thoughts did wander,
> to how ancient peoples, so elevated and famous,
> were touched at times by fortune's caress, at times by its snarling bite;
>
> and these thoughts appeared to me so intriguing
> that I wanted to discover the reason for myself
> of this inconstancy in the affairs of the world.
> (V.28–36)

The theme of change appears again and again. First the wanderings of the stars, then the poet's necessary metamorphosis, and now the "inconstancy in the affairs of the world." Machiavelli's inquiry, therefore, extends from the *varietas* that dominates the macrocosm, to the existential and political vicissitudes of human experience. He seizes the opportunity to stress the weakness of states, paying particular attention to the events in Florence and Venice, and offers general pointers to the causes of their ruin (V.49–72). But even if one cannot escape the necessary reversals of fortune ("And it is, always was and always will be / that bad follows good, good follows bad / and the one is always the cause of the other"; V.103–5), there exist possibilities of accelerating or of slowing down the course of change within kingdoms. If "idleness burns through countries and towns," the virtue of activity and good laws help to put back the day of dissolution:

> It is true that the length of time
> a power lasts, depends on how
> good or bad its laws are.
> That kingdom forced to act
> by virtue or necessity,
> will always rise above the rest. (V.76–81)

Machiavelli insists on the necessity of religion as a moment of co-
hesion, recognizing the positive value of "ceremonies and devo-
tions." However, religion could prove dangerous if, beyond its
unifying function, it should in the name of an afterlife remove man's
desire to intervene in earthly affairs. One must not make the mistake of waiting idly on one's knees for God to help with the problems
of everyday life, thereby renouncing the possibilities of salvation
offered by human industry:

> To believe that without effort on your part God fights for
>   you,
> while you are idle and on your knees,
> has ruined many kingdoms and many states.
> And prayer is of great necessity:
> it is quite insane to deny the people
> its ceremonies and devotions;
> for it is from these that comes
> unity and good order, which in turn
> give rise to good fortune and happiness.
> But let no one be of so little brain
> as to believe that, if his house collapses,
> God will be its only secure prop:
> for he will die beneath its rubble. (V.115–27)[37]

After political reflections, we find the meeting with the "two thousand beasts" of the closed convent. The maiden, in her role as

guide, accompanies the poet to Circe's lair, where there are various
animals that, before their metamorphosis, belonged to the human
race. In the wide review that makes up chapters VI and VII, Machiavelli, by describing the different animals, offers us a rich catalog of human characteristics.[38] The figure of the beast therefore
lends itself to the contemplation of positive and negative moral qualities, wherein, with an inverted model, the same values as those of
the sphere of *humanitas* are to be found. At the close of this ''co-
pious lineup,'' Machiavelli's dialogue with the pig marks the end of
The Ass. The conversation, which is based on one of Plutarch's most
famous dialogues in his *Moralia,*[39] is initiated by the poet asking the
''fat piggy,'' ''do you want to return to your previous form?''
(VIII.21). The animal's reply turns into a lengthy monologue con-
demning the arrogance of humanity and its closed unidimensionality, based on the concept that nothing of value can exist outside
of ''the human essence'':

> I do not want and refuse to live with you,
> and well I see you are in that same error,
> which held me fast for such a long time.
>> Your love of self so deceives you all
> that you believe there is no other good
> but your own human essence and your value.
>> But if you would but hear me,
> by the time you leave my side,
> I will hope to have freed you from this error.
> (VIII.28–36)

The pig's arguments, aimed directly at showing that animals are
superior, exalt the dimension of *feritas* as the epitome of a perfect
balance with nature. The capacity to change with the seasons shows
how animals are willing to ''change skin,'' to move from one place
to another in order to escape the cold of the snows or the heat of

the sun, and to reject a monomaniacal vision of the relationship
with nature. Here, fixed norms crumble before the willingness to
follow the movements of the "weather" and to search for a continual "encounter" with the "inconstancy in the affairs of the world":

> We move ground from bank to bank,
> and it does not pain us to leave our abode,
> as long as we live in abundance and happiness.
> Some flee the snows, some flee the sun,
> learning to live with the weather as our friend,
> just as nature wants to teach us. (VIII.49–54)

Even as regards the use of the senses, the pig reaffirms that "We
are nature's best friends." Although animals, according to their
particular bodily makeup, know how fully to exploit their sight,
hearing, and taste, man, on the contrary, is incapable of gaining
any benefit from touch and relegates the hand to being merely an
instrument of sensual pleasure:[40]

> We are nature's best friends;
> and it seems that it is we who most enjoy its gifts,
> while you are sadly lacking.
> If you want proof of this, just look at our senses,
> and you will easily be persuaded
> that the opposite of what you might be thinking is true.
> The eye of the Eagle, the ears and nose of the Dog,
> and even our taste can be proved superior,
> while touch is all that retains any advantage in you;
> which was granted you not as an honor,
> but simply for the appetites of Venus
> to cause you great bother and trouble. (VII.106–17)

The theme of the hand, which I have already discussed in relation
to Bruno,[41] is still presented with its positive connotations, whereby

humanity can use it to honor its own kind. The pig's criticism does
not diminish the value of the organ in itself, but aims to attack the
obtuseness of those men who cannot live in harmony with nature.
This inability is expressed by not even recognizing the potential of
their own bodies, as they abandon themselves solely to the unleashing of negative qualities, like avarice and ambition, which drag them
into the abyss of destruction:

> Nature gave you hands and speech,
> but it also gave you ambition
> and avarice, which erase these gifts. (VIII.130–32)

The exaltation of *feritas* is posited not as a euphoric adherence to
the myth of the golden age,[42] but is presented solely as the positive
exemplum of a happy "encounter" with nature, of pluridimensional stances aiming to harmonize with the *varietas* that dominates
the universe. Opulence and idleness, together with avarice and ambition, move in the opposite direction, becoming the evidence of a
choice made within a space wholly out of balance with the laws of
nature. These dichotomous positions represent the dual connotation of asininity: on the one hand, negative asses enclosed in their
static unidimensionality, and on the other, positive asses capable of
"changing skin" and having a happy "encounter" with fortune.
Pino's hypothesis based on the model of the ass-centaur, as set out
in the *Ragionamento*, does not appear groundless, since in a comic
context the myth of the man-ass takes on the same positive dignity
given to the centaur. *The Ass* and *The Prince* use different linguistic
forms to express the need to find a reasoned balance between *feritas*
and *humanitas*. The comic and serious styles autonomously posit
themselves as opposing but equally traversable spaces.

The positive model of the ass-centaur exists in opposition to
the *Asinus* by Pontano,[43] which relegates the animal to a place of
blind irrationality. Here the humanistic concept of *feritas* finds its

maximum expression in the image of an ungrateful ass that wastes no time in revealing its uncouth nature. The dialogue, situated within a free *divertissement*, recounts the misadventures of the author, who, having accomplished important tasks in his civil life, decides to take to the idleness of the countryside with an ass in tow. But Pontano's attempts at forming a relationship with the animal end tragically with a barrage of kicks:

> Back, back! most lazy animal, most ungrateful beast! it almost ripped off my hands with its bite! with its obstinate head it threw me to the ground and forced me into the mire! This shrub only just stopped it from trampling me as I lay helpless on the ground, and from crushing me to pieces with its hooves! Back, most villainous animal! This is what it means to be an improvident old man, who has learned too late, this is what it means to be a man completely lacking in foresight. As I have just said, this is what always happens to those who want to wash the ass's head: apart from the trouble it takes, they also lose the soap! who takes delight in the ass shall turn into an ass![44]

A prolonged relationship with *feritas* can only lead to negative results, for "who takes delight in the ass shall turn into an ass." There is no chance of mediating with values that are directly opposed to those of humanity. In short, Pontano reaffirms maintaining a distinction between two antithetical and wholly unrelated universes.

This model is later broken down in the Renaissance literature on the ass. In their own quite different ways, each of the examples we have looked at betray a pluridimensional and ambiguous use of the symbol. These texts are situated within a twin-track structure, where the *double face* nature of asininity creates the possibility of changing position, thereby facilitating the crossover between opposites. The play of reversals becomes a kind of electric arc that works only when its two poles make contact. The absence of one end could shut down the force energizing the text. This could result in losing the sense of the work or, at least, of diminishing it. Beyond this hypothesis, formulated on the basis of the materials with which I have dealt, one ought to study and compare other unpublished works, in order to present a more complete picture of sixteenth-century literature on the ass; a picture, however, that will have to come to terms with this ambiguous image of our four-legged friend, as experienced in the *Attabalippa dal Perù: La nobiltà dell'asino*, attributed to Banchieri:

> But I judge what I have said to be worth nothing com-
> pared to my intention of granting humanity so many dif-
> ferent qualities, which contradict each other in every way
> and cannot be part of the same subject, just as fire cannot
> accommodate both cold and heat. And yet, I find them to
> be in this ASS; nor could I ever have imagined such a
> thing possible, for I have heard people say: he is as hand-
> some as an ass, and as ugly as an ass; as sensible as an
> ass, and as crazy as an ass; as gentle as an ass, and as
> rough as an ass; as wise as an ass, and as ignorant as an
> ass.[45]

The Literature of Paradox. The play on the theme of ignorance—one of the fundamental *topoi* of the literature of the ass—
appears also within its own autonomous space, constituted by a
number of texts that form part of the widespread "genre" of
"praises" and paradox. There can be no doubt that in this case
Bruno was able to dig out material that could easily be adapted to
his discourse on asininity. Indeed, the functioning of these "ora-
tions" is based exclusively on the model of ambiguity. The exaltation of ignorance always conceals a dual connotation, where the
road divides into the negative and positive paths. Giulio Landi, in

his *Orazione della ignoranza*,[46] challenges the exclusively negative use of this concept: "But clearly these men do not understand the power of the word, and they abuse the name of 'ignorance' and 'ignorant,' always taking it in the wrong way, as meaning something bad. They do not consider the extent and size of its jurisdiction, which contains the way of knowing well, as well as that of knowing bad, as I can easily explain."[47] For Landi, the fundamental principle of knowledge is to be found in "the ignorance of deprivation." It is precisely the awareness of "not knowing" that triggers humanity's knowledge-acquiring mechanisms, in the constant realization that yet another road is in sight: "This is why such deprivation of understanding incites [humanity] and is almost an acute stimulus to acquire knowledge; and we have said above that such deprivation of knowledge is ignorance itself. Ignorance, therefore, is a most powerful and sharp spur to the desire to understand and to know, which is not a bad or a sad thing, but a good one that does much good and produces many beneficial effects."[48] In direct opposition are the views of false scholars who, lacking any knowledge whatsoever, point a finger at the ignorance of others without recognizing their own. And in a catalog of negative uses of the arts and professions,[49] Landi does not spare the "grammatical Pedant who, when teaching his disciples the active and passive forms of Latin, is so convinced of and pleased with his abilities, that everyone else appears worthless to him."[50] The text is also full of allusions to "holy ignorance," which is presented as "divine knowledge";[51] ironic allusions accompanied by quotations from the Gospels, a great number of which Bruno includes in the *Cabala*. Within this ambiguous context, Landi assigns knowledge a space characterized by dynamism, while ignorance is relegated to the static contentment of idleness. One has only to turn the connotations upside down to grasp the meaning of this dual opposition:

There is absolutely no doubt that all this knowledge and esteemed wisdom are nothing more than a bother, a worry, a pain in the neck, an attack on body and soul, almost like a plague on unhappy mortals. On the other hand, however, ignorance is a healthy thing, it is truly ignorance that grants the mind eternal rest and sweet tranquillity; and ignorance is not just the veritable way of preserving body and soul, but also a great source of happiness for man while he lives in this world.[52]

Ortensio Lando employs a not dissimilar tone in one of his paradoxes entitled *Meglio è d'esser ignorante, che dotto* [It is better to be ignorant than learned].[53] The author starts from the conviction "that it is better not to know letters than to know them, for those who devote the best part of their lives to them, in the end feel only remorse and pain."[54] There follows a stream of quotations, proverbs, and lessons from the Gospels, reaffirming the need to renounce study because "who adds science, adds pain."[55] In the end, the author seeks to console the ignorant because it is better "to be ignorant than learned, it is better to hate letters than to love them; so let them no longer be ashamed or blush, our ignorant ones, whose ranks (thanks be to God) appear infinite; indeed, let them heartily rejoice, giving thanks to God and deeming it fortunate to know nothing."[56] But what is of greater interest for the purposes of drawing direct comparisons with Bruno's *Cabala* is the paradox *Che Aristotele fusse non solo un ignorante, ma anche lo più malvagio huomo di quella età* [Aristotle was not just ignorant, but also the most wicked man of that time], in which the Stagirite is described as a "filthy animal" quite unworthy "of all the reverence and respect accorded him by fools."[57] Indeed, contrary to current opinion, Aristotle would "steal" from the books that Alexander bought him, and, not "knowing a thing about letters, the rogue" would end up filling his parchments with mistakes.[58] His ignorance was such that he could never express anything clearly, hiding his "knowing nothing" in the obscurity of language:

> For his obscurity he [Aristotle] was known as a squid, since, like the squid, which sprays some sort of ink from beneath its belly to avoid being caught by fishermen, this valiant philosopher to avoid being understood has completely shrouded himself in the darkness of ignorance, and, putting his trust in it, he wrote to Alexander telling him not to be upset at his having published his treatises on *Physics*, for nobody would be able to understand them without first having heard them from his own lips.[59]

Many decades later, two years after the publication of the *Cabala*, Cesare Rao in his *Orazione in lode dell'ignoranza* [Oration in praise of ignorance],[60] redefined the ambiguous space of the concept by identifying two opposing categories: the ignorant wise and the wise ignorant.[61] The former represent arrogant men who hide a profound stupidity behind their apparent omniscience; the latter are identified with those who are aware of their own ignorance, with the truly wise who have understood that "infinite are the things we want to know and very few those we have understood."[62] And to avoid being misunderstood, in an introduction to the oration significantly entitled *A i saggi e giudiciosi lettori* [To wise and judicious readers], Rao gives a key to the reading of his work, which undoubtedly is of interest also in understanding how other texts function:

> Do not (I beseech you, dearest readers) make rash judgments against me and blame me more than I deserve, because when I speak badly of Physicians, Legists, Philosophers, Astrologers, Orators, and other professors

of the sciences, I am speaking only of those who abuse their art. And I have not written this oration with the intention of wanting to praise ignorance, which ever since childhood I have always tried to eradicate from my heart with all my strength and determination, but to reveal some new ideas.[63]

In this chapter I have again limited myself to a few brief observations, with the principal aim of delimiting a "frontier" zone where there is no shortage of material useful to my research. "Asininity" and "ignorance" lend themselves to possible symbolic interferences, so it is not surprising that Doni, in the dedication to Gregorio Rosario, which precedes Giulio Landi's *Orazione della ignoranza*, situates the ass within "the wheel of ignorance": "In my study I have painted a wheel that in its entirety is called the wheel of ignorance. At the bottom there are men; in the middle their top half becomes an animal, and at the top they become full-fledged asses. Then, as they go down and they pass through the middle, the bottom half becomes human."[64]

CHAPTER 13

The Entropy of Writing

So far, by means of an analysis of the symbol of the ass, I have attempted to elucidate certain fundamental traits of Bruno's concept of knowledge. The infinity of the universe and the infinity of the processes of acquiring knowledge have become the two parallel tracks of my study of the dual nature of asininity. The cosmological path has never become separate from the gnoseological one, thereby creating an inexorable process of continuous reciprocal interference.

The same questions can also be found at the level of writing: What kind of language can express the break from the closed universe of the Aristotelians? What kind of language can exalt the infinity of different worlds? Which literary models can provide stylistic elements harmonious with Bruno's gnoseological and cosmological concepts? The brief *excursus* into the literature of the ass undertaken in the preceding chapter, apart from being simply a thematic comparison, served above all as a partial outline of some of the works Bruno could possibly have read; in other words, a small, ideal "library" revealing his particular interest in certain authors and in the specific literary areas they represent. This cultural background requires further investigation. One has only to look through the index of the catalog of books analyzed by Florio for his Italian-English dictionaries, *A Worlde of Wordes* (1598) and *New World of Words* (1611), to obtain a precise picture of the Renaissance works that Bruno could have had at his disposal in England; and once again comic and satirical writers are represented in force (Aretino, Berni, Doni, Franco).[1] But it is Bruno himself, as occurred in the case of the literature of the ass,[2] who implicitly reveals his interest in burlesque literature:

> It is permitted and possible for princes to praise low things; and if they do so, these will pass for noble things, and will be such in truth. . . . Now see by what comparison you can understand this, since Teofilo grossly exaggerates this subject matter; and his argument, however uncouth it might appear to you, is quite different from ancient authors celebrating sauces, little kitchen gardens, mosquitoes, flies, nuts, and things of that ilk; or authors in our time celebrating posts, sticks, fans, roots, mercenaries, candles, bed-warmers, figs, quintan fever, hoops, and other things deemed not just ignoble, but downright disgusting. (*Cena*, pp. 64–65)[3]

The apparently polemical tone of this passage reveals, however, Bruno's interest in exalting "low things," an interest strongly reaffirmed in the *Spaccio* when Sophia explains to Saulino that the gods, apart from studying Aristotle, are also just as happy to read and benefit also from Aretino and burlesque poetry:

Saulino. What are you telling me, Sophia? The gods, therefore, sometimes pick up Aristotle? They study the philosophers, for example?

Sophia. I shall tell you no more than what there is on Pippa, Nanna, Antonia [characters in Aretino's *Ragionamenti*], Burchiello, Ancroia, and another book, either by Ovid or by Virgil, whose title I cannot remember, and other similar books.

Saulino. So now they discuss such momentous and serious things?

Sophia. Do you think that such things are not serious, not momen-

tous? Saulino, if you were more of a philosopher, more aware,
you would believe that there is no lesson, no book that has not
been examined by the gods, and that what is not completely
without salt is not molded by the gods; and that what is not
completely senseless is not approved and chained into the communal library. For they take pleasure in the multiform representation of all things and the multiform fruits of all mental
ingenuity, and they delight in all that is, and in all the representations that are made, just as they ensure that they exist,
and give the order and permission for them to be done. (*Spaccio*, pp. 673–74)

Bruno raises satirical and burlesque literature from a subordinate
position, placing the "serious" and the "comic" on the same level
of dignity,[4] since both spheres express the *varietas* that dominates
the universe. The nullification of vertical relationships is testimony
to the existence of a single horizontal space that goes beyond all
false hierarchies to express "the multiform representation of all
things and the multiform fruits of all mental ingenuity." Bruno
questions the supremacy enjoyed by institutionally established literature: there are other stylistic forms and other paths of inquiry
that cannot be ignored or wiped out in a single stroke. Thus Bruno,
by means of a sharply polemical approach, elevates burlesque literature to the same status as Petrarchism:

And by my faith, if I want to defend the nobility of the
mental ingenuity of that Tuscan poet, who, on the banks
of the Sorgue, showed such yearning for a woman of Vau-
cluse, and I do not mean to say he was a madman to be
chained, I will have to believe and force myself to persuade others that he, lacking the talent for better things,
wanted studiously to feed his melancholy, by celebrating
not least his own intelligence through working on that

skein, explaining the affections and obstinacies of a love that is vulgar, animal, and bestial, just as others have sung the praises of the fly, of the cockroach, of the ass, of Silenus, of Priapus; and, in our time, those who have aped them with poems praising chamber pots, bollocks, pricks, beds, lies, dishonor, ovens, hammers, famine, plague—all of which are no less worthy of being proud and haughty of the illustrious mouths of their singers than the women mentioned above and others should and can be of the poets who sing their praises. (*Eroici*, p. 935)

I will discuss later the points of divergence that characterize Bruno's relationship with these two opposing but complementary poles of sixteenth-century literature; this is an ideological clash that also justifies, on a plane other than the strictly literary one, Bruno's by then outdated polemical anti-Petrarchism. What is important now is to underline how so-called anti-classicism weighed on Bruno's stylistic development.[5] Bruno's interest in these irregular writers is marked by a common denominator—the opposition to and revolt against the literary models celebrated by classicism. The poetry and prose produced by such diverse writers find a broad common ground in the rejection of certain artistic norms in the name of "nature," a "nature" defined by *varietas* and, hence, the guarantor of the experimentation that characterizes this anti-classicist school.[6] The literary experiences of Folengo, Aretino, Doni, Berni, and Franco offer Bruno a richly variegated field in which to find a new language capable of expressing clearly and forcefully the breakdown of the ordered stability of Renaissance Aristotelianism.

In this regard, the studies by Giorgio Bárberi Squarotti, thirty years later, remain fundamental for anyone wishing to do detailed research into the influence on Bruno of every single author in this realist and burlesque field. I limit myself to a brief summary of the stylistic elements that Bruno reworked in an original way in his writings.[7] Berni provides a wide-ranging sample of obscene metaphors, popular proverbs, and vulgar terms as a clear rejection of Petrarchan lyricism, in the name of a new concept of the comic that is much more elastic than the provincial burlesque code.[8] Aretino provides anti-academic prose, which is presented as a break with the tradition of Boccaccio; a prose constructed around various expressive registers that act upon vocabulary (an exaggerated play of metaphors sometimes leading to quite unexpected results) and upon syntax (breaking up sentences into numerous subordinate clauses).[9] Doni, going even further than Aretino, provides a particular interpretation of Tuscan "chatter" through a syntax in which the gap between the main clause and subordinate clauses becomes increasingly wider, and long lists of oppositions break from the central nucleus to become isolated in an autonomous space.[10] Franco provides an aggressive use of caricature and a peculiar technique of parody.[11] And, finally, Folengo gives refined examples of lexical and syntactical experimentation in the context of a decidedly antihumanist perspective.[12]

But it must be stressed immediately that Bruno's interest in these authors is not born of a particular concern with literary experimentation. Bruno saw the anti-classicist tradition as a reference point for his linguistic research, tending to create expressive modes capable of translating the violent revolt against the "Ptolemaic" system in philosophy and literature. Every element of writing (from grammar to syntax, from the dialogic structure to rhetoric, from the lexeme to the sentence) has to conform to the concept of an infinite universe where life pulsates within the smallest element and the *varietas* reigns supreme. One could begin with the vocabulary: scholarly words inhabit the same space as obscene and dialectal terminology; at their side are made-up words, the fruit of a pastiche of different languages. One has only to read this passage from the *Spaccio* to see the skillful way in which Bruno handles language, as if it were a moldable material:

Now what shall be done with the Cup? asked Mercury. What shall be done with the jar? Let it be given, said Momus, *iure successionis, vitae durante,* to the greatest drinker produced by high and low Germany, where Gluttony is exalted, praised, celebrated, and glorified among the heroic virtues, and Inebriation is numbered among the divine attributes; where by *treink* and *retreink, bibe* and *rebibe, ructa reructa, cespita recespita, vomi revomi usque ad egurgitationem utriusque iuris* [by drinking and drinking again, imbibing and imbibing again, belching and belching again, rolling on the ground and rolling again, vomiting and vomiting again to the point of a double regurgitation of soup], that is to say, to the point of regurgitating broth, soup, brain, soul, and sausage, *videbitur porcus porcorum in gloria Ciacchi* [the drinker will appear in all his glory as the pig of pigs]. Let him take Inebriation away with him. Do you not see her in German costume, with such huge breeches that look like the buckets of the abbot of Saint Antony when he goes begging, and those knickers billowing all over the place, as if wanting to fly up to heaven? . . . The standard-bearer Zampaglion carries a scarlet banner on which appear two starlings in the color of their own feathers; and joined by two yokes, four superb and glorious pigs—one white, one red, one mottled, and one black—cheerfully pulling the tiller; the first is called *Grungarganfestrofiel,* the second *Sorbillgramfton,* the third *Glutius,* and the fourth *Strafocazio.* (*Spaccio,* pp. 821–22)

Syntax, too, has to conform to these new demands. The use of hypotaxis sometimes leaves the reader breathless; the numerous subordinate clauses appear to take on an independent value under the effect of a centrifugal force that tends to break their link with the main clause. Similarly, the devices of *accumulatio* and *enumeratio* split sentences into a thousand rivulets, where long lists (sometimes made up of adjective/noun and verb/adjective pairings) end up creating a series of independent nuclei, a complex archipelago of meanings. The sentence tends to break up, as everything can be simultaneously at the center or on the margins. The sentence becomes an infinite universe—it is transformed into a plurality of worlds that are independent but linked by continuous processes of reciprocal interference. At times, the verb's preeminence is the deciding factor in the makeup of the sentence: in this amplified accumulation each component has its own autonomous existence, so that amplification does not appear to be a stylistic medium, but by means of its insistence reveals and important reality of thought:

> Behold the one who has crossed the air, penetrated the sky, wandered past the stars, crossed the limits of the world, broken down the imaginary barriers of the first, of the eighth, of the ninth, of the tenth sphere and more that could be postulated by vain mathematicians or blind and vulgar philosophers. With perfect sense and reason, it was he who used the key of his most diligent inquiry to open these two cloisters of knowledge to which we had no access. He has revealed nature, which was covered and veiled; he has endowed moles with sight, opened the eyes of the blind who were unable to look at their own image in the multitude of mirrors that surrounded them; he has untied the tongues of the dumb who knew not and dared not express intricate feelings; he has put the lame back

on their feet, they who with their spirit were unable to walk the path closed to the ignoble and dissoluble body; he renders the sun, the moon, and the other known stars as familiar as if we were their inhabitants; he shows how similar and dissimilar, better or worse are those bodies we can see far away from the one near us, the one to which we are joined; and he forces us to open our eyes and see our divine mother who carries us on her back, feeding and nourishing us after we leave her bosom, to which we always return, and he forbids us to see her as an inanimate and lifeless body, and nothing more than the dregs of corporeal substance. (*Cena*, p. 33)

Very often, on the other hand, there follow on from each other long sentences marked by the absence of a verb. The opening of the *Proemiale epistola* of the *Cena* unfolds into a long succession of oppositions. The two components of the antithesis, separated into two uniform blocks, speak to each other from a distance, almost as if to eliminate any element of conflict. And the fact that the tension in the first section is then resolved in the second, which in turn is totally dominated by micro-oppositions, betrays the reader's expectations by neutralizing them in a play that blurs any contrast. Antithesis breaks down as a rhetorical device and becomes something else; it is transformed into a many-sided prism that can polarize the different aspects of a complex and contradictory reality:

Behold, Sir, this banquet of nectar does not have the majesty of Thundering Jupiter; nor the disastrous effects for humanity of our first parents' meal; nor the mystery of that of Assuerus; nor the opulence of that of Lucullus; nor the sacrilege of that of Lycaon; nor the tragedy of that of Thyestes; nor the torment of that of Tantalus; nor

> the philosophy of that of Plato; nor the destitution of that
> of Diogenes; nor is it the bagatelle of that of leeches; nor
> a Berni-esque farce like that of an archpriest of Pogliano;
> nor a comedy like that of Bonifacio in the *Candelaio*; no,
> it is a meal both grand and humble; magisterial and un-
> learned; profane and sacred; gay and choleric; bitter and
> merry; slim as a Florentine and fat as a Bolognese; cynical
> and sardanapalian; trifling and serious; grave and clown-
> ish; tragic and comic; so that, I am sure you will have
> many opportunities to become heroic and humble; master
> and disciple; believer and nonbeliever; gay and sad; sat-
> urnine and jovial; light and heavy; rabid and liberal;
> as mocking as an ape and as stern as a consul; sophist
> with Aristotle, philosopher with Pythagoras; ready to
> laugh with Democritus and to cry with Heraclitus. (*Cena*,
> pp. 7–8)

Much could also be said about Bruno's ability to create variations
on an image through the subtle use of adjectives and verbs, wherein
the stylistic tension expresses the total rejection of a universe
shrouded in the darkness of ignorance:

> Here, thank God, I have been spared the sight of the cer-
> emony of the jug or the glasses that are passed around
> the table, from top to bottom, from left to right, and from
> other sides, following no other rule but that of who you
> know and the rudest of manners; when the ringleader has
> taken the vessel from his mouth, leaving it smeared with
> a film of fat which could easily be used as glue, the next
> person drinks from it and drops a crumb of bread into
> it; the next drinker leaves a tiny morsel of meat on the
> rim; the next one drops a bristle from his beard into it;
> all regale themselves thus amid merry chaos, never being

so impolite as not to enrich the communal drink with some
leftover caught in their moustache. Now if anyone—because they do not have the stomach, or because they feel
it is beneath them—is unwilling to drink, they merely
have to put the cup to their mouth and lightly blot their
lips upon it. There is a good reason for this practice; just
as everyone has come together, transforming themselves
into a single carnivorous wolf by feasting on the same
piece of lamb, of goat, of mutton, or of suckling pig
[Grunnio Corocotta], so, by drinking from the same cup,
they turn into a single leech, as a sign of their fraternal
union into one civility, one disease, one heart, one stomach, one throat, and one mouth. (*Cena*, pp. 82–84)[13]

Bruno's interest, in other words, is focused on a style of prose that
adds color and movement to the sentence, at times by the impact of
an incessant rhythm, at times by an explosive vocabulary and syntax. Language must reveal its infinite capacity to translate the complexity of reality.

Within this context, the *genera elocutionis* become ineffective.
They are incapable of expressing the *varietas* of the universe. They
offer only the ordered image of fixed and clearly defined spaces
where no interference can occur and where opposites remain tied
to precise rules. But what would be the point of the opposition between the *genus humile* and the *genus sublime* in a world where
tragedy and comedy, laughter and tears, the high and the low continually interact? Why would one want to preserve within distinct
spheres elements that testify to the instability and contradictory
nature of a reality in continuous motion?

The dialogic structure itself is based on choices and strategies
that repudiate the techniques of reasoning sanctioned by rhetoric.
We are faced not with a slow exchange of opinions leading to a final

resolution, but with a feverish dialogue made up of deviations, anticipations, interruptions, and afterthoughts. Bruno's dialogues are represented by the metaphorical image of the supper, where the variety of tastes and stomachs illustrates the variety of minds and desires:[14]

Filoteo. Do not be surprised, my brother, for this was nothing other than a supper, where minds are controlled by the desires aroused by the effects of taste and the influence of drink and food. The material and corporal supper, therefore, can be compared to the verbal and spiritual one; thus our conversation has its various and different courses, just as the other is wont to have its own; similarly, the conditions, circumstances, and means of this one are the same as those the other one might have.

Armesso. For pity's sake, speak so that I might understand you.

Filoteo. As is usual and fitting, this supper consists of salad and main courses, fruit and simple food, cuisine and spices, dishes for the healthy and for the sick, cold food and hot food, cooked food and raw food, fish and meat, home produce and game, roasts and boiled meat, the ripe and the unripe, the purely nutritious and gourmet dishes, substantial meals and light meals, flavorsome dishes and insipid dishes, sour food and sweet food, bitter food and savory food. In the same way here [in the dialogue], its contradictions and differences have appeared, made fit for contrasting and different stomachs and tastes that might like to take part in our symbolic banquet, so that nobody might complain of having come along in vain, and who dislikes this dish might take from another.

Armesso. That's true, but what will you say if your feast, your supper includes things that are good neither for salad nor main courses, neither for fruit nor simple food, neither for hot food nor for cold food, neither for raw food nor for cooked food, things that satisfy neither appetite nor hunger, that are good neither for the healthy nor for the sick, and that come from the hand neither of the chef nor of the spice seller?

Filoteo. You will see that in this regard, too, our supper is no different from any other. In the same way as there, in the finest of meals, either a mouthful that is too hot burns your mouth so that you have to spit it out, or, weeping tearfully, you roll it around your palate until you can manage that accursed gulp which sends it down your gullet. Or, indeed, one of your teeth makes you wince, or you bite your tongue while chewing on bread, or a little stone breaks off and becomes lodged in your teeth causing you to spit everything out, or one of the cook's hairs gets into your mouth almost making you vomit, or a fishbone gets stuck in your windpipe making you cough slightly, or a small bone lodges in your throat putting you at risk of choking; similarly, to our general displeasure, our supper includes things that correspond and are comparable to those. All of which is the result of the sin committed by our first parent Adam, on account of whom perverse human nature is condemned always to know pleasure at the same time as displeasure. (*Causa*, pp. 197–99)

The dialogic structure is undoubtedly conditioned by the variety of superimposed arguments and reflections placed within a pluridimensional text—within an enormous banquet where everyone takes "the fruits they can, according to the capacity of their stomach" (*Spaccio*, p. 555). The perfect circularity of Bembo's dialogic structure is dissolved with the disappearance of the symmetries between the length of the arguments and the duration of the various parts of the dialogue, between the characters' roles and their language, between the description of the milieux and the truths to be celebrated. The epideictic elements that had characterized the dialogue in the early sixteenth century (Bembo and Castiglione) are completely absent from Bruno's dialogues. There is no longer a homogeneous audience and milieu as in the *Asolani* and in the *Cortegiano* (epideictic discourse, in contrast to judicial and deliberative discourse, characteristically celebrates the values that the audience already accepts; as a result, the attention is focused on the message itself, on its aesthetic function, in an attempt to increase the intensity of shared values). Similarly the privilege of *elocutio* is completely absent (the leading role of this aspect of rhetoric in Bembo's and Castiglione's literary output has been amply documented).[15] The same diagetic technique, which characterized the dialogue in the early sixteenth century and responded perfectly to contemporary demands for accurate descriptions of milieux and of the social characters' status, no longer has any reason to exist. Bruno's dialogues are set in unspecified locations and, very often, are between deliberately unspecified characters.[16] The choice of a mimetic technique, taken to its extremes, is well suited to a systematic elimination of spatiotemporal coordinates, within a dialogic structure in which "where" and "when" have no meaning, precisely because our attention is concentrated on quite different elements. The aesthetic appreciation of truths accepted from the outset by the community to which they belong (very often, in Bembo and Castiglione, disputes and disagreements are resolved in the ultimate "conversion" of all the characters, thereby revealing them as the product of pure literary fiction)[17] gives way to troubled reflections on a problematic vision of a far from balanced world. Bruno's assured attack on all-encompassing false values, his demolition of philosophical positions that refute the inexorable process of acquiring knowledge, does not fashion yet another unidimensional stance or create one absolute truth. During the phase of positive resolution, destructive fury gives way to an enthusiasm that spasmodically elucidates a mode of thought that, despite being quite unsystematic, nevertheless manages to reveal its profound motivations. Within a dialogic structure that negates all final resolutions, Bruno's idea of truth becomes fluid, is scattered into tiny fragments, and lives in a climate of perfect harmony with an unstable and precarious universe. In the *Epistola dedicatoria* of the *Spaccio*, Bruno addresses his readers with a request: "may nobody have such a wicked heart and such a malicious spirit as to want to explain, and allow themselves and others to believe, that what is written in this book is a statement of fact" (p. 553). In the *Cabala*, too, Bruno stresses the impossibility of bringing his "descriptive horse" to an end, an impossibility virtually decreed by "the order of the universe," according to which things are seen only in part and not in their totality: "Now I believe the occasion will pass to express many more thoughts on the cabala of the said horse. For, as I see it, the order of the universe requires that in the celestial region this horse be seen only as far as its navel (and there is a dispute over whether the star at its end is the head of Andromeda or the trunk of this venerable beast), similarly, by way of analogy, it means that this descriptive horse cannot reach completion" (*Cabala*, pp. 911–12).

The main characters themselves do not progress in a strictly linear fashion. At times, they reveal conflicts and contradictions that, their particular role unobscured, are posited as elements of reflection, as evidence of a pluridimensional reality. Hence the importance of the Onorio-Aristotle character who is presented in the dual role, first, of mouthpiece for Bruno's philosophy, and, second, of former Aristotle responsible for a thousand abuses of power.[18] Just as, in the *Candelaio*, Gioan Bernardo, initially having attributed the world's degeneracy to fortune, soon after changes his mind and extols the possibility humanity has of shaping reality according to its own will, of molding its own destiny.[19] Jupiter himself, in his authoritative position as father of the gods, at the beginning of the

Spaccio, attacks Chiron but, by the end, grants him a prestigious role in the zodiac.[20]

The way in which Bruno proceeds is marked by a constant invitation to consider things in their complexity, thereby abandoning positions that are not justified by profound and considered reflection. Bruno's statements, in a passage from the *De minimo*, explicitly reveal the importance, in his concept of philosophy, of the search for comparison and for dialogue; indeed, for a dialogue in which listening comes first:

> Who desires to philosophize, beginning by doubting everything, must not decide in favor of one side of the contradiction, before having heard the counterarguments, and, after having carefully considered and weighed up all the reasons, let him judge and pronounce, not from hearsay, from rumor, according to the number, the seniority, the repute, and the dignity [of the arguments], but according to the constancy of the doctrine to itself and all things, and, yes, even according to the light of reason, illuminated by truth. (*Opp. lat.*, I, III, p. 137)

Not a single element, therefore, can escape Bruno's philosophical design. Even his concept of language, as we have partly seen, expresses a strict relationship with philosophy. Words and terminology become malleable materials that are controlled and shaped to express a view of the world.[21] Humanity must not give up its power over language, because "we ought not to be like them [grammarians], the slaves of certain terms and of certain words, but by the grace of the gods, we are permitted and have the freedom to make them our servants, taking them and accommodating them at our convenience and at our pleasure" (*Spaccio*, pp. 552–53). In the *De minimo*, by taking his proposition to its extremes, Bruno reaffirms

the possibility of inventing new words, whenever the demands of a
new way of thinking call for this:[22]

> We will be the usage and the principle, when we will drag
> From the depths of the darkness with ancient words
> The most celebrated dogmas of the Ancients,
> If it is needed, we will be the inventors of new words
> For new things, wherever these words might come from.
> Let Grammarians be the servants of words, we will have
> words serve us,
> Let them observe the usage we have attached to them.
> (*Opp. lat.*, I, III, p. 135)

Bruno's philosophical design, therefore, opens up new lines of research. "[Bruno's concept of] language," writes Ciliberto, "is an
expressive reality, but not of 'grammatical' or merely linguistic
meanings; it becomes the expression of ethical, religious, and political values. The linguistic plane becomes interwoven with the
essential planes of human history, fusing with them completely. . . .
The new vision of the world becomes interlaced with a new concept
of language. Out of this new way of thinking there blossoms a struc-
turally anti-pedantic language, capable of expressing, pliantly and
flexibly, the infinite plurality of human and natural languages, the
variety of reality, and the wealth and complexities of humanity and
its experiences, highlighting those peculiar and specific characteristics that grammarians, the cultivators of abstract synonymies, ig-
nore and progressively annihilate.[23]

Bruno attacks a "Ptolemaic" view of language and blames Aristotle, but above all the Aristotelians of his own time, for the unidimensionality of a philosophy that, from cosmology to language,
has negated the existence of multiplicity.[24] Thus, along with Skep-

tics, Aristotelians, and evangelical reformers,[25] Bruno includes
grammarians and pedants on the side of negative asininity:

> He is one of those who, having made a nice construction,
> produced an elegant little epistle, cadged a pretty phrase
> from Cicero's breast, believes that now Demosthenes is
> resuscitated, now Tullius thrives, now Sallust lives again;
> here is an Argus who sees every letter, every syllable,
> every word; here Rhadamanthus *umbras vocat ille sil-*
> *entum;* here Minos, king of Crete, *urnam movet.* He calls
> for the examination of orations, discusses phrases and
> says: 'this is by a poet, this by a comic, this by an orator;
> this is serious, this is lighthearted, that is sublime, and
> that is *humile dicendi genus;* this oration is harsh, it
> would be lighthearted if it were composed thus; this
> writer is a child, barely versed in Antiquity, *non redo-*
> *let Arpinatem, desipit Latinum* [He is not the Arpin-
> ian (Cicero), he is clumsy with Latin]. This word is
> not Tuscan, it is not used by Boccaccio, Petrarch, or
> other proven authors.' . . . Endowed with such self-
> importance, while each of us is one, he alone is every-
> thing. When he laughs, he is called Democritus; when he
> grieves, he is called Heraclitus; when he disputes, he is
> called Chrysippus; when he discourses, his name is Aris-
> totle; when he indulges in idle fancy, he is known as Plato;
> when he bellows a little sermon, his title is Demosthenes;
> when he constructs some Virgil, he himself becomes Maro.
> Now he corrects Achilles, approves of Aeneas, draws on
> Hector, exclaims against Pyrrhus, laments over Priam,
> blames Turnus, excuses Dido, commends Achates; and,
> finally, while *verbum verbo reddit* and throws in barbaric
> synonyms *nihil divinum a se alienum putat.* Thus, full of

conceit, he gets down from his podium, like one who has
sorted out the heavens, organized senates, subdued ar-
mies, reformed different worlds; it is certain that, but for
the ravages of time, he would put his thoughts into practice. (*Causa*, pp. 215–17)[26]

Bruno's anti-pedantic critique, despite at times having recourse to
elements already exploited in previous works of literature, is not
resolved by deliberately creating a comic character as an end in
itself or by clearly revealing a sense of disgust. It embodies, in
fact, an ideological condemnation of a universe that confuses
knowledge and eloquence, since it moves only along the surface of
the grammatical meaning of things without grasping their deeper
content.[27]

Grammarians and pedants (with their philological and linguistic apparatus) are situated opposite philosophers: the former
play with words and remain within the darkness of ignorance; the
latter go beyond words, toward the difficult paths of knowledge.
The role of the pedant Poliinnio, in the *Causa*, cannot be analyzed in a superficial manner, for behind the caricature of a
grammarian lies a carefully drawn picture of what Bruno really
means by doctor/pedant. What strikes one most forcefully is the
figure of "the rigid censors of philosophers" (*Causa*, p. 215), of
those who think that "from the knowledge of languages . . .
comes the knowledge of every science" (*Causa*, p. 257), of those
"doctors [who] come cheap like sardines, because with little effort they multiply, are found and caught, and so can be bought at
a low price" (*Causa*, p. 212).[28] In the massed ranks of pedants,
Poliinnio explicitly embodies also Petrus Ramus and Francesco
Patrizi:

It is easy for all to see that the former most eloquently
shows himself to be none too wise; the latter, to put it

simply, shows that he has much of the beast and the ass
in him. One could even say that the former understood
Aristotle, but understood him wrongly, for if he had understood him rightly, perhaps he would have had the good
sense to wage glorious war against him, as was done by
the most judicious Telesio of Cosenza. Of the latter, one
cannot say he understood him either wrongly or rightly,
but that he read and reread him, sewed and unsewed
him . . . ; and, in the end, he put in a huge effort, which
not only proved unprofitable but *etiam* was a great waste,
so that whoever wishes to see to what depths of madness
and presumptuous vanity the cloak of the pedant can
lead, only has to look at this book, before its seed dis-
appears. (*Causa*, pp. 260–61)[29]

But the fundamental element that characterizes the condition
of pedant asses is their wasting time searching for futile things, in
a life that passes so quickly, where not even a single moment must
be lost. Intellectual idleness only reproduces itself, in a negative
process of self-germination in which superfluities grow on superfluities. And there is no chance of escaping the darkness of this vicious
circle. However, the position of those who "by scaling the high rock
and lofty tower of contemplation" take up "arms against dark ignorance" is quite another matter:[30]

They do not spend their time—whose speed is infinite—
on frivolous and vain things, for the present passes with
such astonishing speed, and the future approaches at
the same pace. What we have lived is nothing, what we
are living is a moment, and what we are to live is not
yet a moment, but can be a moment, which both will be
and will have been. And meanwhile, this one burdens
his mind with genealogies, that one devotes himself to

deciphering writings, and the other is busy drawing up
infantile sophisms. . . . Here they do not eat, here they
lose weight, here they grow weak, here their skin wrin-
kles, here their beard grows long, here they rot, here
they drop the anchor of supreme good. In the name of
these futilities they scorn fortune, they use them as a
defense and raise their shield against the onslaught of
fate. With these and other most vile thoughts they believe they can reach the stars, be the equals of the gods,
and understand the beauty and good promised by philosophy. (*Eroici*, pp. 1116–17)

And it is precisely within this merciless condemnation of intellectual
idleness[31] that Bruno attacks Petrarchan literature. His invective
does not assume the mantle of a fierce criticism of a particular type
of literature from a purely literary point of view. Bruno does not
set one poetic against another. His severe judgment is born of ethical and ideological motivations, which lead to the rejection of a
language that is impoverished, repetitive, and lacking any edifying
content.[32] Only in light of this position is it possible to understand
the significance of this late anti-Petrarchan polemic in a historical
context, where anti-Petrarchism had already been "metabolized"
and Petrarchism had begun to break up.[33] Indeed, in a famous
passage from the *Eroici furori*, Bruno presents, and corrodes from
the inside, a wide-ranging sample of Petrarchan language—a code
based exclusively on the repetition of commonplaces—with the intention of showing just what literature, according to Bruno's view,
ought not to be:

Behold traced on paper, enclosed in books, put before
one's eyes and intoned to one's ears a sound, a din, an
uproar of emblems, of devices, of mottos, of epistles, of
sonnets, of epigrams, of tomes, of prolix notebooks, of

agonized sweats, of worn-out lives, accompanied by
screams that deafen the stars, wailing that resounds
through the caves of hell, sufferings that stupefy living
souls, sighs that make the gods collapse with compassion.
And all that for those eyes, for those cheeks, for that bust,
for that white and for that vermilion, for that tongue,
those teeth, those lips, that hair, those clothes, that cloak,
that glove, that shoe, that slipper, that parsimoniousness,
that pretty smile, that little sulk, that widowed window, that eclipsed sun, that hammering, that disgust, that
stink, that sepulcher, that cesspit, that menstruation,
that carcass, that quartan fever, that terrible injustice
and wrong of nature, which by means of a surface, a
shadow, a phantom, a dream, a spell cast by Circe in the
service of generation, gives us the illusion of beauty.
(*Eroici*, pp. 928–29)[34]

Bruno's dissent extends to the whole process of normalization and
codification of genres that had characterized the debate surrounding Aristotle's *Poetica* during the sixteenth century. The future of
literature could not be left to pedantic asses, incapable of any action
outside the complicated universe of rules. In other words, Bruno
contested the notion that it is possible to provide, by means of man-
uals of rhetoric and grammar, precise canons and clear boundaries
between one genre and another, between what is poetry and what
is not. Within such prefabricated grids there is no chance of opening
up new areas of research, of offering a natural picture of the variety
of "poets" and of "minds":

Cicada. So, there are different kinds of poets and crowns?

Tansillo. Not just as many as the Muses, but a great deal more; for,
although certain genres exist, specific types and kinds of human intelligence cannot be determined.

Cicada. There are certain people who draw up rules for poetry and
have great difficulty in accepting Homer as a poet, while rejecting Virgil, Ovid, Martial, Hesiod, Lucretius, and many
other verse writers, having examined them according to the
rules of Aristotle's *Poetica*.

Tansillo. Be sure, my brother, that these are truly beasts, for they do
not consider these rules as principally serving to describe what
Homeric poetry is, or other similar types in particular; they
do not understand that they are there to describe an epic poet
like Homer, and not to establish others who, using other veins,
constructions, and inspirations, could be equal, comparable,
and greater in other genres.

Cicada. Indeed, Homer, in his genre, was not in any way a poet who
relied on rules, but it is in·the nature of rules that they serve
those who are wont to imitate rather than create; and they
have been collated by one who was not a poet at all, but knew
how to assemble rules of that one kind, in other words, of
Homeric poetry, to serve someone who would want to become,
not another poet, but a poet like Homer, not his own muse,
but the ape of another's muse.

Tansillo. You are right to say that poetry is not born of rules, unless
by a slight accident, but that rules derive from poetry; and
thus there are as many types and kinds of true rules as there
are types and kinds of true poet. (*Eroici*, pp. 957–59)

In this passage Bruno clearly distinguishes the work of the "critic"
and that of the "poet"; the former identifies poetic modes and
forms, and the latter concentrates on artistic creation. Bárberi
Squarotti states that "there are as many varieties of 'rules' as there
are varieties of poet and of poetic genres, and these can be traced
back through the centuries, given that 'rules' were nothing more
than critical classifications, instruments of exegesis, explanations

justifying every author and every work.''[35] Bruno situates the problem of the misinterpretation of the *Poetica* in a historical context:
one cannot consider Aristotle's description of the Homeric epic as
an absolute and universal norm of how to write poetry. In doing so,
one loses sight of the sense of history and grants pedantic asses the
final judgment, the possibility of excluding "certain [writers] from
the circle of poets, . . . because the opening of their books and poems does not conform to those of Homer and Virgil, or because they
do not observe the custom of introducing an invocation, or because
they interweave one story or fable with another, or because they
end their verses with a summary of what has been said and with a
description of what is to come" (*Eroici*, p. 959).

Bruno's affirmation ("poetry is not born of rules, unless by a
slight accident, but rules derive from poetry") acquires its true
meaning only within the context I have outlined so far: it is not a
prelude to the romantic glorification of the "rebel genius" who rejects every rule,[36] but it becomes a polemical formula with which to
reaffirm the need to abandon a literature of sterile imitations, in
the name of a new line of inquiry aimed at shedding light on important realities of thought. Once again, Bruno confines himself to
demolishing absolutist positions, without offering universal pre-
cepts: in reply to Cicada's question ("So how will true poets be
recognized?"), Tansillo answers with a tautology: "By the singing
of their verses." The real difference, for Bruno, can be grasped
only in the content, in the teleology of the poem: "Worthy of their
laurels are those who fittingly sing heroic things, either by instructing heroic souls in speculative and moral philosophy, or by celebrating them and presenting them as an exemplary mirror for
political and civil acts" (*Eroici*, p. 957). Literature cannot be separated from the course of philosophy and of knowledge; it has to
be an instrument of social and civil progress, it must serve a more

open vision of the world, it must translate the totalities of a constantly changing reality. This is why Bruno situates canonical and anti-classicist literature on the same plane: both lack any design, and tensions and frictions arise and subside within their literary codes. On this basis Bruno draws a distinction between "poets" and "versifiers": the latter, condemned to live within the space of negative asininity, roam the realm of idleness, and it is precisely these "vain versifiers who, to the detriment of the world, want to pass for poets" (*Spaccio*, p. 744), who are identified with grammarians and pedants.[37] Poets and philosophers, on the other hand, dwell on the opposite bank. They dedicate themselves to study and to research, they strive to penetrate the meaning of things, because knowledge comes not from above but is the fruit of one's own intellectual labors: "One does not become a poet or a philosopher out of mere talent, but also by hard work and by study" (*Opp. lat.*, III, p. 142).

Bruno sees literature as a form of philosophical painting, a representation of reality in all its different aspects, an artistic operation in the service of knowledge. The philosopher/painter relationship appears many times in Bruno's works: the use of imagery is strictly linked to the concepts it represents, and it is precisely by means of imagery that we can grasp the mediation between object and concept.[38] It is not necessary to reproduce reality in its totality, but it is also possible to shed light on some of its aspects from "certain obscure and confused outlines and shadows, like those of painters" (*Spaccio*, p. 554). Bruno aims to specify the fragmentary nature of his philosophical painting by presenting in the *Cabala* a description of asininity made up of details, where, despite not seeing the whole image, the reader/spectator is nevertheless able to grasp a deep significance in the fragments of the text/picture:

And if this reason does not satisfy you, you must also consider the fact that this short work contains a description, a painting, and that in portraits more often than not it is enough to show only the head and no more. I grant you that sometimes one can see the perfect execution of a single hand, a foot, a leg, an eye, a slender ear, half a face visible behind a tree, or in the corner of a window, or as if sculpted on the side of a cup, whose base is the foot of a goose, or the claw of an eagle, or of some other animal; however, it is not condemned or devalued by this, but its workmanship is all the more appreciated and approved. (*Cabala*, pp. 843–44)[39]

It is the ass, in the dialogue appended to the *Cabala*, who clarifies a fundamental element of Bruno's reflections on aesthetics. Bruno rejects the absolutist universal categories of the beautiful, substituting for them a set of new criteria based on the fluid laws of relativism. Objective beauty does not exist; instead, aesthetic communication comes about by means of a complex web of relationships between "the charming subject" and "the charmed object."[40] Thus the Cyllenean ass explains to Micco, the academician, that "the pig does not have to be a handsome horse, nor the ass a beautiful human; but the ass a beautiful ass, the pig a handsome pig, the human a beautiful human. That if, to continue in this vein, the horse is not attractive to the pig, then neither is the pig attractive to the horse; if the ass is not attractive to the human, and the human does not fall in love with the ass, then similarly neither is the human attractive to the ass and the ass does not fall in love with the human. So that, in considering this law, when things will be examined and weighed up with reason, the one will concede to the other, according to their own affections, that there are different kinds of beauty depending on how one sees the proportions of different beings, and that nothing is truly and absolutely beautiful" (*Asino cillenico*, pp. 919–20).[41] From such a perspective, even what is usually called "ugly" can belong to art, and all things that exist in the universe live in a condition of equal dignity.

The subject returns once again to the figures of the ass and of Mercury. Indeed, Bruno does not refrain from using two symbols that under certain conditions, are certainly not incompatible with what is commonly defined as "little dignity."[42] Bruno's concept of literature itself is closely associated with the meaning of the proverb *asinus portans mysteria:* one must adore not asses, but the divinities they carry, just as one must see literature purely in terms of its precise function as a "vehicle" for thought. One's attention cannot be concentrated only on the medium, because what it "transports" is essential. Bruno's writing, in all its aspects, expresses philosophical thought and stylistically exists in strict harmony with its "content." It is a form of writing that, under the sign of Mercury/Thoth, embodies *coincidentia oppositorum* and the *varietas* of the infinite universe; just like Mercury, it does not allow itself to be assigned a fixed position, but finds its roots in the perpetual play of differences.[43] In an infinity of worlds without a center, nothing can have fixed coordinates, and everything can be sometimes here, sometimes there, sometimes above, sometimes below.[44] Bruno's writing reflects the instability and the unrest characteristic of the precarious nature of the universe, which, way out of balance, appears to be running toward entropy; an entropy that does not renounce meaning, but proposes a new search for meaning: "meaning does not limit itself, for wherever it goes, always and everywhere it is visible at the center of the horizon, whether it shifts its observation point on the surface of the earth or on the edges of the universe as it crosses other worlds" (*Opp. lat.*, I, I, p. 204). The old cosmological concept that relegated the "edges" to a perpetually marginal position falls to pieces, for everything can become the center, every element can occupy a different place. Thus, what yesterday might have been deemed meaningless, today becomes meaningful, given all the possible different angles, and this meaning sometimes appears precisely where nobody would have thought it possible: "Consider, too, that there is no word that is idle, for everywhere one has to reap and dig up things of great importance, and perhaps even more so there where one least expects it" (*Cena*, p. 15).

CHAPTER 14

Natural Science and Human Science:
A "Nouvelle Alliance"

The opposition established by Bruno in the field of human science between the philosopher and the grammarian, which I addressed in the previous chapter, corresponds, in the field of natural science, to the opposition between the philosopher and the mathematician. Bruno draws a distinction between the position of the philosopher, who seeks to penetrate the deeper meaning of things, and the different but complementary stance of mathematicians and grammarians, who move along the same plane of superficiality, providing an exclusively descriptive reading of phenomena, which does not grasp their deeper meaning or, at best, does not deduce the necessary consequences arising from them. As Ciliberto has rightly pointed out, Bruno also translates the terms of this opposition onto the linguistic plane, through two antithetical pairings: "words"/"feelings" ("Philosophies and laws do not go to ruin for lack of interpreters of words, but for lack of those who deeply penetrate feelings"; *Causa*, p. 258) and "signs"/"verifications" ("Signs you will find in mathematics, verifications in the other moral and speculative faculties"; *Causa*, p. 335).[1] If grammarians turn their attention to "words" and mathematicians to "signs," the philosopher's task is to go beyond "words" and "signs" and to probe "feelings" and "verifications."

This distinction utilized by Bruno will help us to understand

better his relationship with Copernicus. Bruno, in fact, despite singing the Polish astronomer's praises, does not fail to underline that
"he trusted his own eyes and not those of Copernicus, nor those of
Ptolemy, as regards making judgments and reaching conclusions."
Indeed, Bruno so appreciated Copernicus that he gets angry with
the ass Osiander who, in the foreword to the *De revolutionibus*,
undermined the importance of the innovative aspects of his work.[2]
At the same time, he claimed for himself the possibility of going
further than Copernicus precisely on the basis of the astronomer's
theories:

> A few days ago, two men came to see Bruno on behalf of
> one of the royal squires, with the request that the king
> would like to speak to him: he wanted to understand his
> Copernicus and other paradoxes of his new philosophy.
> To which Bruno replied that he trusted his own eyes and
> not those of Copernicus, nor those of Ptolemy, as regards
> making judgments and reaching conclusions. Although,
> as regards observations, he was most grateful to these
> and other great mathematicians whose succession of
> works and accumulated discoveries have given us a solid
> base on which to found our judgment, which was made
> possible only after numerous centuries of toil. He added
> that, in effect, they are like interpreters who translate
> words from one idiom into another; but then it is others,
> not they themselves, who go on to probe feelings. (*Cena*,
> pp. 26–27)

Mathematicians, like the translators of "words,"[3] are content to
act only on the surface of things. They carry out an operation that,
being an end in itself, cannot translate the complexities of what they
are working on: "it is one thing to play with geometry, it is quite
another to verify things with nature" (*Cena*, p. 148).[4] Bruno's phi-

losophy goes beyond the "signs" identified by Copernicus's genius: the Copernican solar system can occupy any point of the infinite universe, since there is no necessity that the sun be at the center of a cosmology wherein centers no longer have any meaning. Infinite space radically replaces finite space, and new possibilities arise in a world where the mind may wander limitlessly, where thought is freed from the narrow prison of the old philosophy and heads toward the discovery of new horizons:[5]

> Persevere, my good Filoteo, persevere; do not lose courage and do not fall back saying that, with intrigue and machination, the great and grave senate of foolish ignorance threatens and attempts to destroy your divine enterprise and admirable work. . . . Continue to teach us what the skies really are, what the planets and all the stars really are; how the infinite worlds are all distinct from each other; how an infinite space is not impossible, but necessary; how such infinite effect befits the infinite cause; what is the true substance, matter, act, and efficient cause of everything, and how every sensible and complex thing is formed by the same principles and elements. Persuade us of the knowledge of the infinite universe. Rend asunder the concave and convex, which surfaces mark the limits, inside and out, of so many elements and heavens. Ridicule deferential orbs and fixed stars. Break and hurl to the ground with a crash and an avalanche of excellent reasons what the blind vulgar herd holds to be the adamantine wall of the Primum Mobile and ultimate convexity. Destroy the idea that this earth is the only true center of the universe. Reject the ignoble faith in this quintessence. Give us the science with which to recognize that this our star, our world has the same composition as every other

star and world we can see. Let every infinitely great and
vast world nourish and feed, according to its successions
and orders, other infinitely small worlds. Smash extrinsic
motors along with the limits of these heavens. Open the
door through which we might see that this star is no different from any other. Show the consistency of the other
worlds in the ether, which is the same as this one. Make
clear that the motion of all things comes from their inner
soul, so that in light of such contemplation we might proceed with a surer step toward the understanding of nature. (*De l'infinito*, pp. 534–36)[6]

Bruno is aware of the innovative weight of his philosophy. The series of verbs used in this passage from the *De l'infinito* repeatedly
stresses the violent break with Aristotelian cosmology: "Rend asun-
der," "Ridicule," "Break and hurl," "Destroy," "Reject." This
destructive rage translates the need for liberty, the absolute urgency of breaking down the barriers that separate man from the
infinite universe. "Knowledge," observes Biagio De Giovanni,
"cannot be written in terms other than these; the characteristics of
knowledge are the same as those of infinite life. A knowledge that
forgets its vital roots could become illusory; Copernicus, who grasps
and calculates the motion of the earth, nevertheless ties his discovery to a fixed point in the universe and thus remains confined within
the prejudices of vulgar philosophy. But this comes about for a
reason that Bruno's philosophical "candor" declares unequivocally: nature cannot be written in mathematical and geometrical
terms. Whosoever claims to exhaust the writing of the world with
mathematical language may be able to calculate motion, but not
"verify" the subject of this motion; they may be able to measure
the harmony and the precision of the universe, but not grasp its
infinite and unrestricted dimension."[7] Within this context, Yates's

criticism of Bruno appears all the more unjustified. Bruno does not "relegate Copernicus's scientific work to a pre-scientific stage," but shifts the Polish astronomer's discoveries to a different plane; a plane that, beyond pure mathematical calculation, undoubtedly opens up new areas of research.[8]

Bloch's reflections on Renaissance philosophy help to give us a better understanding of Bruno's position. Between a "qualitative philosophy" (which sees man as an incomplete being, troubled by conflict and contradiction, and matter as "being-in-possibility," in constant tension and development) and a "quantitative philosophy" (which favors calculation, domination, and artificiality), Bruno belongs to the former tendency.[9] This tendency, when analyzed in light of certain categories proposed by Bloch, reveals its full novelty. The concepts of *Zwischenwelten* ("the theoretical interstices present in every philosophy in which the new inadvertently makes headway," that is, "seeds of the future, unconsumed thoughts that will ripen later, once the right climate and soil are found"), *Ungleichzeitigkeit* ("the asynchrony that implies an articulated concept of historical time as a set of different levels and temporal distortions, in which the past is not always dead and inert, but can be charged up with the future like a loaded spring"), and *Multiversum* ("reality impregnated with possibles," "negation of a predetermined *Universum* devoid of the openings and 'surprises' of the future") reveal that aspects of thought considered "unscientific" and "irrational," because they are alien to the Weltanschauung of an age tied to the *quantitas* of calculation and profit, nevertheless contain "truths" that will come to light once analyzed with the instruments of a new *ratio* based on different premises.[10]

In Bruno's thought, "science" and "literature" do not correspond to the "signs" of mathematicians and the "words" of grammarians, but fuse and become indistinguishable in a process that identifies them with philosophy and with life. In the *Proemiale epistola* to the *Cena*, the reader is warned that "this may appear to be less a science than a mixture of dialogue, of comedy, of tragedy, of poetry, of eloquence; that praises, accuses, demonstrates, and teaches; that sometimes refers to physics, sometimes to mathematics, sometimes to morals, and sometimes to logic. In a word, every shred of science is included" (*Cena*, p. 15). It is precisely these shreds of science that evidence the impossibility of creating totalizing systems and truths in which even humanity becomes the object of the pretension to quantify everything. And the full force of Bruno's attack against those who "measure humanity with the same yardstick as that used for velvet, and weigh human souls on scales made for metal" (*Cena*, p. 15) could not be understood outside of this context.

Knowledge has to translate the complexity of the world. It cannot be described as if it were heading toward a final accomplishment. Its destiny is directed toward the infinite, toward an interminable path to which every age bears witness. For this reason we are more knowledgeable today than were the scholars of the past, just as our successors will know more than we do:

Prudenzio. However that may be, I do not want to remove myself from the opinions of the Ancients, for the wise man says, in antiquity lies knowledge.

Teofilo. And he adds that prudence comes with age. If you really understood what you are saying, you would see that from the basis of your thought, one infers the opposite of what you are thinking. I mean to say, we are older and of a more advanced age than our forebears; at least as regards certain questions, such as the one we are discussing. The judgment of Eudoxus, who lived shortly after the rebirth of astronomy, could not have been as mature—even if astronomy were not born with him—as that of Calippus, who lived thirty years after the death of Alexander the Great and accumulated observations as he accumulated years. Hipparchus, for the same reason, must have known more than Calippus, because he could see the changes that had occurred one hundred and ninety-six years after the death of Alexander. Since Menelaus, the Roman geometer, could see different movements in the sky four hundred and sixty-two years after Alexander's death, it would be reasonable to say that he knew more than Hipparchus. Muhammad of Arata [al-Battani] must have known yet more one thousand two hundred years later. Copernicus, almost in our time, knew more about it one thousand eight hundred and forty-nine years later. It is true that some others were no more discerning than their forebears, and that most of our contemporaries have lost all insight; the reason being that the former did not and the latter do not live the years of others, and, what is worse, they all lived their own years as if they were dead. (*Cena*, pp. 39–41)

Bruno's original development of the theme *veritas filia temporis*[11] exalts the progressive nature of knowledge. The infinite universe becomes the theater of infinite dynamic processes. The torment of matter in its search for a definite "form" and the torment of humanity in its search for an absolute "truth" offer a new, unified image of nature.[12] Humanity's anthropological dimension reveals its essence in its imbalance, just as the vicissitudes of matter are also way out of balance. Philosophy, life, science, literature, physics, and ethics all speak the same language, the language of the precarious nature of the universe and of its deep complexity.[13]

The division between "human science" and "natural science" is healed by a deep-seated union, since all that exists is subject to the same vicissitudes. Bruno formulated what today certain scientists and philosophers of science call the "nouvelle alliance," a space of interdisciplinary exchange wherein physics and the poetic observation of nature move over the same ground.[14]

Using this as our point of departure, we may be able to discover some openings toward new avenues of research. A possible reference point could be the studies of Michel Serres, in particular, as far as I am concerned, his fascinating reading of Lucretius's *De rerum natura*.[15] The French philosopher sees the poem as one of the great examples of the "alliance" of science, philosophy, physics, ethics, and nature. Within an infinite universe, Lucretius's atomism becomes a science of turbulence, a science of complexity, where everything is unstable and precarious, where everything runs toward death and toward life. Going beyond deterministic, universal, and eternal laws, a reality appears that is fragmented, way out of balance, and rich in qualitative differences. It is necessary to analyze, bearing in mind the relevant differences, how much influence, from the epistemological point of view, Lucretius's model exerted on Bruno. The philosopher refers frequently to the *De rerum natura*, and in some cases it deeply conditions the choices he makes. Lucretius's influence may be felt in Bruno's thinking on spontaneous generation, the plurality of worlds, atomism, the eternal nature of matter; Lucretius even affects the very structure of the Latin poems (*De monade, De immenso, De minimo*).[16] But at this point, the relationship becomes more complex as it takes on the pluridimensional role of Lucretianism during the sixteenth century. Many important observations have already been made in this regard by Raimondi, Garin, and Papi, who, with reference to particular authors, have shed light on certain aspects of how the *De rerum natura* was received.[17] There is still much work to be done, especially on clarifying the role of philosophers like Bruno who, having lived on the margins of the so-called science *par excellence*, have nevertheless made, thanks to their intuition, an indispensable contribution to the progress of science, at times rendering its path problematic.[18]

The relationship between Bruno and Lucretius, within this vision based on a single "open" epistemological model in which "human science" and "natural science" converge, for the moment must remain purely hypothetical, or, to be on the safe side, merely a suggestion. This suggestion, to return to the main theme of my inquiry, brings us back to certain key elements of asininity. The symbol of the ass is closely linked to water, and it is water that, according to Michel Serres, forms the basis for Lucretius's epistemological opening.[19] Positive asininity, in Bruno's view, becomes the realm of complexity, of the fluidity of the real and of the perpetual process of change in everything. The open universe of positive asses is contrasted to the closed universe of negative asses, dynamism is contrasted to stability, and perpetual research to the absolute vision of knowledge. Such research, from this perspective, becomes the guarantor of a fruitful relationship between the various kinds of knowledge, where no model can claim absolute legitimacy, where "human science" and "natural science" come together in the infinite universe. The ass takes on the role of Mercury, the god of exchanges, of crossovers, of dealing, and of interferences.[20] Bruno turns his attention toward the search for points of convergence, precisely because knowledge of "nature's greatest secrets" is to be found at "the point of union" (*Causa*, p. 340). True philosophy must enrich itself with every methodological contribution that can open up new areas of inquiry, since "just as sometimes a single path can lead to different destinations, / A single method does not lead to a single outcome" (*Opp. lat.*, I, III, p. 283).[21] Only thus will it be possible to understand the essence of the *varietas*, to which the ass bears witness by embodying, as Farra states in his *Settenario*, the infinite variety of the forms taken by matter and therefore the variety of the entire universe.[22]

The path we have taken has not been easy. The ass and Mercury have shown us their many-sided nature in all its complexity. But this should have been expected: if the former bears secrets, the latter is the god who can lead travelers down the right path or, on the other hand, can make them lose their way.[23] The cabala of the ass, therefore, has revealed its true nature as a "cabala": it has replaced the combinatory play of atoms/words in the Torah with a complex labyrinth of images, myths, and meanings.[24] I conclude by citing a passage from the *Cena*, which recounts Saul's adventures in his search for lost asses. Here, apart from indulging in a subtle polemic against Christianity, Bruno particularly emphasizes the importance of "searching":

> Do you not know that when the son of Quish, named Saul, went in search of the asses, he was judged worthy of being crowned king of the Israelites? Well, go and read the first book of Samuel, and you will see that this noble character set greater store on finding the asses than on being anointed king. Indeed, it appears he would not have been satisfied with the throne without finding the asses. Thus each time Samuel spoke of crowning him, he would reply: "But where are the asses? the asses, where are they? My father has sent me in search of the asses, do you not want me to find my asses?" In short, he could not settle until the prophet told him that the asses had been found, perhaps wanting to say that the kingdom was his and that he could be satisfied, for it was worth much more than his asses. Thus you can see that at times the search for such a thing is worth more than a kingdom. Thus heaven is full

of promises. Now, Teofilo, continue with your speech.
Tell us of the successes of this searching undertaken by
Bruno; let us hear what else happened in the course of
this journey. (*Cena*, p. 66)[25]

And, like Saul, we too have set off in search of asses . . .

The Italian edition of this book contained thirteen xylographs. With one exception (which was taken from the German translation of Petrarch's *De remediis ultriusque Fortunae*), all the xylographs came from the same source: Sebastian Brant's *Stultifera navis*. As I have already mentioned, these sources are not enough to make a true iconographical collection.

Although the French edition was embellished with new illustrations and new authors, to speak here of an "iconographical collection" would be to overstate the case. Indeed, I am clearly not attempting to provide an exhaustive list of the documentation pertaining to the theme of the ass, for doing so would require a number of other materials—in particular, anthologies of emblems, hieroglyphics, and seals.

My first goal was to extend my study of the symbolic relationships between the ass and fortune by emphasizing the iconographical dimension (see chapter eight). I then proceeded to yield to a veritable "hunt" for the ass. In the past five years, I have been given a great deal assistance from many friends (I would especially like to mention Augusto Gentili) and have had access to a series of "ass" images that have occasionally given me insight into questions posed by my research.

By not placing them in any particular order and by not providing any commentary, I am offering the work of an amateur collector more than of a rigorous scientist. Hence, I appeal to the reader's curiosity and to the iconographer's knowledge and invite them to make their own interpretations.

1. Francesco Petrarca, *Von der Artzney beyder Glück*
(Augsburg: Heynrich Steyner, 1532).

2. *La ruota della Fortuna*, Tarots of the Visconti Dukes, Morgan Library, New York (15th century).

3. Lorenzo Spirito, *Libro delle venture* (Brescia: Boninus de Boninis, 1484).

De fortunę mutabilitate.
Quem rota fortunę cupida spe continet: atcp
Voluit in excelso sors sibi fausta gradu:
Ille etiam metuat lapsus quandocp nocentes.
Perpetuo nescit sors residere loco.

Complures fatuos/latum fortuna per orbem
Efficit instabili voluit eoscp rota.
Fortunam multi sitibundo pectore versant:
Et loca continuo scandere celsa petunt.

4. Sebastian Brant, *Stultifera navis* (Basel: Johann Bergmann, 1497).

De ſęcularis potentię exitu.

Non fuit interris vnꝗ tam magna poteſtas:
   Tempore quę fragili non quoꝗ diffluereet:
Cuncta rapit lœthum: mors vltima linea teru̅ eſt.
   Res hominu̅ nulla conditione manent.

Ad gene-
reris ſine
cede & ſag
uine pauci
Deſcēdūt
reges & ſic
ca morte
tiranni.

O tardos animo fatuos: quos magna poteſtas
Eleuat: & nimiu̅ qui munera vana ſequuntur:
Tanꝗ perpetuis vita hęc ſit firma columnis:
Nec moribunda quidē capiat er tempora fine̅.

Eccle. 9. et 29
Iuuenalis in
ſatyra oibus i
terris

5. Sebastian Brant, *Stultifera navis* (Basel: Johann Bergmann, 1497).

De pluralitate beneficiorum.

Quiſquis cupit poſſidere plura benefitia
Multa ſolus obtinere poſſit & offitia
Plus imponit hic aſello q̄ portare poterit:
Mortem ſaccorum miſello multitudo parturit

Sunt: quibus eſt animus benefitia plura tenere
    Et ſacrum manibus contaminare bonum
Nec ſatis illa valent vigili curare labore:
    Suſceptū nec onus pficere arte queunt.   f.í.

6. Sebastian Brant, *Stultifera navis* (Basel: Johann Bergmann, 1497).

Vxorem ducere propter opes.
Diuitias propter solas: non prolis amor e:
Vxorem ducens/coniugium ve petens:
Hic patitur merito lites: & iurgia/rixas:
Et pacem/& perdit cōmoda connubii.

Impater=
go viro
intolerabi
li⁹ nihil eſt
q̃ femia di
ues.

Aruinam multi quęrunt ſub podice aſelli:
    Et cumulant trullas:ſtercora vana petunt:
Vxorem ducunt vetulam dum turpiter Eglen:
    Qꝛ nūmos habeat/diuitiaſꝗ leues.   h·iiii.

Iuuenalis
l.oratione.ff.
de ri.nup.
i.ad cor.vii
Sapiē.xiiii.

7. Sebastian Brant, *Stultifera navis* (Basel: Johann Bergmann, 1497).

De iracundis mulieribus.
Sunt plęriqʒ mares/afinos equitare frequenter·
Qui cuperent: fi non fœmina prima foret:
Sed qa precipitem mulier contorquet afellum:
Fœmineo hinc generi pareat vfqʒ pecus.

Fœmiɲeū laudare genus mea carmina vellent
Nunc potius: fed me caufa maligna mouet:
Si natura negat: facit indignatio verfum:
Fœmina me patitur praua filere nihil:

8. Sebastian Brant, *Stultifera navis* (Basel: Johann Bergmann, 1497).

De fuppreffis fatuis.
Eft(fcio)turba meo fatuorum picta libello
  Magna: fub infculptis atqʒ locata notis:
In tergum illorum capitofus faltat afellus
  Depreffos monftras / ftultigerofqʒ viros.

Tranftra per & remos collecta eft tanta caterua:
  Et numerum tantum noftra carina vehit:
Vt prope ftultorum fine me difcederet ingens
  Copia: fed monuit nofter afellus herum

9. Sebastian Brant, *Stultifera navis* (Basel: Johann Bergmann, 1497).

De vana ſpe futurę ſucceſſionis.
Rebus in externis eſt qui ſucceſſor haberi
Sperat: & alterius de funere gaudet acerbo.
At ſępe ante illum mortem pręguſtat: & is quem
Ad tumulum deferre putat: ſepelitur ab illo.

In mortez
alteri? ſpē
tu tibi po=
nere noli.

de cóceſ. p̄ē.
c. ii. & c. ꜩe ca
ptande. to. ti.
li. vi.
l. ſtipulatio
ff. de ver. ob.
l. qⁿidã. ff. de
doꞇa.

Quis fatuos tolerare/queat quos ardor habendi
Protinus inſanos: inſipidoſꝗ facit?
Qui cupit alterius rerum ſucceſſor haberi
Et bona nancifci/qui cupit alterius:

10. Sebastian Brant, *Stultifera navis* (Basel: Johann Bergmann, 1497).

De amore venereo.
Infanos fatuos trahimus cū fune ligatos:
  Quifquis amat: paffim retia noftra fubit.
Decipimus plures: & fautia mēbra fagittis
  Percutimus: vulnus nulla medela iuuat.

Qui cytherea venus: fequitur tua iuffa/dolofqȝ:
Et ꝑperat diros temptare Cupidinis arcus:
Is fatuus/miferos cafus/& fata fubibit.
Quas Venus infignes luxu ꝑftrauerit vrbes:

11. Sebastian Brant, *Stultifera navis* (Basel: Johann Bergmann, 1497).

De inutilibus votis & petitionibus
Qui superos passis manibus/votisq; precatur:
Nec tamen ex iusto pectore vota fluunt:
Quod petit a superis votū non percipit illud:
Materiam risus deinde aliquando dabit.

Carpim⁹ hac Satyra optat⁹ quoq; & ipsa vota:
Quę temere a superis nulla ratione precamur.
Voto/homo sepe petit:quę non intelligit ipse.
Sed quę tristia sint discrimina forte datura.

12. Sebastian Brant, *Stultifera navis* (Basel: Johann Bergmann, 1497).

De prȩmio ſapientiȩ.
Poſſumus ad dextram palmȩ ſpectare coronam:
Ad lȩuam mitrȩ cernimus auriculas
Ecce ſiniſtrorſum fatuorum maxima turba
Pergit: & exitii prȩmia iuſta capit:

O ſtulti veniam petimuſcȝ damuſcȝ viciſſim
Parcite ſi vos nunc noſtra thalia ferit:
Iam cano iuſtitiȩ quȩ prȩmia: quanta ſophiȩ
Munera largiri conſtituicȝ valent

13. Sebastian Brant, *Stultifera navis* (Basel: Johann Bergmann, 1497).

De improuidis fatuis.
Qui non prius scit parare
Sellam: q̄ vult equitare.
Si is cadit inconsultus:
Risum mouens: erit stultus.

Sunt alii fatui cupio quos rite docere
Ne semp mentis nubila cęca gerant.
Incautus fatuus/demens/impuidus/atqʒ
Ignauus: curat fata futura nihil.

14. Sebastian Brant, *Stultifera navis* (Basel: Johann Bergmann, 1497).

15. *The Engulfing of Pharoh*, drawing by Lorenzo Lotto for a mosaic in the basilica of Santa Maria Maggiore in Bergamo (1526–1527).

Uod amoʒ mulierú facʒat hoiem beſtiã / inſenſa-
tũ / ſeipſum nõ cognoſcenté / imo ʒ poʒcũ eʒ cer-
ta hyſtoʒia poſſum aſſeuerare. Fuit q̃dã amoʒ ꝟe
diʒ⁹ / ʒ licet oim litteraʒ ignar⁹ ſicut ſtylpho / ſcholas tñ
regédas aſſũpſit ꝟocês pueros ꝓ oia eʒ yſidonio germa-
nico. Et pʒimo in grãmatica in capitulo ꝟe ꝟocalib⁹ A E
J O U. Poſthac in grãmatica poſitiua. pané bʒoʒ. ca-
ſeum keſ, vinum wyn offam ein ſupp, piʒa ein bier. lobi⁹.

q

16. Jacob Wimpfeling, *De fide concubinarum* (Ulm, 1501).

17. Bruegel, *The Ass at School* (1566), Berlin, Kupferstichkabinett.

18. Achillis Bocchii, *Symbolicarum questionum, de universo genere, quas serio ludebat, libri V* (Bologna: Apud Societatem typograhiæ Bononiensis, 1574), bk. III; symb. XC, p. CLXXXIIII.

19. *La nobiltà dell'asino di Attabalippa dal Perù* [attributed to Adriano Banchieri] (Venice: Barezzo Barezzi, 1599).

20. *Roma caput mundi*, etching (1496), London, British Library.

21. *De Deux monstres prodigieux, à savoir d'un Asne-Pape*, Found in the
Tiber River, M.CCCC.XCVI. Jean Crespin, M.D.LVII.

22. Giovanni Battista Nazari, *Della trasmutazione metallica*
(Brescia: Pietro Maria Marchetti, 1572).

Non tibi sed religioni.

Isidis effigiem tardus gestabat asellus,
  Pando uerenda dorso habens mysteria.
Obuius ergo Deam quisquis reuerenter adorat,
  Piasq; genibus concipit flexis preces.
Ast asinus tantum præstari credit honorem
  Sibi, & intumescit admodùm superbiens,
Donec eum flagris compescens dixit agaso,
  Non es Deus tu aselle, sed Deum uehis.
                    C iiii

23. Andrea Alciati, *Emblematum libellus* (Paris: C. Wechelus, 1536).

24. *Le Bon Serviteur* (late sixteenth century). National Library of Paris.

25. Giovan Battista Della Porta, *De humana physiognomia libri III* (Vico Equense: Giuseppe Cacchio, 1586) p. 67.

VN. 'A

POCO VEDETE ET PAR

VI VEDER MOLTO.

VNO

26. Giovan Battista Pino, *Ragionamento sopra del asino*
(n.p., n.e., c. 1551–1552).

27. Giordano Bruno, *Cabala del cavallo pegaseo* (Paris [London : Antonio Baio] J. Charlewood, 1585).

1. When Emmanuel Hatzantonis treats Bruno's *Cantus circaeus* in his work on the metaphor of Circe in the sixteenth century ("Il potere metamorfico di Circe quale motivo satirico in Machiavelli, Gelli e Bruno," in *Italica*, 37 [1960], pp. 257–67), he mistakenly includes the ass in Circe's catalog of the moral qualities of man.

2. This passage is omitted in the Roman manuscript and printed codex (the codex is considered the definitive version of the *Cena*). See Giordano Bruno, *La cena de le ceneri*, ed. Giovanni Aquilecchia (Turin: Einaudi, 1955). On the *Arca di Noè*, see Michele Ciliberto's work, "Asini e pedanti: Richerche su Giordano Bruno," in *Rinascimento*, 24 (1984), pp. 106–19.

3. Domenico Berti, *Giordano Bruno da Nola: Sua vita e sua dottrina* (Turin: Paravia, 1889), pp. 51–52.

4. Francesco Predari, "Le opere di T. Campanella e di G. Bruno edite dai cugini Pompa," in *Bollettino di scienze, lettere, arti, teatri, industrie italiane e straniere*, I, no. 38, March 27, 1854.

5. Rodolfo Mondolfo, "Per la biografia di G. Bruno: La laurea in teologia, il primo viaggio a Roma, l'Arca di Noè," in *Rivista d'Italia*, 10 (1913), pp. 534–50.

6. Vincenzo Spampanato, *Vita di Giordano Bruno* (Messina: Principato, 1921), pp. 155–56; anastatica reprint, intro by N. Ordine, (Roma; Gela).

7. Savolino was a very common last name in the region where Nola and San Paolo are located. Bruno was born in Nola to Flaulisa Savolino and Giovanni Bruno (see Spampanato, *Vita di Giordano Bruno*, pp. 47–49).

8. Bruno also uses the image of the tray in *Cantus circaeus*, recalling the passage from "proportioned to proportionable": "From what is proportioned comes what is proportional, just as the product of the potter is from clay, and contemplation of a universal creator suggests to us a universe that is able to be created. At the great juncture is this proposition" (*Opera latine conscripta*, a cura di F. Fiorentino, F. Tocco, H. Vitelli, V. Imbriani, C. M. Tallarigo [Florence: Le Monnier, 1879], II, I, p. 243).

2 Myths, Fables, Tales: the "Asinine" Materials

1. Waldemar Deonna, "Laus asini: L'âne, le serpent, l'eau et l'immortalité," *Revue Belge de Philologie et d'Histoire*, 34 (1956), pp. 637–38.
2. P.W., *Priapos*, c. 1933 (also P.W., *Esel*, c. 670). Certain sources maintain that Priapus is the son of an ass. See Alexander Krappe, "Appollon onos," *Classical Philology*, 42 (1947), p. 225.
3. P.W., *Esel*, c. 654 (see Krappe, "Appollon onos," pp. 225–26). On the sacrifices of the ass performed in honor of Priapus, see Karoly Kerényi, *The Gods of the Greeks*, tr. Norman Cameron (London: Thames and Hudson, 1951), pp. 175–77.
4. Aphrodite succumbed to the flatteries of Dionysus and gave birth to Priapus. See Robert Graves, *The Greek Myths* (New York: George Braziller, 1955), pp. 67–73.
5. The ass is linked primarily to Dionysus because of its status as a phallic animal. See D.S., *Bacchus*, p. 621; and P.W., *Dionysos*, c. 1041. The episode in which the ass helps Dionysus cross the ocean demonstrates once again the tight symbolic bond between the ass and water (see Deonna, "Laus asini," p. 33). Dionysus and the ass are both linked to the rites of vindication (see George Lafaye, "L'âne et la vigne," *Revue de philologie de littérature et d'histoire anciennes*, 38 [1914], pp. 174–81). Diogenes Laertius recounts that the Stoic philosopher Chrysippus would have died laughing had he seen an ass drinking wine (VII. 185). Apuleius, in his famous episode about the ass in the triclinium, also insists on the comic effect of a wine-drinking ass: "At that time, they who beheld me at the table did nothing but laugh; then one of the wits who was there said to his master: 'I pray you, sir, give this feaster some drink to his supper.' 'Marry,' quoth he, 'I think thou sayest true, rascal; for so it may be that to his meat this our dinner-fellow would drink likewise a cup of wine. . . . ' Then all the bystanders looked on, looking eagerly to see what would come to pass; but I (as soon as I beheld the cup) stayed not long, but at my leisure, like a good companion, gathering my lips together to the fashion of a man's tongue, supped up all the wine at one draught" (*The Golden Ass*, tr. W. Aldington [London and New York: Loeb Classical Library, 1965], X. 16, p. 503).

   Valeriano reports that the ass taught the Ancients how to prune vines: Ioannis Pierii Valeriani, *Hieroglyphica* (Basel: Thomas Guarinum, 1567), p. 90 [copy used: BAV, Chigi I 195]. All quotations are from this edition.
6. Silenus as god-ass: D.S., *Bacchus*, p. 621, n. 1057; Krappe, "Appollon onos," pp. 226–28; P.W., *Marsyas*, c. 1989. For a detailed catalog of the

representations of the Silenus and the ass, see D.S., *Satyri*, p. 1099, n. 31 and 37.

7. Marsyas also comes to be considered a divine ass. See Schiffer, "Marsyas et le Phrygiens en Syria," *Revue des Etudes Anciennes*, 21 (1919), p. 237.

8. Midas appears with ass ears in Ovid's *Metamorphoses*, VI. 146–79. See also P.W., *Midas*, c. 1531 and 1528; Krappe, "Appollon onos," p. 227.

9. Silenus is transformed into a river in a number of ritual games organized by Dionysus. See Nonnos, *Dion.*, XIX.223ff. Marsyas, having lost his musical challenge to Apollo and consequently having been hanged from a tree near a spring, was compassionately transformed from flesh into a river. See Nonnos, *Dion.*, XIX.314ff. See also Ovid's version, *Metamorphoses*, VI.382–400. After Dionysus's gift to Midas of turning everything into gold, the king, out of desperation, succeeds in freeing himself from the magic spell by bathing in the waters of a spring (see Ovid, *Metamorphoses*, XI.85–145).

10. Angelo De Gubernatis, *Mythologie Zoologique* (Paris: Durand and Pedone Lauriel, 1874), p. 389.

11. Ibid., pp. 388–89.

12. The relationship between the ass and Vesta is again affirmed in an episode recounted by Ovid (*Fasti*, VI.321–44). The ass, with its powerful bray, awakens the goddess, who is about to be raped by Priapus. Some sources speak of Vesta as an ancient goddess in an ass's garb (see Deonna, "Laus asini," p. 635, and the references the essay offers). On the presence of the ass in the festivals dedicated to Vesta, see D.S., *Vesta*, p. 757.

13. In pagan processions, the statue of the goddess Cybele came to be transported by asses. See the well-known passages from Apuleius (*The Golden Ass*, VIII.27) and from Lucian (*Lucius or the Ass*, 37ff., in *Una storia vera*, tr. Luigi Settembrini [Bologna: Bompiani, 1983], p. 133). See also Aesop's "The Ass Who Carried a Statuette of God."

14. It is during Isis's procession that Lucius eats the rose and returns to his human form. See Apuleius, *The Golden Ass*, XI.4 and 12.

15. Apuleius stresses the sincerity of the matron's love: "Then she kissed me, not as they are accustomed to do at the stews or in brothel, or in the courtesan schools for gain of money, but purely, sincerely, and with great affection, casting out these and like loving words: 'Thou art he whom I love,' 'Thou art he whom I only desire,' 'Without thee I cannot live,' and other like preambles to talk" (*The Golden Ass*, X.21, p. 509). He also emphasizes the practical worries of Lucius-ass: "But nothing grieved me so much as to think how I should with my huge and great legs embrace so fair a matron, or how I should touch her fine, dainty, and silken skin made of milk and honey with my hard hoofs, or how it was possible to kiss her pretty and

ruddy lips with my monstrous great mouth and stony teeth, or how she, who was so young and tender, could receive my love" (*The Golden Ass*, X.22, p. 511). The tale of Lucius highlights the matron's passion for Lucius-ass, who, returned to being a man, is cast out by the very woman who adored him when he was dressed as a beast (*The Golden Ass*, X.22).

Note the verses of Juvenal that portray women in the absence of men (*Satires*, VI.34–35).

It is not surprising, then, that the ass returns in two of Boccaccio's tales of amorous intrigues: the tale of Gianni Lotteringhi (*Decameron*, VII.1), in which the wife, Monna Tessa, places a skull of an ass in the vineyard to warn her lover that her husband is at home; and that of Pietro di Vinciolo (*Decameron*, V.10) who is inspired by Apuleius's fable of the miller's wife (*The Golden Ass*, IX.14–28). On the latter tale, see Antonio D'Andrea's note, "Avventure letterarie di una asino (*Decameron* V.10)," *Quaderni di italianistica*, 1 (1980), pp. 87–91. For a consideration of Aretino, see chapter thirteen, note 9.

Bruno also stresses the phallic qualities of the ass. See the sonnet "A l'asino cillenico" (*Cabala*, p. 913) and the fable of the ass and the lion told in *Candelaio* (pp. 65–66).

16. The milk of the female ass is a superb skin cream (see Pliny, *Hist. Nat.*, XXVIII.47–50), and the ashes of the ass's genitals renew hair growth and help to deter graying (Pliny, *Hist. Nat.*, XXVIII.46); the ass's bile diluted with water deters rashes on the face (Pliny, *Hist. Nat.*, XXVIII.50).

17. The ashes of the ass's excrement aid in the birthing process (Pliny, *Hist. Nat.*, XXVIII.77); the milk of the female ass heals sensitive breasts and regulates the menstrual cycle (ibid.); excrement, on the other hand, lessens menstruation (ibid.), and the spleen aids in stimulating lactation (ibid.). In addition to Pliny's catalog, see Ulyssis Aldrovandi, *De asino*, in *De quadrupedibus solidipedibus* (Bologna: Victorium Bonatium, 1616), esp. the paragraph *Usus in medicina*, pp. 343–46.

18. *The Golden Ass*, VI.18.

19. Aelian speaks of Scythian asses that have horns filled with water from the Styx (*De nat. anim.*, X.40).

20. Marius Schneider, "La simbologia dell'asino," *Conoscenza religiosa*, 2 (1980), p. 129.

21. Deonna, "Laus asini," p. 648.

22. Ibid., p. 649.

23. P.W., *Esel*, c. 652; G. Daressy, "L'animal séthien à tête d'âne," *Annales du Service des Antiquités de l'Egypte*, 20 (1920), p. 165; René Guénon,

Symboles fondamentaux de la science sacrée (Paris: Gallimard, 1962), pp. 157–62.

24. Plutarch, *Isis and Osiris*, 50.371 C. Like the ass, Set is inherently ambiguous. At times, Set is also considered a benefactor (Deonna, "Laus asini," p. 360).
25. Typhon, a monster with an ass's head, has been compared to Set. See Graves, *Greek Myths*, pp. 13–16.
26. De Gubernatis, *Myth. Zoolog.*, p. 393.
27. Eliphas Levi, *Mysteries of the Qabalah*, tr. Alphonse L. Constant (Wellingborough: Thorsons Publishers, 1974), p. 59.
28. Deonna, "Laus asini," pp. 649–50.
29. Exod. 4:20.
30. Judg. 5:10. In the *Cabala*, Bruno interprets this passage as follows: "But when the Book of Judges sings of Deborah and Barac, son of Abinoen, it says: 'Listen, kings; prick up your ears, princes—you who mount adorned asses and sit in judgment,' the holy rabbis interpreted, 'O governors of the earth, you who are superior to the generous people and whom you govern with your holy whip, punishing the guilty, rewarding the good, and dispensing all things fairly' " (p. 849).
31. Gen. 20:3.
32. Judg. 12:14.
33. I Sam. 25:20.
34. II Sam. 16:2. See also II Sam. 17:23; I Kings 2:40, 13:13; Josh. 15:18.
35. C. Renel, *L'évolution d'un mythe: Açvins et Dioscures* (Paris: Masson, 1896), p. 99, as cited by Krappe, "Appollon onos," p. 233. See also De Gubernatis, *Myth. Zoolog.*, p. 394.
36. De Gubernatis, *Myth. Zoolog.*, p. 394.
37. Aelian, *De nat. anim.*, XII.34.
38. Strabo, *Geographica*, XV.727.
39. Herodotus, IV.129.
40. "As Eratosthenes says, at the time when Jupiter, who had declared war against the giants, had called all the gods together for the attack, father Liber came, along with Vulcan, the Satyrs and the Sileni, who rode on asses. When the asses were not far from the enemy, they are said to have taken fright, and thus each made a great clamor, the likes of which had never before been heard by the giants. At this, all the enemy hurled themselves into flight from the asses' clamor and were thus defeated" (Pseudo-Eratosthenes, *Catasterismi*, 11). Cf. *Scholia vetera latina in Caesaris Germanici Aratea Phaenomena*, II.51.

The episode is recalled not only in *Causa* (p. 193), in *Spaccio*

(p. 597), and in *De imaginum compositione* (*Opp. lat.*, II, III, p. 238) but also in *Cabala:* "These have been the meanings expressed through the allegory of the ancient wise men (to whom the divine spirit sought to reveal something, at least in order to make them impeccable), in that sententious apology of the gods who fought against the rebellious giants, sons of the earth and ardent predators of the sky; those who, with the voice of asses, confused, terrorized, frightened, triumphed, and dominated" (p. 852).

41. De Gubernatis, *Myth. Zoolog.*, p. 394.
42. P.W., *Esel*, c. 672.
43. Fedro, *Asinus inridens aprum*, I.29. The fable had great fortune. In one of its numerous versions, *l'asinus demisso pene* was "moralized" into *demisso pede* (see Ferruccio Bertini, "Fortuna medievale ed umanistica della favola dell'asino e del cinghiale," in *Letterature comparate: Problemi e metodi, Studi in onore di Ettore Paratore* (Bologna: Pàtron, 1981), pp. 1063–73.
44. Homer, *Iliad*, XI.558–65.
45. Gen. 49:14.
46. Judg. 15:14ff. The Samson episode is also related to water. In the *Cabala*, Bruno recounts it in the following way: "The same [the meaning of the war of the giants] is expressed sufficiently, where, upon raising the veil of the sacred figure, one fixates one's eyes on the anagogic meaning of that divine Samson, who took the lives of a thousand Philistines with the jaw of a she-ass. This means, according to the holy interpreters, that with the jaw of the she-ass (or that is to say, with the preachers of the law and ministers of the synagogue) and with the jaw of the baby-ass (that is, with the preachers of the new law and ministers of the militant church) *delevit eos*, a thousand people (that perfect number) were obliterated and, as is written: *From your left side a thousand fell, and from your right, ten thousand*; and the place where they fell is called *Ramath-lechi*, namely, the exultation of the jaw. Such a jaw is followed not only by ruin of its adversaries as fruit of its preaching, but also by the health of those who have been regenerated, because from the same jaw, that is, by the virtue of preaching, those waters that proclaim divine wisdom, that dispense celestial grace and render its drinkers capable of eternal life, have flowed in and out" (*Cabala*, pp. 852–53).
47. Lucius's exhausting experience inside the mill remains exemplary (*The Golden Ass*, IX.11–12). Many of Aesop's fables also emphasize the ass's hard work (see "The Asses to Zeus"). In antiquity, men who carried weights were sometimes thought to resemble asses (see P.W., *Esel*, c. 640).
48. Ariosto revives this relationship by transforming it into the "courtesan-ass" relationship. The ass thus becomes a servant of the court: "Once there was

a donkey, so thin that he displayed his every bone and sinew. One day he entered through a hole in the wall into a place where there was a mighty heap of grain. He ate so much that his belly grew bigger than a tun, and he guzzled until he was full, which was not within a short time. Fearing afterward that he might be beaten for his temerity, he strained to get out where he had entered, but he could no longer fit through the hole. While he puffed and panted and tried in vain to squeeze through, a tiny mouse said to him, 'If you wish to get through that hole, cousin, remove your belly-armor first. You must begin by vomiting up all you have taken into your carcass, and get thin again, otherwise you will never manage to get out of the hole you are in.' Now, in conclusion, I declare that, if the reverend Cardinal thinks he has purchased me with his gifts, I find it neither bitter nor harsh to return them and to resume my former freedom" (Ludovico Ariosto, *The Satires of Ludovico Arisoto: A Renaissance autobiography*, tr. Peter DeSa Wiggins [Athens: Ohio State University Press, 1976], I.251–65, p. 21). The "ass-servant" relationship reappears in a different context in Giulio Camillo's *L'idea del theatro* (Florence: Lorenzo Torrentino, 1550), p. 86: "Being a Saturnian animal, an ass is born for toil, which means being condemned to the same things as servants: driving coaches, being porters, and milling." On Camillo, see Lina Bolzoni's important work, *Il teatro della memoria: Studi su Giulio Camillo* (Padova: Liviana, 1984).

49. Gen. 12:14–16.
50. Job 1:3.
51. II Kings 4:2ff.
52. Zach. 9:9–10.
53. In the following chapters we will see how this pair of contraries is pertinent to Bruno's concept of asininity.
54. Buddha has large ears; in China, the statues of emperors are often given big ears; in Africa, the god Leza has long ears; among the Incas and in Babylon, the people of the highest ranks have large ears (Deonna, "Laus asini," p. 640, n. 2). Bruno, too, in the sonnet "A l'asino cillenico" (*Cabala*, p. 913), recalls "Long ears, a royal hearer."
55. De Gubernatis, *Myth. Zoolog.*, p. 397, n. 2.
56. Schneider, "La simbologia dell'asino," p. 139.
57. "Neither could I see any comfort in my transformation, save that the nature of my members was increasing likewise to the great discomfiture of Fotis" (*The Golden Ass*, III.24, p. 137).
58. Ibid., IX.15.
59. Ibid., XI.23.

60. Rémy de Gourmont, *Le latin mystique* (Paris: Les Editions Crès, 1922), p. 183. See also chapter twelve, note 21.

61. Valeriano, *Hieroglyphica*, p. 91.

62. Cicero, *Ad Pisonem*, in *The Letters to His Friends*, tr. W. Glynn Williams (Cambridge: Harvard University Press, 1927), p. 43.

63. Deonna, "Laus asini," p. 639.

64. "There are so many things said about the stupidity of asses that we must come back to that topic presently. If the Egyptians wanted to describe it more clearly, they chose it to be the most docile animal of all, and they imagined a group of monkeys among which an ass might dance or sing with flutes or even debate, something that is indeed as ridiculous to recount as it is to watch, but that may be worthy of consideration when one has retired into the country" (Valeriano, *Hieroglyphica*, p. 88).

65. For a detailed bibliography on the terra-cotta images and figures of the ass appearing in the clothes of the master, see Deonna, "Laus asini," p. 639, n. 2.

66. Aesop, "The Ass Dressed in the Skins of a Lion and the Wolf," in *Aesop's Fables*, based on the trans. by George Fyler Townsend (Garden City, N.Y.: Doubleday, 1976).

67. De Gubernatis, *Myth. Zoolog.*, pp. 401–2.

68. Deonna, "Laus asini," p. 652. De Gubernatis mentions the symbolic ambiguity of the ass in Vedic India, which also corresponds to the ambiguity of the terms that designate it.

69. See Francesco Zambon's introduction to *Il bestiario di Cambridge* (Parma and Milan: Franco Maria Ricci, 1974), p. 32.

3 The Ass and Mercury: A Key to *Coincidentia Oppositorum*

1. The nymph Maia gives birth to Mercury, son of Zeus, in a cave on Mount Cyllene (Kerényi, *The Gods of the Greeks*, p. 162).

2. On Valeriano, see Gennaro Savarese's introduction to *La letteratura delle immagini nel Cinquecento*, ed. Gennaro Savarese and Andrea Gareffi (Rome: Bulzoni, 1980), pp. 15–23.

3. Valeriano, *Hieroglyphica*, pp. 246r–47.

4. Ibid., p. 247.

5. On the ass, see the references in chapter two, notes 15 and 57. Hermes' phallic nature is widely attested: see Callimachus, *Diegemata*, 8.33; and Herodotus, II.51 (Kerényi, *The Gods of the Greeks*, p. 171). In the Museo Archeologico Nazionale di Napoli (in the secret Gabinetto) there is a statuette of Hermes with a large phallus. For a psychoanalytic interpretation

of the complex meanings of Mercury's sexuality, see Rafael Lopez Pedraza, *Ermes e i suoi figli* (Milan: Edizioni di Comunità, 1983).

6.   After he sprang forth from his mother's immortal limbs,
      he did not remain for long lying in his holy cradle,
      but he leaped up and searched for the cattle of Apollon,
      stepping over the threshold of the high-roofed cave.
      There he found a tortoise and won boundless bliss,
      for Hermes was the first to make a singer of a tortoise

("To Hermes," in *The Homeric Hymns*, tr. Apostolos N. Athanassakis [Baltimore: Johns Hopkins University Press, 1976], p. 31).

The mythologema of the "rascal" Hermes, who steals cows from Apollo, also appears in the Homeric hymn. Jung explores the nature of the "rascal" (*The Trickster: A Study in American Indian Mythology*, ed. Paul Radin, with commentaries by Carl Gustav Jung and Karoly Kerényi [New York: Greenwood Press, 1956]) and reveals how it can embody a double valence within itself (part "clever" and part "stupid"). Jung notes these qualities in Mercury, as well as in the medieval *festum asinorum* (pp. 195–211). In short, the medieval carnival brings the "rascal-like" elements of antiquity into an ecclesiastic setting (see chapter thirteen, note 42).

7.   This study will not address the exceptions to the proverb *asinus ad lyram*. On this theme, see the following essays: Alessando Vitale Brovarone, "The Asinus Citharedus in the Literary and Iconographic Tradition of the Middle Ages," *Marche Romane*, 28 (1978), pp. 121–29; Martin Vogel, *Onos lyras* (Düsseldorf: Verlad der Gesellschaft f. system, Musikwissenschaft, 1973); W. Stander, "Asinus ad lyram," in *Festschrift Helmuth Ostoff zu 70 Geburtstag* (Tutzing: Frankfurter Musikhistoriche Studien, 1968), pp. 25–32; H. Adolf, "The Ass and the Harpe," *Speculum*, 25 (1950), pp. 49–57; R. Hammerstein, *Diabolus in musica* (Bern and Munich: Francke, 1974), pp. 73–75; Schneider, "La simbologia dell'asino," pp. 132–37; and Louis Charbonneau-Lassay, *The Bestiary of Christ*, tr. D. M. Dooling (New York: Parabola Books, 1991), pp. 106–11.

8.   Valeriano, *Hieroglyphica*, p. 348.

9.   Ibid., p. 347.

10. The theme of music in relation to "variety" also appears in Ariosto:

      But here, sir, it behoves me shift my ground,
      like him that makes the sprightly viol ring,
      who often changes chord and varies sound,
      And now a graver strikes, now sharper string

(*Orlando Furioso*, VIII.29, tr. William Stewart Rose [Indianapolis: Bobbs-Merrill, 1968], p. 65). On these verses, see the references furnished by Carlo Muscetta in his introduction to "*Orlando furioso*" *e una scelta delle Opere minori*, ed. Carlo Muscetta and Luca Lamberti (Turin: Einaudi, 1962), vol. I, pp. xvii–xviii. The concept of *varietas*, however, is not only relevant to the narrative structure of the poem. It also becomes an expression of a vision of a world where nature and man are in a constant process of mutation. It is not by chance that Bruno often cites the *Furioso* in his Italian dialogues.

11. Martin Vogel offers further references to the relationship between Mercury and the ass (*Onos lyras*, pp. 388–90). Here, in addition to a rich catalog of mythological references, Vogel postulates a close etymological relationship between the Greek term *harmonia*, the asinine term *imeru-himaru*, and *Hermes*, the Greek name of Mercury (the symbolic relationship with the lira could function as a common denominator). Continuing his etymological analysis, which is at times disputable, Vogel derives the term *hermetic* from *hermèneús*, which also designates "the man who guides the ass" (that is, the ass-owner).

4 The Ambiguous Space of Asininity

1. Saulino, corroborating with Sophia's thesis, adds: "*Saul*. So it seems to me; because justice has no act except where there is error, harmony is not effectuated except where there is contrariety. The spherical does not repose on the spherical, because they touch each other at a point; but the concave rests on the convex. And morally, the proud man cannot get together with the proud man, the poor man with the poor man, the greedy man with the greedy man; but the one is pleased with the humble man, the other with the rich man, the latter with the splendid man. However, if the matter is considered physically, mathematically, and morally, one sees that that philosopher who has arrived at the theory of the 'coincidence of contraries' has not found out little, and that that magician who knows how to look for it where it exists is not an imbecile practitioner. All, then, that you have uttered is most true. But I should like to know, O Sophia, for what purpose, toward what end, you say it" (*The Expulsion of the Triumphant Beast*, tr. Arthur Imerti [Lincoln: University of Nebraska Press, 1964], p. 90; *Spaccio*, p. 573). In the *Eroici*, Tansillo also maintains that "all things are made of contraries, and because of this composition in all things, the affections never bring us delight without also bringing something bitter. In fact, I shall go further; if it were not for the bitter in things there would be no delight

in rest; separation is the cause of our finding pleasure in union; and if we investigate the matter generally, it will always be found that one contrary is the occasion for the other contrary's desirability and pleasure" (*The Heroic Frenzies*, tr. Paul Memmo [Chapel Hill: University of North Carolina Press, 1964], p. 98; *Eroici*, p. 974).

2. See chapter two, note 40, and the passage in *Asinus cyllenicus* in *Opp. lat.*, II, III, p. 238.

3. See chapter one for the passages in *Spaccio* (pp. 808–9) and *Cabala* (pp. 862–63).

4. "And to whom shall I dedicate my *Candelaio?* To whom, O great destiny, would you like me to consecrate my beautiful paranymph, my good leader? To whom will I send that which the heavenly influences of Sirius—in these most sweltering days and stinging hours, which they call canicular—had the fixed stars rain down in my brain; whose wandering fireflies of the firmament have riddled me, whose decan of the twelve signs has struck me in the head, and whose seven wandering stars have blown into my internal ears? To whom, I ask, is this work to be dedicated, to whom does it concern, who does it target? Your Holiness? No. Your Imperial Highness? No. Your Highness, most illustrious and reverent Lordship? No, nix. Indeed, it is not prince, nor cardinal, nor king, nor emperor, nor pope that will take this candle from my hand, in this most solemn offertory. It is your turn. It is to you that one must give it; and you will either stuff it into your cabinet, or thrust it in your candlestick; you who are, to a superlative degree, learned, wise, beautiful and generous, my Signora Morgana" (*Candelaio*, p. 21).

5. Spampanato, *Vita di Giordano Bruno*, p. 61.

6. In *Spaccio*, Bruno clearly demonstrates the game between "high" and "low" through his ambivalent use of the symbols "Poverty" and "Wealth": "You, Poverty, when you are a part of inferior beings, will not be permitted to be joined, bound, and locked to Wealth in superior things, just as your contrary, Wealth, could not be joined, bound, and locked to you in inferior things; because no one who is wise and wishes to know will ever deem it possible to associate himself with great things in the company of the latter, inasmuch as riches offer an impediment to philosophy, and Poverty gives us a sure and expeditious path. . . . I want that man to be great who in his poverty is rich because he is content; and I want that man to be a cowardly slave who in his wealth is poor because he is not satisfied" (*Expulsion*, p. 162; *Spaccio*, p. 677).

7. For the symbolism of the sephiroth in Bruno, see Frances Yates, *Giordano Bruno and the Hermetic Tradition* (Chicago: University of Chicago Press, 1964), pp. 100–103. In chapters 7 and 14, Yates emphasizes the influence

of Agrippa's works (*De occulta philosophia* and *De vanitate*) on the formation of Bruno's hermeticism. The concept of the ass as knowledge can be found in *Ad encomium asini digressio*, the final chapter of *De vanitate*. See Yates's study on Brunian mnemonics in *The Art of Memory* (Chicago: University of Chicago Press, 1966), pp. 199–319. On the relationship between mnemonic technique and the theater in Bruno, see Daniela Quarta, "Sul *Candelaio* di Giordano Bruno," in *Il mago, il cosmo, il teatro degli astri: Saggi sulla letteratura esoterica del Rinascimento*, ed. Gianfranco Formichetti (Rome: Bulzoni, 1985), pp. 179–97.

5 Man and the Ass, between "Bestiality" and "Divinity"

1. Bruno also refers to the importance of the hand, at least twice, in *De monade:* "Therefore man does not have greater foresight than other animals; in fact, many animals surpass him in a variety of things—even those animals who seem to be of no importance because of their small size. To man a kinder Fortune has yielded hands as a gift" (*Opp. lat.*, I, II, p. 331); and "Whatever it is, the serpent considers all things from the point of view of the serpent, and the raven from the point of view of the raven, and they make their own species the measure of all things, and set it in the center, just as we do with our own species by setting it in the center (a race confused and mixed, endowed with voice and with wit, which we use to praise our hands)" (*Opp. lat.*, I, II, p. 329). In the different context posed by the *Cantus circaeus*, the hand takes on a negative connotation; see M. Ciliberto, "Giordano Bruno 1582–1583: Da Parigi a Oxford," *Studi Storici*, 26 (1985), pp. 141–43.

2. Fulvio Papi, *Antropologia e civiltà nel pensiero di Giordano Bruno* (Florence: La Nuova Italia, 1968), p. 240.

3. It is also worth citing other verses by Ronsard:

> Les seules Mains qui en dix doigts s'allient,
> Comme il nous plaist qui s'ouvrent et se plient,
> Nous font seigneurs des animaux, et non
> Une raison qui n'a rien que le nom,
> Bien qu'arrogante et venteuse se fie
> Aux sots discours de la philosophie,
> Laquelle en vain au ciel veut faire aller
> Nos corps bourbeux qui ne peuvent voller. . . .
>
> Si les sangliers, les tigres et les loups
> Avoient des mains et des doigts comme nous,

Ils seroient Rois des terres où nous sommes,
Et donneroient commandement aux hommes;
Mais bien peu sert un coeur superbe et haut
A l'ennemy quand la main luy defaut. . . .

La Main, bien jointe en cinq souples rameaux,
Commence tout, parfait tout, et ne cesse
De travailler, des mestiers la princesse,
Qui peut son oeuvre aux estoiles pousser,
Royne des arts, ministre du penser.
Les Mains font l'homme, et le font de la beste
Estre veincueur, non les pieds ny la teste. . . .

J'ay, mon grand Prince, en ce vers memorable
Escrit des Mains la loüange admirable;
Car peu vaudroit l'entendement humain,
Bien que divin, sans l'aide de la Main

(Ronsard, *Paradoxe,* in *Oeuvres complètes,* ed. Gustave Cohen [Paris: Gallimard, 1950), vol. II, pp. 470–71).

In addition to showing its affinity with Bruno's *Cabala,* Ronsard's position contains elements that contrast with Bruno's text (see Papi, *Antropologia e civiltà,* pp. 244–45). To the eulogy of work, he juxtaposes the celebration of the golden age in his *Discours contre Fortune.* Here, as Papi observes (*Antropologia e civiltà,* pp. 355–56), themes are found that are nearly literal renditions of the critique Idleness makes of work in *Spaccio* (pp. 726–29) (on the theme of *yours* and *mine,* see chapter seven, note 3):

Docte Villegaignon, tu fais une grand' faute,
De vouloir rendre fine une gent si peu caute,
Comme ton Amerique, où le peuple incognu
Erre innocentement tout farouche et tout nu,
D'habit tout aussi nu qu'il est nu de malice,
Qui ne cognoist les noms de vertu ny de vice,
De Senat ny de Roy, qui vit à son plaisir
Porté de l'appétit de son premier désir,
Et qui n'a dedans l'ame ainsi que nous emprainte
La frayeur de la loy qui nous fait vivre en crainte,
Mais suivant sa nature est seul maistre de soy,
Soy-mesmes est sa loy, son Senat et son Roy;
Qui de coutres trenchans la terre n'importune,
Laquelle comme l'air à chascun est commune,

Et comme l'eau d'un fleuve, est commun tout leur bien,
Sans procez engendrer de ce mot *Tien* et *Mien*.
Pource laisse-les là, ne romps plus, je te prie,
Le tranquille repos de leur première vie;
Laisse-les, je te pri', si pitié te remord,
Ne les tourmente plus et t'enfuy de leur bord.
Las! si tu leur apprens à limiter la terre,
Pour agrandir leurs champs ils se feront la guerre,
Les procez auront lieu, l'amitiè defaudra,
Et l'aspre ambition tourmenter les viendra
Comme elle fait ici nous autres, pauvres hommes,
Qui par trop de raison miserables sommes

(Ronsard, *Discours contre Fortune*, in *Oeuvres complètes*, vol. II, p. 407).

4. Alfonso Ingegno's hypothesis that there is a connection between the *Cabala*, where human knowledge and animal knowledge are fused, and a few verses of the *Zodiacus vitae* seems quite convincing. The comparison of Palingenius's verses to Onorio's discourse (*Cabala*, pp. 885–87) removes all doubt: "For if speech had not been conceded to man as a gift of the gods, nor the two hands by which all things are accomplished, no animal on earth would be more miserable and unhappy than man. Our nature is nobler and better because of these two items. In them is all our pride, from them come the arts. For a man who is present is warned by voice what to do and what to avoid, but written words speak to him who is absent. If other animals were able to make known the movements hidden in their chests by speaking, as we do, and to address words to each other and respond, and to write different books with able fingers, then the ass would be wiser than us, and other races would possess more intelligence than us and dare to place their own kind above all else: even the ass would say that he was more noble than us. Therefore, as they say, it is speech and hands that make everything succumb to us, not intelligence. They add that if men were born with maimed hands and from mute parents, and if they spent time in the forests and remote fields, and were themselves deprived of hands and speech in the same way as other animals, what, I ask, would human character be worth? What intelligence would be apparent in them? Would they not live as other animals with unadorned bodies? How would they be any wiser than the rest of the crowd of beasts? The life force is one and the same in all animals. Nevertheless, it seems to be dissimilar and varied because bodies are not equal among all animals, and different faculties are conceded to different limbs" (Marcellus Palingenius, *Zodiacus vitae* [Lyons: Apud Ioannem Tornaesium, 1576], pp. 105–6 [copy used: BCC per 176]). The *Zodiacus vitae*

has Epicurian-Lucretian echoes, and Bruno himself makes these "echoes" explicit in *De monade*, thereby proffering a similar "poetic vision of the world" (Eugenio Garin, *Storia della filosofia italiana* [Turin: Einaudi, 1978], vol. II, pp. 665–70).

5. For an analysis of the theme of the hand in antiquity (Anaxagoras, Aristotle, Cicero), in Sansovino (*L'edificio del corpo umano* [Venice, 1550], p. 375), in Du Bartas (*La sepmaine ou Création du Monde* [Paris, 1585]), and in texts other than Bruno's, see Papi, *Antropologia e civiltà*, pp. 237–47. On the theme of the hand in Machiavelli, see chapter twelve.

6. Papi, *Antropologia e civiltà*, pp. 241–42.

7. Lucretius critiques final causes as follows: "There is a fault in this regard which we earnestly desire you to escape, shunning error with exceeding fearfulness: do not suppose that the clear light of the eyes was made in order that we might be able to see before us; or that the ends of the calves and thighs were jointed and placed upon the foundation of the feet, only to enable us to march forward with long strides; that the forearms again were fitted upon sturdy upper arms, and ministering hands given on either side, only that we might be able to do what should be necessary for life. Such explanations, and all other such that men give, put effect for cause and are based on perverted reasoning; since nothing is born in us simply in order that we may use it, but that which is born creates the use" (Lucretius, *On the Nature of Things*, tr. W. H. D. Rouse [Cambridge: Harvard University Press, 1982], IV.823–35, pp. 342–43).

8. Papi, *Antropologia e civiltà*, p. 242.

6   Positive Asininity: Toil, Humility, Tolerance

1. Enrici Cornelii Agrippae, *De incertitudine et vanitate scientiarum* (Cologne, 1531), ch. CII [copy used: BAV, Palatina V 940]. On the influence of Agrippa's works on Bruno, see chapter four, note 7.

2. Valeriano, *Hieroglyphica*, p. 91.

3. In his Italian dialogues, Bruno often cites Book VI of the *Aeneid*. On the relationship between Bruno and Virgil, see Michele Ciliberto, "Giordano Bruno," in *Enciclopedia virgiliana* (Rome: Istituto dell'Enciclopedia Italiana, 1984), vol. I, pp. 537–39.

4. "Whatever kind of good it was that I possessed this evening, it was not given to me by God and nature. Although fortune denied me, justice showed me the opportunity, diligence made me take her by the hair, and perseverance had me keep her" (*Candelaio*, p. 151).

In *Candelaio*, the ass also becomes an example of how to take advantage of a situation: "If you do not have some evils, you have others, or others still; and if you are not refined, like I am, you are refined like another. Now, let us leave these words to the wind: let us come to our point. —There was a time when the lion and the ass were friends. On a pilgrimage together, they decided to take turns carrying each other when they crossed a river: that is to say, one time the ass would would carry the lion, and the next time the lion would carry the ass. Since they had to go to Rome and they had neither boat nor bridge to assist them, when they reached the Garigliano River, the ass pulled the lion onto his back. Yet the lion, afraid of falling into the water as the ass swam toward the riverbank, sank his claws deeper and deeper into the ass's skin, so much so that he penetrated right down to the poor animal's bone. The miserable ass, being one who makes a profession out of patience, proceeded as best he could, without uttering a word. When, out of the water safe and sound, the ass shook himself off a little and rubbed his back on the warm sand three or four times, they proceeded on their way. Upon their return eight days later, it was the lion's turn to carry the ass. The ass, now on top and wanting to avoid falling into the water, grabbed the lion's neck with his teeth. But this was not enough to keep him from falling, so he thrust his instrument, or, how shall we put it, his . . . you know what I mean, frankly speaking, into the space underneath the tail, the space that lacks skin, which made the lion feel more pain than a woman giving birth, and scream: 'Ouch! Ouch! Yow, yow, yow, yikes! Ouch! Traitor!' To which the ass responded in a serious and grave tone, 'Have patience, my brother: you realize that I do not have other nails than this one by which to attach myself to you!' And so the lion had to suffer and endure until they had crossed the river. As far as this is concerned: *Omnio rero vecissitudo este* [deformation of *omnium rerum vicissitudo est*]; the ass has such a big member that, at times, if the occasion presents itself, nobody will refuse it" (pp. 65–66).

5. "I certainly think that it is better to be impetuous than cautious, because fortune is a woman, and if you want to control her, it is necessary to treat her roughly. And it is clear that she is more inclined to yield to men who are impetuous than to those who are calculating" (Niccolò Machiavelli, *The Prince*, ed. Quentin Skinner and Russell Price [Cambridge: Cambridge University Press, 1988], chap. 25, p. 87). Besides the obvious similarities, Machiavelli's influence on Bruno is worthy of investigation. Ciliberto (in his introduction to *Spaccio della bestia trionfante* [Milan: Rizzoli, 1985], pp. 54–57) highlights a few points of convergence between Bruno's concept of religion and Machiavelli's *Capitoli* (which were printed by John Wolf's press in 1584, when Bruno was still in England). See Ferdinando D'Amato's

note on the relationship between Bruno and Machiavelli, "Giordano Bruno," *Giornale critico della filosofia italiana*, II (1930), p. 92. Similarly, I have noted a close relationship between a few verses of the *Asino* (which was also printed by John Wolf in 1588) and the sonnet "In lode de l'asino," appended to the *Cabala* (see chapter seven, note 9).

7 Negative Asininity: Idleness, Arrogance, Unidimensionality

1. In the sixteenth century, the plethora of travelogues contributed to the dissemination of information concerning the lives of primitive people: Villegagnon describes the bestial life of Brazil's indigenous people to Calvin (J. De Lery, *Histoire d'un voyage fait en la terre du Brésil, autrement dit Amérique* . . . [La Rochelle: Antoine Chupin, 1578]); the same theme can be found in *Les singularitez de la France Antarctique, et de plusieurs Terres et Isles decouvertes de nostre temps* (Antwerp: Christopher Plantin, 1558), and in Girolamo Benzoni, *La Historia del mondo nuovo la quale tratta dell'isole e mari nuovamente ritrovati e delle nuove città da lui proprio vedute, per acqua e per terra in quattordici anni* (Venice, 1565). For an analysis of this theme, see Papi, *Antropologia e civiltà*, pp. 195–200.

2. Papi, *Antropologia e civiltà*, p. 199. Yet in addition to the impact that the rebirth of the golden age had on the biblical principle of humanity's monogenesis, the theory was also put into question by the discovery of the New World. "Throughout the sixteenth century," Papi observes, "the origin of the American people was always tied to the theory of the antipodes. The existence of the antipodes was refuted by two of the great Church Fathers, Lactantius and Augustine. The fact that the existence of the antipodes was proved by recent voyages, however, not only discredited the two Church Fathers' geographical notions (which is not in itself so significant), but brought to light the reasons why Lactantius and Augustine had denied the existence of the antipodes, reasons that are far from scientific, and were derived from religious faith. If it were accepted that men existed on the other side of the earth, it would have raised the problem of reconciling this concept with the biblical tale of creation" (p. 202).

The Nolan does not miss the chance to mock those who believe in human monogenesis. In *Spaccio*, Jupiter gives Aquarius (who is displaced from his celestial throne) the task of explaining the universal flood to man: "Let him go to visit men and unravel that question of the deluge and declare how it was possible that it was universal, and why it was that all of heaven's cataracts burst loose. And let it no longer be believed to have been a particular deluge, since it is thought impossible that the sea and the rivers could have covered both hemispheres, or even one on this side of, and beyond, the Tropics or the Equator. Then he should make them understand how this remnant of the human race, swallowed by the waves, went to our Olympus of Greece, and not to the mountains of America or to Mongibello of Sicily, or any other place. Then he should make them understand that the generations of men are found on various continents, not in the manner in which are found so many other species of animals that have come forth from the maternal bosom of Nature, but by dint of migration and by virtue of navigation. And he should tell them, for example, that they were transported by those ships which existed before our first one was invented. . . . He should make them understand that a new part of the earth, called the New World, has been recently discovered, that there they have memorials of ten thousand years and more. . . . But let him, in order to avoid the inconveniences that you yourself might contemplate, go and skillfully preserve this belief, finding a suitable manner in which to adjust those years; and that upon which he cannot comment and for which he cannot find an excuse, let him boldly reject, saying that more faith must be placed in the gods (whose letters, patents and seals he will carry) than in men, who are all liars" (*Expulsion*, pp. 249–50; *Spaccio*, pp. 797–98).

Jove's proposal ridicules the notion of "migration and navigation," to which the supporters of human monogenesis referred in order to justify that men existed on other parts of the hemisphere. Here, too, the Nolan confirms that the generation of man is spontaneous, like that of "many other species of animals that have come forth from the maternal bosom of Nature." Momus's envisioned solution, however, that "it seems better to excuse the belief in this manner, that is, by saying for example that the people of the new land do not belong to the human species because they are not men, although they are similar to men in parts, shape, and brain. On many occasions they prove to be wiser and not at all ignorant in their dealings with their gods" (*Spaccio*, p. 798), seems to be too bold for Mercury: "But I think that it is advantageous to find some good reason, to explain a few gusts of wind or some abductions by whales which have swallowed up persons of one country and have gone to vomit them alive upon other parts and other continents. Otherwise we Greek gods will be confused, because it will be said that you, Jove, through Deucalion are the restorer not of all men, but only of a certain part of them" (*Expulsion*, p. 250; *Spaccio*, pp. 798–99).

According to Nicola Badaloni, "The piercing irony of Deucalion's myth makes those arguments ridiculous that often reintroduced the explanation of the origin of men on the new continent without significantly altering the biblical explanation. When the myth of Deucalion is transferred to Noah, however, it poses the problem in a radically different manner from that of the Christian myth. Bruno bases his thoughts on a materialistic concept of the origin of man as deriving from the breast of nature, which is of extreme importance" (N. Badaloni, *La filosofia di Giordano Bruno* [Florence: Parenti Editore, 1955], pp. 131–32).

These pages of the *Spaccio* are linked to the thesis that Bruno puts forth in the *Cabala*. Jove and Onorio affirm the theory of spontaneous generation as well as the common natural root of all living beings (see chapter five). Here, Bruno's anti-teleologic materialism recalls (not without substantial differences) the Lucretian concept of the genesis of life. On the other hand, as Bruno tried to defend himself from the accusations of the Inquisition, he justified his theories as being simple philosophical expositions of Lucretius: "I believe that this is Lucretius's opinion, and I have read this opinion and heard it spoken about, but to my knowledge, I do not think I have referred to it as my opinion, nor have I ever held it as my own, nor have I believed in it, nor in all that I have reasoned or read that referred to Lucretius the Epicurian's opinion and similar ones; and it is not possible to see in this opinion, which does not conform to my own, the principles and conclusions of my philosophy, as it may easily appear to him who reads it" (Vincenzo Spampanato, *Documenti della vita di Giordano Bruno* [Florence: Olschki, 1933], pp. 59–60). Notwithstanding the contrasting evaluations that Badaloni (p. 133) and Papi (p. 11) make of this declaration by the Nolan, they both insist on Bruno's deep knowledge of *De rerum natura* and on Lucretius's influence on Bruno's theories of genesis. Bruno also emphasizes the monogenesis of humanity and its spontaneous generation, in *De immenso* (*Opp. lat.*, I, II, p. 282) and in *De monade* (*Opp. lat.*, I, II, pp. 397–98).

3. Idleness's accusations of Toil, who is responsible for having introduced the concepts of *yours* and *mine* into the human vocabulary, recall a number of remarks in Giovan Battista Gelli's *Circe*. Here, the theme of "*yours* and *mine*" recurs as one of the reasons the animals (humans transformed by Circe into beasts) give in order to show Ulysses how unhappy the human race is: "*Lion.* . . . Tell me what cravings you wish there to be between us, being that we are all equal, so that we might never scorn one another; . . . Greed, which has not yet distinguished the *mine* and the *yours* between us, does not have a place among us, and thus many other vices that make your life unhappy" (*Opere*, ed. Delmo Maestri [Turin: UTET, 1976], pp. 379–80; also pp. 349–50 and p. 419). Ulysses himself, however, responds by saying, "As you have not distinguished between *mine* and *yours*, you do not

yet have your own country or place to belong" (p. 423). Gelli avenges, in short, the superiority of man, who can become "almost a God" (p. 444), but not without allowing for the criticism of a number of negative contradictions to *humanitas,* well evidenced by the animals' argumentation. On the theme of *yours* and *mine,* see chapter five, note 3.

4. Gio. Bernardo. What I want to ask is this: What do you think "pedant" means?

   Manfurio. *Lubentissime* I would like to tell you, teach it to you, declare it to you, expose it to you, state it to you, make it *palam* to you, insinuate it to you, *et—particula coniunctiva in ultima dictione apposuta—* inculcate it in you; *sicut, ut, velut, veluti, quemadmodum nucem ovidianam meis coram discipulis—quo melius nucleum eius edere possint,—enucleavi.* Pedant means almost a *pede ante: utpote quia* it is a forward step, which makes the young *erudienti* advance; *vel per strictiorem artioremque aethymologiam:* Pe: *perfectos,* Dan: *dans,* Te: *thesauros.* What do you think of these two etymologies?

   Gio. Bernardo. They are good; but I do not like either one, nor do they seem relevant.

   Manfurio. You have the right to speak, *alia meliore in medium prolata, idest* when you have introduced a more worthy route.

   Gio. Bernardo. Here you go: *Pe:* pecorone [big sheep]; *Dan:* da nulla [from nothing]; *Te:* testa d'asino [ass's head]." (*Candelaio,* pp. 78–79)

   On pedants, see chapter thirteen.

5. Lucian of Samosata, in his dialogue "Philosophies for sale," has Pyrrhus's philosophy follow that of Aristotle in a catalog of philosophies in order to contrast ironically the "I know everything" of the first with the "I know nothing" of the other:

   Zeus. Don't delay; call another, the Peripatetic.

   Hermes. (to *Peripatetic*) I say, you who are handsome, you who are rich! (To the *Buyers*) Come now, buy the height of intelligence, the one who knows absolutely everything!

   Buyer. What is he like?

   Hermes. Moderate, gentlemanly, adaptable in his way of living, and, what is more, he is double.

   Buyer. What do you mean?

   Hermes. Viewed from the outside he appears to be one man, and from the inside, another; so if you buy him, be sure to call the one self "exoteric" and the other "esoteric." . . .

   Buyer. Heracles, what insight!

   Hermes. What if I should tell you of other information demanding far keener vision, about sperm and conception and the shaping of the embryo in the womb, and how man is a creature that laughs, while asses do not laugh, and neither do they build houses nor sail boats. . . .

Zeus. Whom have we left?

Hermes. The Sceptic is still on our hands. Ready, come here and be put up, without delay. The crowd is already drifting away, and there will be but few at his sale. However,—who'll buy this one?'

Buyer. I will. But first tell me, what do you know?

Sceptic. Nothing.

Buyer. What do you mean by that?

Sceptic. That in my opinion nothing at all exists.

Buyer. Then do not *we* exist?

Sceptic. I don't even know that. . . .

Buyer. Of course, for you look to be slow and lazy. But what is the upshot of your wisdom?

Sceptic. Ignorance, and failure of hearing and vision.

(Lucian, *Lucian*, tr. A. M. Harmon [London: Heinemann, 1929], vol. II, pp. 503–9).

There is no doubt that Bruno was thinking of Lucian while he wrote his *Dialoghi*. I will note other textual comparisons between Lucian and Bruno in the course of this study. For an analysis of Lucian's influence on Renaissance authors, see C. A. Mayer, "Lucien et la Renaissance," *Revue de littérature comparée*, 47 (1973), pp. 2–22; Emilio Mattioli, "Il lucianesimo," in *Luciano e l'umanesimo* (Naples: Istituto Italiano per gli Studi Storici, 1980), pp. 71–187; and Guido Manacorda, "Notizie intorno alle fonti di alcuni motivi satirici ed alla loro diffusione durante il Rinascimento," *Romanische Forschungen*, 22 (1908), pp. 733–60.

6. Bruno's aggressive attitude toward skepticism corresponds to an annotation he inscribed in a manuscript that Nowicki discovered in the University Library in Wroclaw (A. Nowicki, "Un autografo inedito di Giordano Bruno in Polonia," *Atti dell'Accademia di Scienze Morali e Politiche*, 78 [Naples, 1967], pp. 262–68). On the frontispiece of a work by the Portuguese philosopher Francesco Sanchez (*Quod nihil scitur* [Lyon, 1581], see the edition by E. Limbrick and D. F. S. Thomson, *That nothing is known* [New York: Cambridge University Press, 1988]), Bruno accuses the author of being an ass. After having added underneath Sanchez's name the titles, *philosophus et medicus doctor*, with great consternation Bruno remarks, *Mirum quod onager iste appellat se doctorem* [Astonishing that this ass calls himself a doctor]. The copy of *Quod nihil scitur* was given personally to Bruno by

Sanchez, whom Bruno had met in Tolosa in 1581, as the manuscript's dedication indicates:

Cl[arissimo] V[iro]
d[omi]no Jordano Br[uno]
Nolano T[heologiae] D[octori]
Ph[ilosoph]o Acutissimo
fam[iliaritatis] g[ratia] h[onoris] c[aus]a
d[ono] d[edi]t
F. Sanchez

Bruno disputes Sanchez's theses, which acknowledge from the very first
pages the impossibility of knowledge—a notion that originates in Sanchez's
own failure in his search for the truth (for a specific analysis of Sanchez's
skepticism, see F. Walter Lupi's exposition, "Quod nihil scitur," *Riscontri*,
3 [1981], pp. 149–62; see also A. Nowicki, "Giordano Bruno nella patria
di Copernico," *Accademia Polacca delle Scienze—Biblioteca e centro di
studi a Roma*, fasc. 54 [1972], pp. 19–25).

A few decades later, in a dialogue by La Mothe Le Vayer (*Des rares
et eminentes qualitez des asnes de ce temps*, in *Cincq dialogues* [Mons: Paul
de la Fleche, 1671]), in which Machiavelli's *Asino* is cited among the ass's
illustrious literary antecedents, the asinine apology portrays (from a perspective tied to skepticism) a fictitious world wherein consciousness is pure
asininity.

7. Already in *The Golden Ass*, Apuleius frequently uses the image of a "Pegasean ass" in comic contexts. Lucius, transformed into an ass and seized
with fear, runs as if he had the wings of Pegasus (VI.30; VIII.16). The
Pegasean ass, however, actually appears to Lucius-ass during Isis's procession, a few moments before his metamorphosis back into a man: "I saw
there . . . an ass had wings glued to his back and went after an old man,
whereby you would judge the one to be Pegasus and the other Bellerophon,
and at both would you laugh well" (XI.8, p. 553).

Aretino also cites the Pegasean ass. In his *Cortigiana* the Pegasean
ass is used to scorn a poet: "And go ahead and accompany the Archpoet
who grooms, waters, and feeds the Pegasean ass, only to win its gift of
manure" (P. Aretino, *Teatro*, ed. Giorgio Petrocchi [Milan: Mondadori,
1971], p. 143).

8. Bruno specifically considers Aristotelian physics in two Latin works: *Figuratio aristotelici physici auditus* (Paris, 1586) and *Acrotismus camoeracensis*
(Wittenberg, 1588). In the dedicatory letter of the *Figuratio aristotelici*, the
reasons why the Nolan wrote this text are explained: "I would like others
to understand the three primary reasons why I undertook this project—

namely, that of casting light on Aristotle's intentions to the extent that I am able to do so. The first of these reasons is that I would not want the same thing to appear to happen to me as has happened to certain writers, who sully absolutely everything with constant observations and discussions, and who, supporting themselves with rash ignorance along with a certain hasty arrogance, take over for themselves the power of censuring those things about which they have no understanding whatsoever.

"The second reason that compelled me here is that among the very large crowd of those who cast themselves not only as philosophers but also in order to increase their dignity as Peripatetics, I see very few who are anything more than pretenders possessing an admirable discipline of this type more through an ignorance that labors out of faith in one man rather than through an intelligence that distinguishes among that man's principles with educated reasoning.

"The third intention that compels me to take up this project is that I may not, by some mistaken idea, appear to be an overbold argumentator who rises up against the majesty of proud things, rather than a frank man legitimately discussing things that (as I seem to believe myself, and rightfully so) have been opened up to me" (*Opp. lat.*, I, IV, pp. 133–34).

The synthesis of Aristotelian physics, as Tocco notes, "is done with great care; none of the Aristotelian arguments is left out, and the most irksome to Bruno, like those against the infinity of the world, are reported with scrupulous exactitude" (Felice Tocco, *Le opere latine di Giordano Bruno esposte e confrontate con le italiane* [Florence: Le Monnier, 1889], p. 104). This work by Bruno has a few obscure points, which Tocco discusses on pp. 104–7 of his essay. These points do not, however, compromise the comprehensibility of the text: "As a whole, the compendium of Aristotelian physics that Bruno published before undertaking the formidable assault against it is such that with opportune adjustments, it could serve us even today" (Tocco, *Le opere latine di Giordano Bruno*, p. 107).

In the *Acrotismus camoeracensis*, Bruno discusses all the principles of Aristotelian physics point by point (*Opp. lat.*, I, I). He disputes the claim that physics can only study nature in its eternal and inalterable essence (p. 83). He contests the fact that Aristotle did not allow for the existence of monstrosity or chance in nature (p. 107). He contests the idea of a finite universe (p. 122). Finally, he contests Aristotle's notions of space and time. For a complete and precise synthesis of Bruno's arguments, see Tocco's critical exposé (*Le opere latine di Giordano Bruno*, pp. 107–18), which defines the Nolan as a "great authority on Aristotelian works who does not fear entering into the most scabrous arguments and almost always gets them right.''

9. The tercet, "Holy asininty does not care about this; / But wants to remain with hands joined and kneeling, / Waiting for God to proclaim her destiny'' seems to utilize the image employed by Machiavelli in the *Asino* (V. 115–17): "To believe that without effort on your part God fights for you, while you are idle and on your knees, has ruined many kingdoms and many states'' (Machiavelli, *The Ass*, in *The Chief Works and Others*, tr. Allan Gilbert [Durham, N.C.: Duke University Press, 1965], p. 764). For a detailed analysis of Machiavelli's poem, see chapter twelve, and chapter six, note 5.

Certain themes appear in this sonnet that were already used by Erasmus in his *Moriae encomium:* "Now the simple people of the golden age, who were not armed with any formal learning, lived their lives completely under the guidance of natural impulses. . . . Then too, they had more reverence than to pry into the secrets of Nature with irreligious curiosity—to measure the stars, their motions and effects, to seek the causes of mysterious phenomena—for they considered it unlawful for mortals to seek knowledge beyond the limits of their lot. As for what is beyond the range of the furthest stars, the madness of exploring such things never entered their minds'' (Erasmus, *The Praise of Folly*, tr. Clarence H. Miller [New Haven: Yale University Press, 1979], pp. 50–51).

10. The episode of Christ's walking on water is found in the Gospels (Matt. 14: 22–23; Mark 6:45–56; John 6:16–21), while the myth of Orion is attested in Hyginus's *Astronomica*, 2.34 (see Kerényi, *The Gods of the Greeks*, pp. 201–4), and in the *Liber monstrorum*, "Orion is said to have been made in such a way that he could cross every sea, and keep his shoulders above the waves of any gulf, no matter how deep,'' *De Orione*, in *Liber monstrorum*, ed. Franco Porsia [Bari: Dedalo Libri, 1976], p. 212). See also Virgil, *Aeneid*, X.763–67.

11. Here we can also hear an echo of Erasmus's irony: "Nor is it merely an accident that fools are so extremely pleasing to God. . . . Paul testifies very clearly on this point when he says, 'What is foolish to the world, God has chosen,' and when he says that God was pleased to save the world through folly because it could not be redeemed through wisdom . . . and again when he gives thanks that the mystery of salvation has been hidden from the wise and revealed to the simple, that is, to fools. Relevant here, too, are his attacks everywhere in the Gospel against the scribes and pharisees and doctors of the law, whereas he carefully protected the ignorant populace. For isn't 'Woe to you, scribes and pharisees' equivalent to 'Woe to you, wise men'? But he seems to have taken the greatest delight in simple people,

women, and fishermen. In fact, even on the level of animal creatures, Christ is most pleased with those who are farthest removed from the slyness of the fox. Hence he preferred to ride on an ass, when if he wished he could have mounted a lion's back with impunity" (Erasmus, *The Praise of Folly*, pp. 128–29).

For the thematic comparisons that follow, it is also useful to cite this passage from the *Cabala:* "Everyone knows that not only in the human species, but in all animal species, the mother loves more, caresses more, contents her child more, and is more apt to let it be lazy. Without being asked or becoming fatigued, she hugs, kisses, squeezes, and protects her youngest child and treats him like a being that does not know good from evil, a being that has a bit of a lamb and a bit of a beast within him, a being that is an ass and does not know how to speak or to discourse; and as he grows in mind and prudence, he is ever diminishing in love, attention, and the pious affection that he received from his parents" (pp. 855–56).

Ciliberto identifies the author of *De serva arbitrio* in the character of Orion-Christ, highlighting passages in the *Spaccio* that echo Luther (See Ciliberto's introduction to *Giordano Bruno, Spaccio de la bestia trionfante,* pp. 37–43 and 51–53). Alfonso Ingegno also aims to explore the influence on the *Spaccio* of the debate between Erasmus and Luther concerning free will (*La sommersa nave della religione: Studio sulla polemica anticristiana del Bruno* [Naples: Bibliopolis, 1985]).

12. The transmigration of the souls of evil men into bodies of asses is also discussed by Plato in the *Phaedo* and by Lucian in *Menippus*. In the *Phaedo* (XXXI), when Socrates explains the transmigration of souls to Cebes, he emphasizes that souls end up in bodies that have characters similar to those they have just left: "I mean, for example, that those who have indulged in gluttony and violence and drunkenness, and have taken no pains to avoid them, are likely to pass into the bodies of asses and other beasts of that sort" (*Phaedo*, XXXI.81e, in *Plato*, tr. Harold North Fowler [London: W. Heinemann, 1960], p. 185).

Lucian, on the other hand, rails against the rich, inventing a decree that constrains them to transmigrate into asses: "Whereas many lawless deeds are done in life by the rich, who plunder and oppress and in every way humiliate the poor, be it then resolved by the senate and people, that when they die their bodies be punished like those of the other malefactors, but their souls be sent back up into life and enter into donkeys until they shall have passed two hundred and fifty thousand years in the said condition, transmigrating from donkey to donkey, bearing burdens, and being driven by the poor; and that thereafter it be permitted them to die"

(*Menippus*, 20, tr. A. M. Harmon [London: W. Heinemann, 1925], pp. 105–7).

Similarly, in Cesare Rao's "Elegy to the ass," Rao notes that "if it is permissible within the opinion of Pythagorism, then the souls of the wisest philosophers, and of great Lords, and of all powerful men who are esteemed in the world, transfer into the bodies of these animals [asses], as if into more worthy subjects, more honorable receptacles, or better yet, superb hotels. Perhaps it is this opinion that has made it possible for villains, uncouth people ill suited for discourse (believing that they are partially avenging the offenses and outrages of Lords and Gentlemen), to torment incessantly these poor and gentle animals with cruel beatings, unbearable burdens, and pathetic food" (Cesare Rao, *L'argute et facete lettere* [Venice: Giovanni Alberti, 1622], p. 101 [copy used: BAV Chigi VI 403]; the first edition, which was printed in Paris, is from 1573).

8 The Oration of Fortune

1. " 'I shall tell you, O Fortune,' said Minerva, 'why you are said to be without discourse and reason. He who lacks a certain sense lacks some knowledge, and especially that knowledge which is dependent upon that sense. Now, take yourself into consideration, you who are deprived of the light of eyes, which are the greatest source of knowledge.' Fortune answered that Minerva either was deceiving herself or wanted to deceive Fortune, and was confident of doing so, because she saw that the other was blind. 'But although I am deprived of my eyes, I am not deprived of ears and intellect,' said Fortune to her" (*Expulsion*, p. 170; *Spaccio*, p. 688). On the relationship between ear and intellect, see chapter two, note 54 (for specific references on the relationship between knowledge and the long ears of the ass, see pp. 13–14).

2. Nicola Badaloni, *La filosofia di Giordano Bruno*, p. 211.

3. Ernst Cassirer, "Freedom and Necessity," *The Individual and the Cosmos in Renaissance Philosophy* (Oxford: Basel Blackwell, 1943), pp. 74–75. For an iconographical summary of the symbol of Fortune in the Renaissance, see A. Warburg, *Francesco Sassettis letzwillige Verfügung* (Leipzig: Kunstwissench. Beiträge, August Schmarsow gewidmet, 1907); A. Doren, "Fortuna im Mittelalter und in der Renaissance," *Vorträge der Bibliothek Warburg*, II (1922–23; Leipzig and Berlin, 1924), p. 71–144. On the symbol of Fortune in sixteenth-century literature, see Mario Santoro, *Fortuna, ragione e prudenza nella civiltà letteraria del Cinquecento* (Naples: Liguori, 1967).

4. See the previous discussion in chapter three, esp. note 7.

5. See the passage of Valeriano cited on pp. 72–75.

6. Ibid.

7. Sebastian Brant, *Stultifera navis* (Basel: Johann Bergmann, 1497 [copy used: BAV, Inc. IV.147 = Hain 3746]). I have consulted the Latin translation of the poem done by one of Brant's students (Jakob Locher) and edited by the author himself, because it is to this work that we owe the European diffusion of the *Narrenschiff* as well as its numerous translations (see Josef Schmidt, "Sebastian Brant," in *Dizionario critico della letteratura tedesca* [Turin: UTET, 1976], p. 100).

8. A substantial portion of the engravings in the *Narrenschiff* belong to Dürer, who worked in Basel in 1493 as an "illustrator" (see Ladislao Mittner, "Brant: La letteratura della 'stultitia,' " in *Storia della letteratura tedesca* [Turin: Einaudi, 1982], vol. I, pt. II, p. 587.

9. I owe these "wheel of the ass" references to the generosity of Giorgio Stabile. In my description of the cardinal points and the course of the wheel, I have followed some of the suggestions offered in Stabile's essays on the wheel of fortune (Stabile, "La ruota della fortuna: Tempo ciclico e percorso storico," in *Scienze credenze occulte livelli di cultura*, Convegno internazionale di Studi, Florence, June 26–30, 1980 [Florence: Olschki Editore, 1982], pp. 477–503). Stabile, because of a series of astrological and cosmological interests, puts into question the traditional reading of the four cardinal points fixed on the wheel. The reader will note the following correspondences: *right* (orient, dawn, spring, generation, birth, innate power); *high* (meridian, noon, summer, culmination of growth, maturity, realized power); *left* (occident, sunset, autumn, decrease, old age, declining power); *low* (north, midnight, winter, corrosion, death, annihilated power). It is for this reason that the "southern" cardinal point of our wheel of the ass corresponds to what we call "north." See my Iconographical Collection.

10. Sebastian Brant, *Stultifera navis*, fols. xlvii and lxiiii. The ass in the *Stultifera navis*, however, also appears in xylographs that treat other themes: *De improvidis fatuis* (f. xxiii), *De amore venereo* (f. xxiiii), *De inutilibus votis et petitionibus* (f. xxxvii), *De pluralitate beneficiorum* (f. xli), *De iracundia ex levi causa* (f. xlvi), *Uxorem ducere propter opes* (f. lx), *De iracundis mulieribus* (f. lxxii), *De suppressit fatuis* (f. lxxxvi), *De vana spe futurae successionis* (f. ciii b), *De praemio sapientiae* (f. cxxi b).

Added to the specific theme of the wheel in Brant's poem is the ass's strong link to madness. The various characters populating the engravings always wear clown's hats that have two big ears attached to them. The xylograph of the ass (*De praemio sapientiae*) represents the ass with a horn on one side and a hat with ass's ears on the other, alluding to the theme of knowledge and asininity (on the relationship between the ass and madness, see chapter twelve, note 34). What is more, *Stultifera navis* is one of the first examples of the literature of the *stultitia* (see Giorgio Sichel, "Letteratura della 'Stultitia,' " in *Dizionario critico della letteratura tedesca*, p. 678).

The same "wheel of the ass" xylograph appears in a volume that includes Johannes Geiler von Kayersberger's sermons on Brant's *Narrenschiff*. The volume contains a series of sermons that use the poem as a textual base from which to discuss religious and political problems with a diverse public. The ass is placed in the context of two terms: *Turba Tristantium* (*Turba* XXXVI) and *In potestate gaudentium* (*Turba* LV) (Joannis Geyler, *Navicula sive speculum fatuorum* [Argentorati, 1511; copy used: BAV, Rossiano 5253]). Geiler's sermons were gathered and published by one of his disciples, Giacomo Other. On the important role of Geiler in the culture of his time, see Josef Schmidt, "Johannes Geiler," in *Dizionario critico della letteratura tedesca*, pp. 337–38.

In one of the many Latin editions of the *Stultifera navis*, the xylograph of the wheel of fortune can once again be found, with only one major difference: the ass is replaced with a figure of a man (see *Stultifera navis* [Basel: ex officina Sebastiani Henricpetri, 1572], p. 73 [copy used: BAV, R.G. Neolat. V.30]).

11. Stabile, "La ruota della fortuna," pp. 482–84.

12. Francesco Petrarca, *Von der Artzney beyder Glück* (Augsburg: Heynrich Steyner, 1532), 1.I, p. 105 [copy used: BAV, Rossiano, 2959]. This engraving seems to have been inspired by Brant himself. See Domenico Rossetti, "Bibliografia petrarchesca," in Francesco Petrarca, *De' rimedii dell'una e dell'altra fortuna*, translated by Giovanni Dassominiato (Bologna: Romagnoli, 1867), p. 42. The xylograph is reproduced in A. Doren, "Fortuna im Mittelalter und in der Renaissance," plate IV (illus. 11c). See my Iconographical Collection.

13. Francesco Petrarca, *De remediis utriusque Fortunae*, in *Opera* (Basel: Henricum Petri, 1554), vol. I, p. 90 [copy used: BCC, Racc. Sal. 5813].

14. On the ability of the ass to "seize the moment," see chapter six, note 4.

9 In the Labyrinth of Truth

1. The proverb *asinus portans mysteria* [the ass carries mysteries] dates back to ancient times when the ass was used as a vehicle of transport for divinities such as Dionysus, Cybele, and Isis (on these figures, see chapter two, notes 5, 13, and 14). The proverb also appears in Aristophanes' *Frogs* (159) in a

context that is linked to the Eleusinian cult. The proverb has since assumed a comic connotation. It illustrates the presumption of the ass, who, upon seeing people bow as he passes and not knowing that he is transporting a sacred image, believes himself to be the cult object. Aesop's fable goes as follows: "An ass once carried through the streets of a city a famous wooden Image to be placed in one of its temples. As he passed along, the crowd made lowly prostration before the Image. The ass, thinking that they bowed their heads in token of respect for himself, bristled up with pride, gave himself airs, and refused to move another step. The driver, seeing him thus, stopped, laid his whip about his shoulders and said, 'O you perverse dullhead! It is not yet come to this, that men pay worship to an ass' " (*Aesop's Fables*, tr. Townsend, p. 105).

In the sixteenth-century tradition, Alciato revives the theme of the proverb in the emblem, *non tibi, sed Religioni* [not for you, but for religion]: "A slow ass carried a statue of Isis, holding on his crooked back the venerable mysteries. Whoever met them respectfully adored the goddess, and down on his knees he piously began to pray. But the ass believed that such an honor was offered to *him*, and he swelled up with pride, becoming reasonably arrogant, until the driver subdued him with blows and said: 'You are not the god, ass, you only carry him' " (Andrea Alciato, *Emblemi* [Padova: P. P. Tozzi, 1626, copy used: BAV, Rossiano 6469]. The first edition of the *Emblemata* is 1531).

In the *Ad encomium asini digressio* (*De vanitate*, caput CII), Agrippa also speaks of the *asinus portans mysteria*. Bruno lends a negative connotation to the proverb in this particular case by indicating those chosen by grace who are bearers of divine truth. Another interesting point is the meaning the proverb assumes with respect to the general establishment of Bruno's conception of asininity, where the symbol of the ass becomes a vehicle for the transmission of the philosophy of knowledge. See chapter eleven.

2. John M. Steadman investigates the symbolism of the ass in Spenser's work, proposing a Protestant reading of the proverb *asinus portans misteria* ("Una and the Clergy: The Ass Symbol in *The Faerie Queene*," *Journal of the Warburg and Courtauld Institutes*, 21 [1958], pp. 134–36). I do not agree with Steadman's interpretation of the symbol of the ass in Bruno here. The ass cannot be considered a mere symbol of sacred ignorance void of worldly erudition and endowed only with the wisdom of the spirit. The problem is much more complex.

3. Nicola Badaloni, *La filosofia di Giordano Bruno*, p. 33.

4. For a discussion of the various positions taken by Bruno scholars (Spaventa, Olschki, Corsano, Guzzo, Garin) on the myth of Actaeon, see Badaloni, *La*

filosofia di Giordano Bruno, pp. 54–65. See also A. Ingegno, *Cosmologia e filosofia nel pensiero di Giordano Bruno*, pp. 245–47. A reference to the myth of Actaeon in relation to Bruno can also be found in Jacques Lacan, "The Freudian Thing, or the Meaning of the Return to Freud in Psychoanalysis" in *Ecrits*, tr. Alan Sheridan (New York: Norton, 1977), pp. 114–45.

5. In the hieroglyphs of Caelius Augustus Curio, which are included in the appendix to Valeriano's *Hieroglyphica*, we can find an engraving of Mercury offering a robe to the naked Diana. The comment is significant: "The maiden to whom Mercury offers a garment is Diana, who represents the changing of things as they undergo increase and decrease. The Greek poets imagined that when Jupiter saw Diana walking nude, which seemed hardly appropriate for a maiden, he ordered Mercury to make her a garment. Although Mercury made many garments for her, he could not make one that was suitable: the reason being that while he was preparing one for her, she was continually changing in size, with the result that she could not put it on. She is, therefore, a figure of increase and decrease, and the hieroglyph of the changing of things, of plans, and of one's mind" (Caelius Aug., *Hieroglyphicorum*, quoted in Valeriano, *Hieroglyphica*, p. 433). See also Giulio Camillo, *L'idea del theatro*, pp. 88–89.

6. Papi, *Antropologia e civiltà*, p. 181.

7. Bruno's dialectic differs from that of Nicholas of Cusa with respect to the concept of unity. Whereas Bruno posits that matter is the point of union, Cusa holds that the highest dialectical conversion takes place in God (see Badaloni, *La filosofia di Giordano Bruno*, pp. 53, 71, 74). The providential finalism of the German philosopher cannot be reconciled with the Democritan and Lucretian concepts of the infinite in the Nolan's philosophy. Furthermore, comparisons between the works of Cusa and the works of Bruno have shown how the Nolan makes use of the mathematical models of the first and second books of *De docta ignorantia* and ignored the third book, which contains the Christological theme (Papi, *Antropologia e civiltà*, pp. 25–27). On the relationship between Bruno and Cusa, see also Ingegno, *La sommersa nave della religione*, p. 97.

8. Papi, *Antropologia e civiltà*, p. 275. Bruno seems to be quite explicit in these verses of *De immenso:* "For nature is more than present to things; nature is innate in them: it is distant from nothing, since nothing is distant from being, except that which is false, which is never nowhere, and nothing. And while the appearance of things varies only on the surface, nature, which is more intimate to all things than each thing is to itself, is

flourishing: nature which is the beginning of being, the source of all forms, Mind, God, Being, One, Truth, Destiny, Reason, Order" (*Opp. lat.*, I, II, p. 314).

9. " 'Does it seem to you, Jove,' he asked, 'that in the house of Leisure there is leisure as regards active life, there where there are so many gentlemen in waiting with servants who arise most punctually in the morning to wash their masters' faces and hands three and four times with five or seven kinds of water, and with a hot iron and with the sap of a fern spend two hours waving and curling their hair, imitating lofty and great providence, by whom there is not a hair of a head that is not examined in order that it be disposed of according to its law?' " (*Expulsion*, p. 210; *Spaccio*, pp. 739–40).

The theme of hair crimping, which establishes a relationship between these two passages from the *Spaccio* and the concept of providence, attacks Lutheran determinism. Bruno implicitly cites the passage from Matthew ("And even the hairs of your head are all numbered"; Matt. 10:30), which seemed favorable to the Lutherans, but turns its senses around with subtle irony (see Ingegno, *La sommersa nave della religione*, p. 38).

10. Papi, *Antropologia e civiltà*, p. 275.

11. Badaloni, *La filosofia di Giordano Bruno*, p. 109.

12. For a commentary on these verses of Book II of *De rerum natura*, see Michel Serres, *La Naissance de la physique dans le texte de Lucrèce: Fleuves et turbulences* (Paris: Les Editions de Minuit, 1977). Serres's interpretation clearly breaks from the traditional reading of this passage, which notes a pronounced selfishness in Lucretius's attitude. See also Hans Blumenberg, *Schiffbruch mit Zuschauer* (Frankfurt am Main: Suhrkamp, 1979), pp. 47–57.

Serres's interpretation of Lucretian epistemology will serve in the final chapter when I set up a number of analogies with Bruno's position.

13. Badaloni, *La filosofia di Giordano Bruno*, p. 174.

10   From Orion to Chiron: Opposing Images of the Religious Cult

1. In a list of negative symbols situated in the sky, Jove also includes the symbol of Chiron: "You know that Chiron and his beast get sixty-six stars in the southern latitude of the sky for having been the tutor of that son born out of the stuprum of Peleus and Thetis" (*Expulsion*, p. 112; *Spaccio*, pp. 606–7).

2. Bruno is particularly ruthless when he attacks superstition. In the *Spaccio*, Saulino mocks those who worship the ass's tail: "In a similar manner, I

have seen the Monks of Castello in Genoa showing the veiled tail for a short time and allowing it to be kissed, saying: 'Touch it not, kiss it. This is the holy relic of that blessed she-ass, declared worthy of carrying our Lord from the Mount of Olives to Jerusalem. Adore it, kiss it, offer alms. *Centuplum accipietis, et vitam aeternam possidebitis* [You will receive a hundredfold, and will possess eternal life]' '' (*Expulsion*, p. 246; *Spaccio*, p. 792). This same episode appears in *Candelaio* (p. 37).

The story Bruno tells of the adoration of Genoa's ass's tail is mirrored in a text that analyzes the symbol of the ass: Johannis Benedicti Carpozovii, *Asino Messiae Christi in urbem ierosolymam vectore* (Leipzig: Friderici Lanckisii, 1671), p. 50.

In *Candelaio*, the Nolan refers to other forms of superstition: "He who wishes for *Agnus dei*, for sacred grains, for the water of Saint Peter the martyr, the seed of Saint John, the manna of Saint Andrew, the oil of the fat of the marrow of the bone shaft of the body of Saint Piantorio; he who wishes to make a vow in order to have a good journey, go find madonna Angela Spigna" (pp. 161–62). See also *Cabala*, p. 836.

3. Papi, *Antropologia e civiltà*, p. 312.
4. Ibid., p. 333.
5. On Henry III's motto, see Frances A. Yates, *French Academies of the Sixteenth Century* (London: Warburg Institute, 1947), pp. 227–28. See also Badaloni, *La filosofia di Giordano Bruno*, pp. 188–92.
6. Badaloni, *La filosofia di Giordano Bruno*, p. 179.
7. Papi, *Antropologia e civiltà*, p. 324.
8. Badaloni, *La filosofia di Giordano Bruno*, pp. 216–17.
9. Ibid., p. 248.
10. The source of the tale *Prometeo, l'asino, il serpente e l'immortalità* is in Nicander (*Scolia in Nicandri Theriaka*, 343ff.). For a detailed reconstruction of the different versions, see Deonna, "Laus asini," esp. pp. 17–21.
11. On the specific relationship between water and fire, see Bruno's analysis in *De immenso* (*Opp. lat.*, I, II, pp. 306–8).
12. Serres, *La Naissance de la physique*, pp. 74–75.
13. R. Trousson, *Le thème de Prométhée dans la littérature européenne* (Geneva: Librairie Droz, 1964), vol. I, pp. 116–17.
14. For an analysis of the Promethean myth in the Renaissance, see Trousson, *Le thème de Prométhée*, pp. 100–141; Cassirer, *Individual and the Cosmos*, pp. 92–98; Paolo Rossi, "La nuova scienza e il simbolo di Prometeo," in *I filosofi e le macchine* (Milan: Feltrinelli, 1971), pp. 174–86; and Papi, *Antropologia e civiltà*, pp. 145–58.

11   The Ass in the Guise of the Sileni: Appearances Are Deceptive

1. For a discussion of this passage in the *Cabala*, see pp. 7–8.

2. The *Explicatio triginta sigillorum ad omnium scientiarum et artium inventionem et memoriam* is a text on the art of memory that was probably published in London in 1583. Bruno revises and discusses all the material included in his other mnemonic texts, with particular reference to the *Cantus circaeus* and *De umbris idearum*.

3. For the relationship between the ass and these works by Bruno (*Spaccio*, *De umbris idearum* and *Arca di Noè*), see chapter one.

4. Desiderii Erasmi, *Sileni Alcibiadis*, in *Adagia*, in *Opera Omnia* (Leiden, 1703), vol. VI, pp. 433–34.

5. Ibid.

6. Ibid.

7. "But if you sometimes see certain serious propositions, which would seem to have to fear coming before the supercilious censure of Cato—have no doubt, for these Catos are quite blind and mad, if they cannot discover what is hidden beneath these Sileni" (*Cena*, p. 14). The theme recurs in his Latin works as well: "For however precious may be the reward hidden under the Sileni, nevertheless the divine example of truth, concealed under the form of what appear to be impossible assertions (a truth that a common and extremely base mode of belief perceives as distorted, as in the curved and oblique surface of a mirror), has come out into the full light of day, and all the fallacies that were standing in the way have been removed, it simply vanishes" (*Opp. lat.*, I, I, p. 62); "Pleasant chestnuts are concealed under the prickles of their shells, and under Sileni the most expensive merchandise is sometimes hidden. *O beautiful youth, do not trust too much in appearances.* It is an opinion that, at first sight, I judged obvious, but from up close I discovered that the opinion was possible, then that it was true, and finally, when it had been examined in depth, that it proved to be both necessary and absolutely evident" (*Opp. lat.*, I, I, p. 208).

8. On the relationship between the ass and the Silenus, see chapter two, note 6.

9. Plato, *Symposium*, 221e–222a, in *Plato*, tr. Fowler, p. 239. Erasmus resumes Alcibiades' discourse on Socrates-Silenus, "Anyone who took him [Socrates] at his face value, as they say, would not have offered a farthing for him. He had a yokel's face, with a bovine look about it, and a snub nose always running; you would have thought him to be a stupid, thick-headed clown" (*The "Adages" of Erasmus; A Study with Translations*, tr. Mar-

garet Mann Phillips [Cambridge: Cambridge University Press, 1964], p. 270).

10. Delio Cantimori, "Erasmo e la vita italiana nel secolo XVI," in *Umanensimo e religione nel Rinascimento* (Turin: Einaudi, 1975), p. 42. Other Renaissance authors have evoked the theme of the Silenus. The first example can be found in Pico della Mirandola's letter to Ermolao Barbaro, in which he defends the primacy of philosophy over eloquence. Pico compares the unadorned speech of the philosopher to the image of the Silenus: "But would you like me to represent to you the idea of our conversation? It is precisely the same as our Alcibiades' idea of the Sileni. For these were statues of these Sileni that had rough features, hideous and repulsive, but within they were full of jewels, and of rare and costly objects. So if you were to look at them from the outside, you would see a wild beast, but if you were to look inside, you would recognize a deity" (*Ioannes Pico Mirandulanus Hermolao Barbaro suo*, in *Prosatori latini del Quattrocento*, ed. Eugenio Garin [Milan and Naples: Ricciardi, 1952], p. 812). In another context, Giulio Camillo also alludes to the Sileni (see *L'idea del theatro*, p. 61). The Occult Academnicians (1564–70) used the image of a Silenus for their emblem, combined with the motto *Intus non extra* (see *Rime de gli Accademici Occulti con le loro imprese e discorsi* [Brescia, 1568]). On the relationship between these authors and the Sileni, see Carlo Ossola's fundamental work: "Les devins de la lettre et les masques du double: La diffusion de l'anagrammatisme à la Renaissance," in *Devins et charlatans au temps de la Renaissance*, ed. M. T. Jones-Davies (Paris: Centre de recherches sur la Renaissance de l'Université de Paris-Sorbonne, 1979), pp. 127–57; see also Ossola's "L'Académie des Occulti: Fonctionnement politique et culturel" (paper presented at the conference "L'état et les forces sprituelles," Tours, May 20–22, 1976, C.E.S. de la Renaissance). Tasso also includes the Sileni in his work:

> They used to marvel in the ancient days
> at rude and rough Silenus coming forth;
> but that great myrtle in its open womb
> made rarer, lovelier wonders manifest:
> there was a lady whose false beauty beamed
> like an angelic loveliness on earth.

(*Jerusalem Liberated*, tr. Joseph Tusiani [Rutherford, N.J.: Fairleigh Dickinson University Press, 1970], XVIII.30.1–6, p. 383). See also the dialogue of Girolamo Vida, *Sileno, dialogo . . . nel quale si discorre della felicità de' mortali, et si conclude che fra tutte le cose di questo mondo l'Amante fruisca solo la vera e perfetta beatitudine humana* (Vicenza: Giorgio Greco, 1589).

A few contemporary critics have used the theme of the Sileni as an interpretive model for understanding how certain texts function. For example, Giulio Ferroni analyzes madness in *Orlando Furioso* (see "Ariosto e la concezione umanistica della follia," in *Ludovico Ariosto*, convegno internazionale, September 27–October 5, 1974 [Rome: Accademia Nazionale dei Lincei, 1975], pp. 73–92); and Silvia Longhi analyzes a number of sixteenth-century burlesque texts (see *Lusus: Il capitolo burlesco nel Cinquecento* [Padova: Antenore, 1983], pp. 123–34). For works not from the sixteenth century, see Roberto Barbolini, *Il sileno capovolto: Socrate nella cultura 'fin de siècle'* (Bologna: Cappelli, 1981).

11. François Rabelais, *Gargantua and Pantagruel*, tr. J. M. Cohen (Harmondsworth: Penguin Books, 1976), p. 37.

12. Ibid., p. 38.

13. "First, it is clear that all human affairs, like the Sileni of Alcibiades, have two aspects quite different from each other. Hence, what appears 'at first blush' (as they say) to be death, will, if you examine it more closely, turn out to be life; conversely, life will turn out to be death; beauty will become ugliness; riches will turn to poverty; notoriety will become fame; learning will be ignorance; strength, weakness; noble birth will be ignoble; joy will become sadness; success, failure; friendship, enmity; what is helpful will become harmful; in brief, you will find everything suddenly reversed if you open the Silenus" (Erasmus, *The Praise of Folly*, p. 43).

14. See, for example, the way Bruno, in a scene in *Candelaio*, describes the conflicting movements that agitate human life: "*Marca*. They left *en masse*, some of them to amuse themselves, some to sadden themselves, others crying, others laughing, some giving advice, others hoping, some reacting in one manner, others in another, some using one kind of language, and others using other kinds: comedy and tragedy came together. In sum, he who wishes to see how the world was made should have been present" (*Candelaio*, p. 82). For *coincidentia oppositorum* in Bruno, see the analysis in chapter four (see also Laura Sanguinetti White, " 'In tristitia hilaris, in hilaritate tristis': Armonie dei contrasti," *Quaderni di italianistica*, 2 (1984), pp. 190–203).

15. In antiquity, Democritus of Abdera (founder of the school of atomism) and Heraclitus of Ephesus (theorist of *panta rei*) became symbols for two opposing attitudes toward life. Democritus laughed at all human preoccupations; Heraclitus cried because he saw the transience of all things (Juvenal, *Satires*, X.28ff.). This image is enhanced in the Renaissance—one fre-

quently finds the terms "to democritize" and "to heraclitize." One of Alciato's emblems, entitled *In vitam umanam*, portrays the two philosophers with their respective attitudes: "You should now cease to lament the misfortunes of human life, more than is customary. Heraclitus: according to you human life teems with many evils. As for you, Democritus, it's now or never: extol laughter, for with laughter life has been made more playful. Meanwhile, seeing this, I wonder to what purpose I might weep with you [Heraclitus], or how heartily I might joke with you [Democritus]" (Andrea Alciato, *Emblemi*, p. 224). On this *topos*, see the preface by Yves Hersant, in *Hippocrate: Sur le rire et la folie* (Paris: Editions Rivages, 1989); P. Guaragnella, *Le maschere di Democrito e di Eroclito* (Fasano: Schera, 1990); D. Arnould, *Le rire et les larmes dans la littérature grecque d'Homère à Platon* (Paris: Belles Lettres, 1990); A. Buck, "Democritus ridens et Heraclitus flens," in *Wort und Text: Festschrift für Fritz Schelk* (Frankfort, 1948); and the recent work of Th. Rütten, *Demokritlachender Philosoph und sanguinischer Melancholiker, Mnemosyne*, supp. 118 (Leiden, 1992).

16. Rabelais, *Gargantua*, p. 79.

17. Ibid., p. 79. Erasmus tells the tale of the ass and the thistle (*Adagia*, I.10.71); Valerius Maximus tells that of the ass and the figs (I.10). It is important to stress that the ass reappears numerous times in Rabelais's work; for instance, the apology in *Pantagruel* (bk. V, chap. VII): "Panurge tells Master Aeditus the Fable of the Horse and the Ass," and the fact that Rabelais pokes fun at Cornelius Agrippa (bk. V, chap. XVIII), describing him as having the large genitals of an ass attached to his belt, lead us to suppose that he knew of the *Ad encomium asini digressio*, as well as other contemporary writings about the ass.

18. Vincenzo Spampanato, *Alcuni antecedenti e imitazioni francesi del Candelaio* (Portici: Della Torre, 1905), pp. 11–35. Spampanato's investigation is limited to a few textual comparisons, which require further research and critical reflection. Other general references are found in Marcel Tetel, *Rabelais et l'Italie* (Florence: Olschki, 1969), pp. 47–59. Tetel's review, while lacking in critical observation, offers a panorama of interrelationships between Rabelais's text and those of other Renaissance authors, such as Lando and Aretino. We shall see that these authors have a rather significant influence on Bruno's Italian dialogues.

19. Giulio Ferroni, "Frammenti di discorsi sul comico," in *Ambiguità del comico* (essays by Della Terza, Ferroni, Gronda, Paccagnella, Scalise), ed. G. Ferroni (Palermo: Sellerio, 1983), pp. 44–45. In his analysis of Bruno's *Candelaio*, Ferroni applies the theme of the Sileni to the concept of the world as theater: "All Brunian philosophy . . . wavers between a total ac-

ceptance of the world theater, its paradoxes and infinite masks, and a fury of negation, a tension toward a truth capable of affirming its own total enlightenment. Science is covered with rags; the wise man caught inside a Silenus is the same as he who continually shifts the surfaces, who endlessly exchanges the internal for the external. And yet the affirmation that this person is torn in half is already a discovery of a truth that brings one far from the scene itself, distances it, and looks at it as if it were foreign to itself" (p. 53).

20. Guazzo recounts a similar anecdote in his *La civil conversazione*. He who finds himself in some sort of obscure difficulty while reading cannot, as Guazzo writes, "pray to the book to reveal itself." Instead, "it is good for you now and then to leave him [the book] reluctantly, telling him that if he does not want to be understood, you do not want to understand him" (Stefano Guazzo, *La civil conversazione* [Venice: Altobello Salicato, 1580], p. 20 [copy used: BAV, Chigi V583]).

21. "And calls bread, bread, a prick, a prick, / and so much the worse for him who does not like it" (Pietro Aretino, *Capitolo al Duca di Mantova*, in *Opere burlesche* [Utrecht al Reno, 1771], vol. III).

In *De la causa*, Bruno also emphasizes the necessity of speaking clearly: "I shall not speak like a holy prophet, an abstract diviner, an apocalyptic visionary, nor like the angelic she-ass of Balaam. I shall not reason as if inspired by Bacchus, nor as if swollen with wind by the strumpet Muses of Parnassus, nor as a Sibyl impregnated by Apollo, nor as an oracular Cassandra, nor as if packed from my toenails to the tips of my hair by Apollonian enthusiasm, nor as a seer illuminated by the oracle or Delphic tripod. . . . No, I'll speak in the everyday and vulgar tongue, as a man who has had thoughts other than going around distilling the juice of the great and small regions of the brain until there is only dryness left to the meninges. I'll speak, I say, like a man who has no other brain than his own" (*Cause, Principle and Unity*, tr. Jack Lindsay [New York: International Publishers, 1962], p. 59, translation altered slightly; *Causa*, pp. 194–95). On Bruno's polemical realism, see Giorgio Bárberi Squarotti "L'esperienza stilistica di Bruno fra Rinascimento e Barocco," in *La critica stilistica e il barocco letterario* (Florence: Le Monnier, 1958), p. 155.

12   The Literature of the Ass before Bruno

1. Among the various Renaissance editions of the *The Golden Ass*, I shall note M. Tuccius, ed. (Florence: P. de Giunta, 1512); Franciscus Asulanus, ed. (Venice: Aldi & Andrea Soceri, 1521); and Bernardus Pisanus, ed. (Flor-

ence: P. Iuntae, 1522). The Beroaldo commentary also went through various editions: (Bologna: B. Ectoris, 1500); (Venice: B. de Zaniis, 1504); (Venice: P. Pincium, 1510); (Venice: I. Tacuini, 1516). The translation into the vulgate by Boiardo (1516) should also be noted, as well as Firenzuola's liberal rewrites (1550), both of which (especially the latter) were reprinted several times. On the influence of the *The Golden Ass* on Renaissance iconography, see Riccardo Scrivano's paper, *"L'Asino d'oro* nel Rinascimento tra racconto scritto e racconto figurato," in *Modi del raccontare*, ed. Giulio Ferroni (Palermo: Sellerio, 1987), pp. 46–52.

2. Niccolò Machiavelli, *The Ass*, in *The Chief Works and Others*, tr. Gilbert. All citations are from this edition.

3. Enrici Cornelii Agrippae, *Ad encomium asini disgressio*, in *De incertitudine et vanitate scientiarum* (Cologne, 1531), caput CII.

4. Merlin Cocai (Teofilo Folengo), *Le maccheronee*, ed. Alessandro Luzio (Bari: Laterza, 1911), 2 vols.

5. *L'asinesca gloria* (Venice: Francesco Marcolini, 1533).

6. Giovan Battista Pino, *Ragionamento sovra del asino* (N.p., n.d.).

7. The ass also appears in a number of "burlesque" works. It suffices to recall del Mauro's *Capitolo in lode di Priapo*, in *Il primo libro delle opere burlesche*, by M. Francesco Berni (Florence, n.d.), and Bino's *In lode dell'asino*, in Berni's *Il secondo libro delle opere burlesche* (Florence, 1555).

8. In most texts that treat the topic of the ass, other illustrious antecedents are often cited (among which Apuleius and Lucian are inevitable figures, and at times the ending of *Lucius or the ass* is even attributed to *The Golden Ass*). On this last feature, see my "Simbologia dell'asino: A proposito di due recenti edizioni," *Giornale storico della letteratura italiana*, 161 (1984), p. 117.

9. Vincenzo Spampanato, *Giordano Bruno e la letteratura dell'asino* (Portici: Della Torre, 1904).

10. At this time there are only four known examples: Biblioteca Nazionale di Firenze (Magl. 3.2.41), British Library (12316. i. 47), Biblioteca Nazionale di Roma (69.7.E:46), and Biblioteca Nazionale di Napoli (S.Q.XXI.C.56).

11. The *Catalogue of Italian Books* of the British Library places a question mark after the 1549 date. This hypothesis, however, is refuted by two textual references that move the date to at least after 1550. The first is a brief parenthesis, "il nostro cinquanta" ("our 1550's"), and the second is a citation from Doni's *Zucca* published in Venice in 1551–52.

12. Giovan Battista Pino, *Ragionamento sovra del asino*, ed. Olga Casale (Rome: Salerno Editrice, 1982), pp. 41–42. All citations are from this edition, and I point out when necessary the passages that depart from the original. Casale's work frequently includes philological selections,

which, in my opinion, may make the text incomprehensible (see my "Simbologia dell'asino," pp. 116–18).

13. Pino, *Ragionamento*, p. 42.
14. Ibid., p. 82.
15. Ibid., pp. 38–39.
16. Ibid., pp. 39–40. On Pino's puns, see my article, "Asinus portans mysteria: Le 'Ragionamenti sovra del asino,' " in *Le monde animal au temps de la Renaissance* (Paris: published under the direction of M. J. Jones-Davies, 1990), pp. 189–217. On the theme of *feritas*, see G. Paparelli, *Feritas, Humanitas, Disunitas: L'essenza umanistica del Rinascimento* (Messina and Florence: Casa Editrice G. D'anna, 1960).
17. Pino, *Ragionamento*, p. 71.
18. "You should know, then, that there are two ways of contending: one by using laws, the other, force. The first is appropriate for men, the second for animals; but because the former is often ineffective, one must have recourse to the latter. Therefore, a ruler must know well how to imitate beasts as well as employing properly human means. This policy was taught to rulers allegorically by ancient writers: they tell how Achilles and many other ancient rulers were entrusted to Chiron the centaur, to be raised carefully by him. Having a mentor who was half-beast and half-man signifies that a ruler needs to use both natures, and that one without the other is not effective" (Machiavelli, *The Prince*, chap. 18, p. 61).
19. Pino, *Ragionamento*, p. 166.
20. Ibid., p. 79.
21. "The veritable ass-man, a seminal figure in the Middle Ages, is often painted or sculpted with the clothes and features of a schoolmaster. This indicates the vain doctrine that is similar to the braying that comes from such a mouth, and implicitly to all purely wordly science" (Rémy de Gourmont, *Le latin mystique*, p. 183). The tradition also offers us an inverted image of the ass-centaur. It is no longer the head of an ass and the legs of a man, but the reverse. In the *Liber monstrorum* (p. 154) it is described as such: "*Onocentauri* [half man, half ass] seem to have the rational body of men down to the navel, and the lower part of the body is represented as having the base shagginess of asses." Even Isidore, referring to a passage of the *Commentarium in Isaiam* by St. Jerome (Hieronymus Stridonensis, *Commentarii in Esaiam*, ed. M. Adriaen [Tornhout, 1963], pp. 422–23), speaks of ass-centaurs and traditional centaurs: "The onocentaur, however, is called that because he is said to be made half in the form of a man, half in that of an ass, just as the hippocentaurs have their name because it is thought that the natures of horses and of men were combined in them" (Isidorus His-

palensis, *Etymologiarum sive Originum libri XX*, ed. W. M. Lindsay [Oxford, 1911], XI.3).

Ulyssis Aldrovandi also speaks of these creatures, paraphrasing Aelian (*De nat. anim.*, XVII.9): "Whoever has seen a donkey-man will not consider incredible the story spread far and wide by rumor: that centaurs existed, and that neither sculptors nor painters were untruthful in their reproduction of them, but rather that they, too, were the products of time. And whoever has seen them will not deny that two bodies of different natures have coalesced into one. Nevertheless, I wish to pass over the question as to whether they actually existed in fact, or whether it was rumor, more malleable than any wax and more adept at modeling, that shaped them (so that two bodies, half the body of a man and half the body of a horse, were intermingled, and were reconciled to each other by one soul). I now intend to discuss the ass-woman, of whom I have come to know the following things through hearsay and rumor. She is similar to man, of course, in features, and her face is framed by long hair. Likewise both her neck and her chest carry a resemblance to human form: her breasts, too, which swell from her chest. Her shoulders, arms, elbows, and hands are by nature like those of humans; her back, sides, stomach, and hind feet are very similar to the ass; and exactly like the ass, she is of an ashy-gray color. Her lower stomach (at the sides) is slightly white. Her hands serve a double purpose, for when she needs to move swiftly, they run ahead of the pair of feet behind; as a result, she is not overtaken by other quadrupeds when she runs. And then again, when she needs to take food, or to pick something up, set it down, seize it, or grasp it, what were previously feet become hands; at that point, she does not walk, but sits still. This animal has an extremely hostile disposition. For if she is captured, unable to bear slavery, she abstains from all food out of longing for liberty, and condemns herself to death by starvation. These things about the ass-woman are reported by Pythagoras, as Crates from Pergamum in Mysia attests" (Ulyssis Aldrovandi, *De asino*, in *De quadrupedibus solidipedibus*, p. 313). For further references to the ass-centaur, see P. A. Robin, *Animal Lore in English Literature* (London: John Murray, 1932), pp. 81–82.

22. Pino, *Ragionamento*, pp. 65–66. The comparison between the assimilation of food and the metabolizing of the contents of a book also recurs in Guazzo (*La civil conversazione*, p. 85).

23. Lucius thanks the ass in the following manner: "Wherefore I do now give great thanks to my assy form, in that by that means I have seen the experience of many things, and am become more experienced (notwithstanding that I was then very little wise)" (*The Golden Ass*, IX.13, p. 421). For a

psychoanalytic reading of Lucius's experience, see Marie Louise von Franz, *The Golden Ass of Apuleius: The Liberation of the Feminine in Man* (Boston: Shambala, 1992).

24. Pino, *Ragionamento*, p. 69.

25. I shall allude to a few themes: the praise of toil (p. 41), the description of the gods' advice (p. 44), Jove's benevolence toward asses (p. 63), the victory over the giants (p. 63), and Prometheus and the ass (p. 85). In telling the episode of Samson, the comparison between Pino and Bruno is more than simply thematic: "One can verify this with Samson's experience: with a mandible, or, rather, a jaw of an ass, he killed a thousand of his enemy Philistines. *Can you imagine what he could have done if he had had the whole ass*" (Pino, *Ragionamento*, p. 94); "With a long, strong jaw, Samson could have killed 1,000 Philistines (What do you think, I said, he could have done with a whole, true, and living ass?)" (Bruno, *Opp. Lat.*, II, III, p. 238).

26. Guido d'Agostino, "Il governo spagnolo nell'Italia meridionale (Napoli 1503–80)," in *Storia di Napoli* (Naples: Società editrice storia di Napoli, 1972), vol. V, pt. I, pp. 66–67.

27. Ibid. On Pino's antigovernment attitude, see Romeo De Maio's interesting, recent proposal (*Pittura e Controriforma a Napoli* [Rome and Bari: Laterza, 1983], pp. 239–42). In a manuscript entitled "Historia di Napoli," a number of figures are mentioned that, on the occasion of the Corpus Domini in 1548, Pino painted precisely to ridicule Viceroy Don Pedro of Toledo.

28. The details of the polemic are also illustrated by Spampanato in his essay, "Una pagina dello *Spaccio*," in *Giordano Bruno e la letteratura dell'asino*, pp. 106–11.

29. See the passages drawn from the *Historia della Città e del Regno di Napoli* by Summonte, which Spampanato cites in order to validate his thesis, in "Una pagina dello *Spaccio*," pp. 107–9.

30. Spampanato defends himself against Fiorentino's objections (who asks, why cite an episode from a distance of nearly forty years?) by furnishing other examples in which Bruno remembers facts and circumstances from the distant past. See Spampanato, "Una pagina dello *Spaccio*," pp. 110–11.

31. The hypotheses on the dating of *The Ass* are based on the famous letter to Lodovico Alamanni (December 17, 1517): "I have just been reading *Orlando Furioso* by Ariosto, and truly the poem is fine throughout, and in many places wonderful. If he is there, give him my regards, and tell him I am sorry only that, having spoken of so many poets, he has left me out like a prick, and has done to me in his *Orlando* what I shall not do to him in

my *Ass*" (N. Machiavelli, "Letter to Lodovico Alamanni," in *The Chief Works and Others*, p. 967, translation altered slightly).

32. Giulio Ferroni, "Appunti sull'Asino di Machiavelli," in *Letteratura e critica: Studi in onore di Natalino Sapegno* (Rome: Bulzoni, 1975), vol. II, p. 5. For further references to this particular anthropological perspective in Machiavelli, see Ferroni's essays " 'Mutazione' e 'riscontro' nel teatro di Machiavelli," in *Mutazione e riscontro nel teatro di Machiavelli* (Rome: Bulzoni, 1972), pp. 17–137; and "Le 'cose vane' nelle *Lettere* di Machiavelli," *La Rassegna della letteratura italiana*, 76 (1972), pp. 215–64.

33. Machiavelli, *The Ass*, I.97–114, p. 752. On the literary project of "dir male" (saying negative things), see Paolo Fazion's citations in "L'Asino da leggere," in *Machiavelli, l'Asino e le bestie*, by Giano Mario Anselmi and Paolo Fazion (Bologna: Clueb, 1984), pp. 29–33. This work by Fazion, rich in interesting observations on the sources and rhetorical structure of the short poem, is firmly situated in literary themes and motivations, and somewhat deprecates the "anthropological perspectives" of Machiavelli. Fazion dedicates a little less than a page to the theme of "comparison" and "mutation," coming to pessimistic conclusions on Machiavelli's anthropological interpretation, which, in his opinion, confirms "the impossibility for the individual to be able to mutate his own 'nature' in order to find parallels with the times, in all circumstances" (p. 126). But even if we accept Fazion's hypothesis as true, this does not mean that one cannot note the continual tension between "mutation" and "verification" in the text. The prospects of *The Ass*, therefore, go further than a simple literary "wager" by Machiavelli, as Fazion maintains. And in this sense, Ferroni's analysis, which departs from precise textual observations, seems to offer us starting points for reflection in that "ideologic" direction that Fazion does not share. Fazion mistakenly burdens the analysis with a negative connotation based on the concept of the preconstructed scheme when, instead, it assumes the characteristics of a problematical horizon of research. Giorgio Inglese thinks along the same lines as Fazion; see "Postille machiavelliane," *La cultura*, 23 (1985), pp. 230–37.

34. In the descent toward Hell, Baldus and his companions reach the realm of Gelfora, where Boccalus surprises a few witches while stealing food from the palace kitchen. As a result, the witches beat him and turn him into an ass. "Lastly Boccalus was moistened with some ointment or other. Look, immediately he extends his long ears little by little. He grows a long moustache, as if to touch the sand. His arms become legs, four in number. Finally all his person is covered with shaggy, gray hair, and he has become an ass, he who was Boccalus before. Now he does not cry, 'Alas!' but only sounds

out 'a.a.' He runs here and there, beaten on all sides with batons. He wants
to remove the shoes that he is not used to wearing, in order to defend himself, but he falls and in falling he knocks against the hard ground. He mar-
vels at himself, amazed that he is not Boccalus, but rather the torso of an
ass, and he is hairier than any ass who roams in Arcadia, as he carries grain
for the mill, and as he rolls on his back in the hot dust. Now he is caught
by the tail, now by the ears, and dust is shaken from his pelt with the harsh
blows of a stick" (*Le maccheronee*, XXIII.601–17). Boccalus's metamorphosis into an ass (his other companions were also transformed into
various beasts) is quite significant. There is a close symbolic relationship
between the character and the animal. Boccalus is described as a clown:
"His name was Boccalus; never was there one among the Gonellas more
learned at the art of clowning than he" (XIII.125–26), and he becomes
absolutely carnivalesque in various episodes: he hurls his wife from a ship
into a stormy sea (XII.574–83); he prepares meals (XV.3–5); he organizes
games (XIII.401ff.); and in a group brawl he even succeeds in punching
himself (XXV.50–70). In short, he becomes the "lowest" incarnation of
materiality, expressing himself through laughter and food. He is a key character who, in his total ignorance, assumes the role of protagonist capable
of causing Lucifer along with his whole infernal army to flee. While his
companions run to help Baldus in the bloody battle against the devils, it is
Boccalus, hidden in a hedge and preyed upon by fear, who, once discovered,
brandishes the sole object that happens to be in his hands—a cross—
thereby creating chaos between the forces of evil (XIX.611–33). It is not by
chance that Folengo entrusts the end of the poem to another clown: he will
lead Baldus and his companions to the inside of the great pumpkin, where
the adventures cease and the ambitious plans to conquer Hell disappear
(XXV.580ff.). Boccalus the clown is a perfect incarnation of the symbolic
qualities of the ass. Both Boccalus and the ass are expressions of the "low
material" of the carnivalesque. In addition to the information that Bakhtin
gives on the ass as a symbol of the low (to which I allude in chapter thirteen,
note 42), it is interesting to observe the close relationship that emerged in
the Middle Ages between the festival of the ass and that of madness. See
Jean Bénigne Du Tilliot, *Mémoire pour servir à l'histoire de la fête des foux
qui se fesait autrefois dans plusieurs Eglises* (Lausanne and Geneva, 1741),
pp. 8–14; Charles Du Cange, *Glossarium mediae et infimae latinitatis*
(Paris, 1884), vol. III, pp. 255–56; F. Bourquelot, *L'office de la fête des
foux* (Sens, 1956); Félix Clément, "L'âne au Moyen-age," *Annales Archéo-
logiques*, 16 (1856), pp. 373–85; and regarding the carnivalesque aspects of
Baldus, see Nino Borsellino, "La letteratura anticlassicista," in *La letter-*

atura italiana, ed. Carlo Muscetta (Rome and Bari: Laterza, 1973), vol. IV, pt. I, pp. 597–623; and Giorgio Bárberi Squarotti, "L'inferno del *Baldus*," in *Cultura letteraria e tradizione popolare in Teofilo Folengo,* ed. Ettore Bonora and Mario Chiesa (Milan: Feltrinelli, 1979), pp. 153–85.

The ass returns in another of Folengo's works. In the *Caos del Triperuno,* the third dialogue of the *Selva II* is called *L'asinaria.* Here there are numerous similarities to Bruno's work. *L'asinaria* is about a talking ass who enters into a dialogue with Fùlica and Liberato on "natural philosophy" (Bruno's Silenic ass also discusses philosophy). The ass condemns Aristotle's concept of the eternity of the universe (I will cite from the text edited by Umberto Renda, "Teofilo Folengo," in *Opere italiane* [Bari: Laterza, 1911], vol. I, p. 318), confirms the material similitude between the body of man and that of animals (p. 318), and lists the places in the Bible where he is assigned a fundamental role of importance (p. 319). He claims that Apuleius and Lucian are his illustrious antecedents (pp. 320–21) and draws from Pythagoras to confirm the theory of metempsychosis (p. 319). More important, however, he lashes out against the corruption of the men of the Church: "I do not bite them, touch them, or punch them. I leave them alone, for I revere them and fear true Christians, priests, and kings. I tell the tales of those who hope to be thought good ministers and want to be commended and revered; those who are, in truth, mercenaries and hirelings, who for the aim of gaining political power and for other vile reasons, feed Christ's sheep and are wolves starved for adventure. Since the necessary ceremonial thing to the good and true ministers and holy prelates of the Church is to give them every honor we possibly can, this 'correct' indignation, therefore, stimulates me to blame the filthy and wicked life of the clergymen and rectors of the Church" (p. 324). *L'asinaria,* like the *Cabala,* also breaks off, leaving meaning suspended. A detailed inquiry into the intricate structure of *Caos* perhaps could furnish us with useful elements to orient ourselves more easily in the dense labyrinth of this work by Folengo. On the *Caos,* besides Cesare Federico Goffis's study (*Teofilo Folengo: Studi di storia e di poesia* [Turin: Bona, 1935]), we should return to Gianfranco Folena's valuable essay, "Il linguaggio del *Caos,*" in *Cultura letteraria e tradizione popolare in Teofilo Folengo,* pp. 230–48.

35. Ferroni, "Appunti," p. 19.

36. On the theme of night as a place of deceit in Machiavelli (in the *Mandragola* and in the *Clizia,* darkness is favored for the mechanics of trickery), see Gian Mario Anselmi, "L'altro Machiavelli," in *Machiavelli, l'Asino e le bestie,* pp. 2–12.

37. Machiavelli, *The Ass,* p. 764. See the comparison with a few verses of Bru-

no's sonnet "In lode de l'asino," in chapter seven, note 9. The opposition between idleness and virtue, proposed by Machiavelli, is one of the principal themes Bruno engages in the *Spaccio* (see chapter seven).

38. On this catalog of animals, see Fazion ("L'Asino da leggere," cit., pp. 95–103) and Ferroni ("Appunti," pp. 25–28).

39. In the sixteenth century, Plutarch's dialogue, known by the title *Gryllus*, appeared in Latin and vulgate versions in the *Moralia* (see Ferroni, "Appunti," pp. 29–31).

40. These verses by Machiavelli on the erotic use of the hand seem to allude to the modalities of the amorous relationship between the poet and the woman. Having conquered his initial shyness and his interlocutor's explicit "invitation," the Florentine secretary describes the scene of approach, insisting heavily on the "hand" and on "touch": "And I moved near her, extending my cold hand between the sheets. And when I touched her body, a sweetness came to my heart so pleasing that I do not believe I shall ever taste greater. Not in one place did my hand remain, [and] as it ran all over her body, my lost vigor quickly returned" (IV.122–29, p. 761).

41. On the theme of the hand, see chapter seven.

42. On this aspect, see Anselmi, "L'altro Machiavelli," p. 15.

43. On Pontano's *Asinus*, see the observations of F. Tateo, "L'umorismo di Giovanni Pontano e l'ispirazione etica dell'*Asinus*," in *Tradizione e realtà nell'Umanesimo italiano* (Bari: Dedalo Libri, 1967), pp. 319–54. See also Ferroni, "Appunti," pp. 4–5.

44. G. Pontano, *I dialoghi*, ed. C. Previtera (Florence: Sansoni, 1943), p. 305.

45. *Attabalippa dal Perù: La nobiltà dell'asino* (Venice: Barezzo Barezzi, 1592), p. 67 (copy used: BAV, Capponi V 318 int. 1, 2). To conserve space, I have arbitrarily listed the opposing qualities in paragraph form instead of in columns as in the original text.

46. Giulio Landi, *Orazione della ignoranza*, in *La vita di Cleopatra reina d'Egitto* (Venice, 1551; copy used: BAV, Capponi V 833). Citations are to this copy.

47. Ibid., p. 53.

48. Ibid., p. 54.

49. Ibid., pp. 56–57.

50. Ibid., p. 57v.

51. Ibid., p. 59.

52. Ibid., p. 58.

53. Ortensio Lando, *Paradossi* (Venice, 1545; copy used: BAV, Capponi VI 59). Citations are to this copy.

54. Ibid., p. 12.

55. Ibid., p. 12v.
56. Ibid., pp. 16v–17.
57. Ibid., p. 76v.
58. Ibid., p. 77.
59. Ibid., p. 79v. On this image of Aristotle-cuttlefish, see Charles B. Schmitt, "Aristotle as Cuttlefish," *Studies in the Renaissance*, 12 (1965), pp. 60–72, and Schmitt's *Gianfrancesco Pico della Mirandola (1469–1533) and His Critique of Aristotle* (The Hague: Martinus Nijhoff, 1967), pp. 69–73. The episode of the letter to Alexander and the theme of Aristotle's ignorance recur in Onorio's discourse-confession in *Cabala* (pp. 895–96). See also Bruno's discussion of anti-Aristotelianism, discussed in chapter seven.
60. Cesare Rao, *Orazione in lode dell'ignoranza*, in *Invettive, orazioni, discorsi* (Venice: Damiano Zenaro, 1587; copy used: BAV, R.G. Lett. Ital. IV 166). Citations are from this copy.
61. Ibid., pp. 183–84.
62. Ibid., p. 179v.
63. Ibid., pp. 156–156v.
64. Anton Francesco Doni, "Al Signor Gregorio Rosario di Pordenone," in Giulio Landi, *La vita di Cleopatra reina d'Egitto*, pp. 50–50v.

13   The Entropy of Writing

1. On this subject, see Giovanni Gentile's review of Longworth Chambrun, *Giovanni Florio: Un apôtre de la Renaissance en Angleterre à l'epoque de Shakespeare* (Paris: Payot, 1921), *Critica*, 19 (1921), pp. 366–68. For an analysis of the words recorded by Florio, and thus of the works and their authors, see Vincenzo Spampanato, "Giovanni Florio: Un amico del Bruno in Inghilterra," *Critica* 21 (1923), pp. 56–60, 113–25, 189–92, 313–17; and 22 (1924), pp. 56–61, 116–24, 246–53. See also Giovanni Aquilecchia's introduction to *Cena*, pp. 26–27.
2. See the remarks in chapter twelve.
3. Bruno omits this passage in the final draft of *Cena*, which Giovanni Aquilecchia edited with great competency, reproducing the Roman codex in printed and in manuscript form. Bruno includes a brief dialogue before Teofilo's journey to the dinner (*Cena*, pp. 127–28). See also Aquilecchia's "La lezione definitiva de la *Cena de le Ceneri* di Giordano Bruno," in *Atti dell'Accademia Nazionale dei Lincei*, Memorie, Classe di Scienze morali, storiche e filologiche, 8th ser., 3:4 (1950), pp. 207–43.

On the significance of this passage's omission, see Giorgio Bárberi Squarotti's review of Aquilecchia's edition, *Lettere Italiane*, 8 (1956), pp.

340–41. Besides Tissoni's contributions on the *Cena* ("Bruniana: Note sulla grafia e la punteggiatura bruniana a proposito di recenti edizioni," *Giornale storico della letteratura italiana*, 135 [1958], pp. 156–65; "Lo sconosciuto fondo bruniano della Trivulziana," *Atti dell'Accademia delle Scienze di Torino*, 93 [1958–59], pp. 431–72; and "Sulla redazione definitiva della *Cena de le Ceneri*," *Giornale storico della letteratura italiana*, 136 [1959], pp. 558–63), see also Luigi Firpo, "Per l'edizione critica dei dialoghi italiani di Giordano Bruno," *Giornale storico della letteratura italiana*, 135 (1958), pp. 587–606; and "Correzioni d'autore coatte," in *Studi e problemi di critica testuale*, Convegno di studi di Filologia italiana nel Centenario della Commissione per i testi di lingua, April 7–9, 1960 (Bologna: Commissione per i testi di lingua, 1961), pp. 143–57; and Aquilecchia's thoughts ("Redazioni a stampa originarie e seriori," in *La critica del testo: Problemi di metodo ed esperienze di lavoro*, Atti del Convegno di Lecce, October 22–26, 1984 [Rome: Salerno Editrice, 1985], pp. 67–80.

4. "To come then to my further comments—leaving on one side the remarks and opinions on the theme of light and the clarifications your philosophy may bring us—I'd like you to state the sort of voices with which you'd wish us to greet in particular that brilliance of doctrine emanating from the book *Ash Wednesday Supper*. What animals are those that perform in the Supper? I ask you: are they aquatic, aerial, earthly, or lunatic? And putting aside the observations of Smith, Prudenzio, and Frulla, I'd like to know if those critics are incorrect who assert that you bark like a rabid and demented dog in addition to sometimes playing the role of monkey, sometimes of wolf, sometimes of magpie, sometimes of parrot, now this creature and now that, mixing up all kinds of discourses, grave and serious, moral and natural, ignoble and noble, philosophic and comic?" (*Cause*, p. 60; *Causa*, pp. 196–97). On the relationship between the serious and the comic, see chapter eleven.

5. On the various denominations ("disorderly," "irregular," "restless," "polygraphs," "journalists," etc.) used by literary criticism to indicate this group of anti-classical writers, see Nino Borsellino, "La letteratura anti-classicista," pp. 541–42.

6. Ibid., p. 542. On the concept of "nature" in Aretino, see Giulio Ferroni, *Le voci dell'istrione: Pietro Aretino e la dissoluzione del teatro* (Naples: Liguori, 1977), pp. 153–56.

7. I will follow Squarotti's line of thought in "L'esperienza stilistica di Bruno," pp. 154–69.

8. On Berni, see Giorgio Bárberi Squarotti's introduction to the *Rime di Francesco Berni* (Turin: Einaudi, 1969), pp. viii–xxvii; and Nino Borsellino,

"La letteratura anticlassicista," pp. 573–89, esp. the bibliography on pp. 669–70.

For a broad thematic and stylistic assessment of erotic poetry from Burchiello to Marino, see Jean Toscan's voluminous work, *Le carnaval du langage: Le lexique erotique des poètes de l'équivoque de Burchiello à Marino (XV–XVIIe siècles)* (Lille: Atelier Reproduction des Thèses Université de Lille III, 1981), vols. I–IV.

In his dialogues Bruno frequently alludes to a number of Berni's works: for instance, *Il capitolo del prete di Povigliano (Cena*, p. 8); *Vaghezze di maestro Guazzaletto medico (Cena*, p. 55; *Spaccio*, p. 736); *Sonetto della mula (Cena*, p. 58); *Capitolo secondo della peste (Cena*, p. 170); *Capitolo primo alla sua innammorata (Causa*, p. 196); *Sonetto delle puttane (Eroici*, p. 929).

9. On Aretino's production in general, see Giorgio Petrocchi's study, *Pietro Aretino tra Rinascimento e Controriforma* (Milan: Vita e Pensiero, 1948); Paul Larivaille's monograph, *L'Arétin entre Renaissance et Maniérisme (1492–1537)* (Lille: Service de reproduction des Thèses, 1972), vols. I-IV; and the bibliography in the *Nota bio-bibliografica*, in *Folengo, Aretino, Doni*, in *Opere*, ed. Carlo Cordiè (Milan and Naples: Ricciardi, 1976), vol. II, pp. 16–46. Nino Borsellino's recent introduction to *P. Aretino, Ragionamento e Dialogo*, ed. Paolo Procaccioli (Milan: Garzanti, 1984), pp. vii–xxx, offers interesting perspectives. For a specific analysis of theatrical production, see Ferroni, *Le voci dell'istrione*.

Aretino also appears often in Bruno's Italian dialogues. In addition to the passages already pointed out in my study, and the references to the *Ficheide* and the *Filosofo (Spaccio*, p. 820), Bruno explicitly cites three verses from the *Capitolo all'Albicante* in the *Eroici*: "crowns for poets are made not only of myrtle and laurel, but also of the vine branch for scurrilous verses, of ivy for Bacchic verses, of olive for sacrifices and laws, of the poplar, elm, and corn for agriculture, of cypress for funerals, and other garlands without number for as many other occasions; and, if you will permit, even of that material which a gallant gentleman designated, when he said: O brother Porro, poet of flukes, / in Milan you girdle yourself with a garland / of pudding, tripe, and sausage" (*Heroic Frenzies*, p. 84; *Eroici*, p. 960). On the debate concerning the significance of this citation, see G. Bárberi Squarotti, "Per una descrizione e interpretazione della poetica di Giordano Bruno," *Studi Seicenteschi*, 1 (1960), p. 41.

Returning to the specific theme of asininity, note that Aretino places the ass in a fundamental role in one of the two stories that weave through the *Filosofo* (quotations are from Aretino, *Teatro*, ed. Petrocchi). The conflict between Plataristotele (who loses all touch with reality because he encloses himself in speculative abstraction) and his wife Tessa (who scolds her husband for not fulfilling his conjugal duties because he is chasing after pedantries: "Look at him, by calling himself a philosopher he excuses himself for not having deflowered his wife," p. 540; "The nature between the thighs, and not that which you see in things, should content you," p. 541; "Caress me; you should flirt with me and not with your pompous books and papers," p. 553) is resolved through a joke that the wife will orchestrate to cause harm to her husband. In place of the lover that Plataristotele believed was imprisoned in his study, Tessa puts an ass. When the tricked philosopher discovers that an ass has soiled his books and is now standing in the midst of them, he realizes his stupidity: "I am beginning to believe that astrologers are actually asses. Besides rubbing their snout on the wall as they leave the stall in order to make their peasant-owner understand that rains are coming the following day, the ass, having defecated in my 'thinking place,' predicts my desire to be stupid no longer. Consequently, I draw considerable utility from what I have just experienced" (p. 552). Here, too, the figure of the ass reveals its double connotation. On the one hand, it presents itself as a mirror through which Plataristotele sees his own stupidity, and on the other, it serves as a legitimate symbol of "nature," as a guarantor of a material relationship with reality (and here the allusion to the ass's sexual potency is in perfect harmony with the reasons that agitated the conflict between Tessa and her husband), and as opposite to the philosophers' pedantry. Plataristotele's self-reflection ("I reproach, or better yet, accuse the knowledge derived from study to be ignorance; due to them I have fallen into an error that requires emending," p. 555) is transformed into a new relationship with reality, precisely in the direction indicated by the ass: "I think about enjoying the woman who has been enjoyed by others, while I was raving about the intelligibility of beauty, and not of the palpable good" (p. 549). The abandonment of pedantry thus reestablishes a priority of "natural things" over "supernatural things": "I free myself from the presumption that since philosophic study and its audacious penetrations into the intelligence of natural cause is not satisfactory, it cannot rise into supernatural understandings either" (p. 556). On these themes, see Ferroni, *Le voci dell'istrione*, pp. 323–25.

In addition to these brief considerations (the comedy certainly merits a more profound analysis), I would like to digress further. It is not by chance that three centuries later, in Dostoevski's *Idiot* (1868), the bray of an ass is precisely what illuminates Prince Myshkin's mind: "the thing that roused me was the braying of a donkey in the market-place. I was struck with the donkey, and for some reason very pleased with it, and at once everything in my head seemed to clear up" (*The Idiot*, tr. David Magarshack [New York: Penguin Books, 1955]. p. I, chap. V, p. 83).

10. For a bibliography of relevant works and criticism, see Cecilia Ricottini Marsili-Libelli, *Anton Francesco Doni scrittore e stampante* (Florence: Sansoni, 1960). For an up-to-date list of critical contributions, see, however, the *Nota introduttiva* and the *Nota bio-bibliografica* in *Folengo, Aretino, Doni*, in *Opere*, vol. II, pp. 571–96. For the presence of the ass in the works of Doni, see the remarks in chapter twelve.

11. For a philosophical analysis of Franco's works, see Paul Grendler, *Critics of the Italian Worlds, 1530–1560: Anton Francesco Doni, Nicolò Franco, and Ortensio Lando* (Madison: University of Wisconsin Press, 1969).

    Nor does Nicolò Franco disdain asses. One of his sonnets appears in Giovan Battista Pino's *Ragionamento sovra del asino:* "PINO, in the immortal shadow of your genius, / In which the three Graces have seat and love, / Where the Hours reign in Hippocrene, / And pass their time in sweet dance, // Silenus is now permitted to come and rest, / And at such a sight valor cannot diminish, / To be seen with him, raised to a new place of honor, / The ASS-FOUL supports the old way; // So that while it is praised by you, / It grows and changes its vile appearance / Leaving behind its usual unworthiness, // It is pitiful to see him stripped of his honors / As if he came to be translated to heaven / Ornea's idol to whom I write a thousand letters" (Pino, *Ragionamento*, p. 28).

12. On the relationship between Bruno and Folengo, see G. Bárberi Squarotti, "Bruno e Folengo," *Giornale storico della letteratura italiana*, 135 (1958), pp. 51–60. Among the general studies of Folengo's production, see *Cultura letteraria e tradizione popolare in Teofilo Folengo*. For the presence of the ass in Folengo's work, see chapter twelve, note 34.

13. Bruno omits this passage in the final draft of *Cena*.

14. "It is not right that we deprive the asses of their lettuce, nor that we wish their taste be similar to ours. The diversity of genius and intellect is no less great than that of spirits and stomachs" (*De l'infinito*, p. 466).

15. These general hypotheses, extremely synthetic, are at the base of my research for "Teoria e situazione del dialogo nel' '500' " (Doctoral thesis, Cosenza, 1987). See "Il dialogo cinquecentesco tra diegesi e mimesi," *Studi e problemi di critica testuale*, 37 (1988) pp. 155–79, as well as the introduction to Tasso's *Discours sur le dialogue* (Paris: Belles Lettres, 1991), pp. 9–61. On the close relationship between epideictic genre and *elocutio*, see *Dialogo della retorica*, by Sperone Speroni and Heinrich Lausberg, *Elementi di retorica* (Bologna: Il Mulino, 1969), p. 20; see also Mario Pozzi's

introductory note to the *Trattatisti del Cinquecento* (Milan and Naples: Ricciardi, 1978), pp. 498–500. For an analysis of the position of the listener in the epideictic genre, see Chaïm Perelman and Lucie Olbrechts-Tyteca, *The New Rhetoric: A Treatise on Argumentation*, tr. John Wilkinson and Purcell Weaver (Notre Dame: University of Notre Dame Press, 1982), pp. 47–51. On Bruno's dialogic technique, see Giorgio Bárberi Squarotti, "Alcuni temi di un saggio su Giordano Bruno," *Il Verri*, 2 (1958), pp. 92–98.

16. The difference between the "diagetic" dialogue and the "mimetic" dialogue is discussed in Sperone Speroni's *Apologia dei dialogi* (which distinguishes the "referred" dialogue from the "represented" dialogue) and in Torquato Tasso's *Discorso dell'arte del dialogo*. On the relationship between the court environment and diagetic dialogue in the early sixteenth century, see Piero Floriani, "Il dialogo e la corte," in *I gentiluomini letterati: Studi sul dibattito culturale nel primo Cinquecento* (Naples: Liguori, 1981), pp. 33–49.

17. On this subject, see Riccardo Scrivano, "Nelle pieghe del dialogare bembesco," in *Il dialogo: Scambi e passaggi della parola*, ed. Giulio Ferroni (Palermo: Sellerio, 1985), pp. 101–9.

18. See chapter seven.

19. "*Gio. Bernardo.* You have understood well. All the mistakes that happen are because of this traitor, Fortune: those good things that she gave to your father, Malefacio, she has taken away from me. She honors those who do not deserve it, she gives good fields to him who does not sow them, good gardens to him who does not plant them, money to him who knows not how to spend it, many children to him who cannot raise them, a healthy appetite to him who has nothing to eat, biscuits to him who has no teeth. What can I say? Fortune, the poor dear, should be pardoned, for she is blind and she gropes as she goes looking to give out the goods she carries in her hands. What's more, she runs into the imbeciles, fools, and scoundrels, of which the world is full. It is a great twist of fate when she touches worthy people, of whom there are so few, even greater when she touches one of the most worthy, who are even fewer. It is greatest and most extraordinary if she touches, or prepares herself to touch, one of the most truly worthy, of whom there are the fewest. Thus it is not her fault, but the fault of him who has created her. Jove denies having done it; and yet whether she was created, or not, either she was guilty, or we cannot find who is guilty for her creation" (*Candelaio*, p. 150). Further on: "*Gio. Bernardo.* . . . What you say is true, and I have presently experienced it. Whatever kind of good it was that I possessed this evening, it was not given to me by God and nature. Although Fortune denied me, justice showed me the opportunity, diligence

made me take her by the hair, and perseverance had me keep her" (*Candelaio*, p. 151). On the role of Fortune, see chapter eight.

20. See chapter ten.

21. For an analysis of the concept of language in Bruno, see Michele Ciliberto's introduction to the *Lessico di Giordano Bruno* (Rome: Edizioni dell'Ateneo & Bizzarri, 1979), pp. ix–xlv; Giorgio Bárberi Squarotti, "Alcuni temi di un saggio su Giordano Bruno," pp. 89–92; Patrizia Bertini Malgarini, "Giordano Bruno linguista," *Critica letteraria*, 8 (1980), pp. 681–716 (the appendix contains numerous passages from Bruno of linguistic and rhetorical interest); and Giovanni Aquilecchia, "L'adorazione del volgare nei dialoghi londinesi di Giordano Bruno," *Cultura Neolatina*, 13 (1953), pp. 165–89.

Cesare Segre offers a useful survey of language in the sixteenth century: "Edonismo linguistico nel Cinquecento," *Giornale storico della letteratura italiana*, 130 (1953), pp. 145–77 (now available in *Lingua, stile e società* [Milan: Feltrinelli, 1963], pp. 355–82). On the concept of literary pluralism, see the superb work by Ivano Paccagnella, *Il fasto delle lingue: Plurilinguismo letterario nel Cinquecento* (Rome: Bulzoni, 1984).

Useful insights into Bruno's language are developed in a few essays on the stylistics and rhetoric of *Candelaio*. See Roberto Tissoni, "Saggio di commento stilistico al *Candelaio*," *Giornale storico della letteratura italiana*, 137 (1960), pp. 41–60; and also by Tissoni, "Appunto per uno studio sulla prosa della dimostrazione scientifica nella *Cena de le ceneri* di Giordano Bruno," *Romanische Forschungen*, 78 (1961), pp. 346–88; Carla De Bellis, "Giordano Bruno: La parola e il vedere nei prologhi del *Candelaio*," *Filologia Moderna*, 1:2 (1980), pp. 43–109; Clara Borelli, "Spoglio linguistico del *Candelaio* di Giordano Bruno," *Misure Critiche*, 10 (1980), pp. 25–67 (on this last essay, see Luca Serianni's critique in *Studi di linguistica italiana*, 8 [1982]).

22. Fiorentino writes about the originalities of Bruno's use of Latin in his poems: "Lucretius, from whom he borrows most of the language he uses, cannot completely suffice: new ideas require new words, and the Nolan does not hesitate to coin them; and not only nouns, but epithets, verbs, and constructions, with a liberty that at times gives the impression he is taking poetic license. He is well aware of this, and if he had ignored it, there would have been no lack of grammarians to point it out to him; but instead of hiding the license he takes, he justifies it and arrogates the right to himself. . . . I do not know how far this Brunian theoretic can go, nor if the right measure dictated by urgent need was surpassed by chance. It is certain, however, that there is a specific arrangement to his verses, a style that cannot be

confused with anyone else's, because it is not an outline or collection of other people's phrases. This originality, this freedom of movement, makes you rise above the violated purity" (Francesco Fiorentino, *Al chiarissimo comm. Francesco De Sanctis, deputato al Parlamento*, in *Opp. lat.*, I, I, p. xl).

23. Ciliberto's introduction to *Lessico*, p. xxvii.

24. For an analysis of the Aristotelian concept of language, see Tullio De Mauro, "L'aristotelismo linguistico nella storia e nel *Tractatus* di Wittgenstein," in *Introduzione alla semantica* (Bari: Laterza, 1975), pp. 42–72.

25. See chapter seven.

26. "You will again see the pomp and circumstance of a man, *masculini generis*. Someone who gives you two kisses that would turn the stomach of a pig or a chicken; an establisher of the ancient Latium, an emulator of Demosthenes, a type that stirs Tullius from the deepest and darkest center, a bard of the hero's gestures. Here is an acuteness that brings tears to your eyes, makes your hair curl, makes your teeth gnash and bang, gives you an erection, and makes you cough and sneeze. Here is a composer of books well deserving the attention of the republic, of annotators, glossers, constructors, methodical people, adders, translators, interpreters, compendium makers, new dialecticians, those armed with a new grammar, a new dictionary, a *lexicon*, a *varia lectio*, an approver of authors, an authentic authority; with epigrams in Greek, Hebrew, Latin, Italian, Spanish, and French placed *in fronte libri*. . . . Oh how these people warm my heart when either by force or by good will, speaking or writing, they inspire a verse of Homer, of Hesiod, or a scrap of *Plato* or the Greek *Demosthenes*. How clearly they prove that they are the only ones upon whose heads Saturn has pissed judgment, and the only ones on whom the nine damsels of Pallas have heaped a cornucopia of words between their pia and dura maters. And yet it is quite suitable that they walk with that mien, with a slow and measured gait, with chest up, head and neck straight, and eyes inspecting with a modest arrogance" (*Candelaio*, pp. 34–35).

On the various meanings of the pedant in Bruno's works, see Michele Ciliberto, "Asini e pedanti: Ricerche su Giordano Bruno," pp. 83–88.

27. Bruno attacks the humanistic concept that relates knowledge to eloquence. The humanists believe that knowledge of a language is not enough to understand the philosophical content of a text. In *De la causa*, Bruno objects to this notion: "For some time I have thought this dexterity the main thing; for even if one does not know Greek, one can still understand all the meaning of Aristotle and recognize many errors in him. One sees clearly that the idolatry surrounding the authority of that philosopher, especially in natural

science, has been abolished among those who grasp the ideas of this other school. Also, a man who knows no Greek, no Arabic, and perhaps no Latin, like Paracelsus, can yet have a better knowledge of medicaments and medicine than Galen, Avicenna, and all the others who were acquainted with the Roman tongue. Philosophers and laws fall into perdition, not through the lack of interpreters of words, but through the lack of men who are profound thinkers" (*Cause*, p. 97; *Causa*, pp. 257–58). The same concept returns with regard to Averroes, "Averroes partly meant this. An Arab and ignorant of the Greek tongue, he yet understood the Peripatetic doctrine better than any Greek we have read and he'd have understood it still better if he had not been so dedicated to his deity Aristotle" (*Cause*, p. 128; *Causa*, p. 306). See Bertini Malgarini, "Giordano Bruno linguista," pp. 697–700; and Ciliberto's introduction to *Lessico*, pp. xv–xvi.

Bruno's position authoritatively enters the Renaissance debate on the necessity of translation. From Speroni: "God wants, for the good of those who come after me, that some educated and pious person dedicate himself to the task of translating all the books of every science into the vulgate, as many as there are in Greek, Latin, and Hebrew. Perhaps, then, the number of good philosophers would be greater than it is in our day, and their excellence would become even more rare" (S. Speroni, *Dialogo delle lingue*, in *Trattatisti del Cinquecento*, p. 621); to Gelli: "Grammar, or rather for me, Latin, is a language, and languages are not what makes men wise, but rather concepts and sciences do, because otherwise it would follow that today's Jew, who is a goldsmith next to de' Pecori, and who knows eight or ten languages, would be the wisest man of Florence" (G. B. Gelli, *I capricci del Bottaio*, in *Opere*, p. 178); not forgetting the fifteenth-century disputes between the Ciceronians (see the letter, *Ioannes Picus Mirandulanus Hermolao Barbaro suo*, in *Prosatori latini del Quattrocento*, pp. 804–23), where the necessity of abandoning the old conceptions of language, based on the sacred nature of Greek and Latin, is confirmed. On these themes, see Ettore Bonora, "Dallo Speroni al Gelli," in *Retorica e invenzione* (Milan: Rizzoli, 1970), pp. 37–43; E. Bonora, "I grandi traduttori," *Storia della letteratura italiana* (Milan: Garzanti, 1966), vol. IV, pp. 531–61. See also my essay, "Théorie de l'imitation, rapport *res/verba*, traduction autour de quelques aspects du débat sur la langue en Italie au XVIe siècle," in *Langues et Nations au temps de la Renaissance*, ed. M. T. Jones-Davies (Paris, 1991).

28. On the relationship between Poliinnio in *Causa* and the *Cena*, see Papi, *Antropologia e civiltà*, pp. 45–47.

29. See Ciliberto's introduction to *Lessico*, pp. xxiv–xxv. On Bruno's judgment,

see G. Aquilecchia, "Ramo, Patrizi e Telesio nella prospettiva di Giordano Bruno," in *Atti del Convegno internazionale di Studi su Bernardino Telesio*, Cosenza, May 12–13, 1989 (1990), pp. 181–91; and by the same author, "Ancora su Bruno e Telesio," in *Bernardino Telesio e la cultura napoletana*, ed. R. Sirri and M. Torrini (Naples, 1992), pp. 191–202.

30. This "high rock and lofty tower of contemplation" (*Eroici*, p. 1116) recalls Lucretius's *templa serena* (see chapter nine).

31. *Spaccio*, pp. 739–44 (see chapter seven).

32. Giulio Ferroni situates the repetitive nature of Petrarchism with respect to the anthropological conception of a society that "inhales" the immobility of time, the negation of the future: "The tautological nature of Petrarchism is clearly demonstrated through the schema of human behavior, through central and totalizing linguistic norms, and through proceedings of multiplication and repetition. This is affirmed, nonetheless, by Bembo himself in his aspiration toward a literature that is rescued from the devastation of time and inclines toward becoming classical and eternal. That which must be eternal must *per force* be defined once and for all. This repeating necessarily equates to saying always the same thing, folding thought and discourse into an apparently plural movement, but in reality, continually spinning upon itself" (G. Ferroni, *Introduzione* to *Poesia italiana del Cinquecento* [Milan: Garzanti, 1978], pp. x–xi). See also Bárberi Squarotti, "Per una descrizione," pp. 52–57.

33. For an analysis of late Petrarchism, see Ettore Bonora, "La dissoluzione del petrarchismo," in *Storia della letteratura italiana*, vol. IV, pp. 545–50. See also the chapter on Tansillo, pp. 538–44.

    Bruno's use of Tansillo's and Epicurus's compositional schemes as reference points for his verses in the *Eroici* to support the structure of the dialogues does not contradict his anti-Petrarchism, since the Petrarchist language is broken and bent "into a metaphysical ideal, distant from organically serving the social forces in power and their anthropology, aiming toward revolutionary hypotheses that the society of the time could not recognize nor accept; hypotheses with respect to which poetry could be but a mere, accidental instrument" (G. Ferroni, *Introduzione* to *Poesia italiana del Cinquecento*, p. xxvi). On the instrumental use of literature in Bruno, see Bárberi Squarotti, "Alcuni temi," pp. 98–100.

34. "You will see how in a lover there are sighs, tears, clashing, trembling, dreams, excitement, and a heart that burns in the fire of love; there are thoughts, abstractions, fits of anger, melancholies, envies, quarrels, and the least hope for what he desires the most. In this part of the heart you will find his soul in shackles, chains, captivity, prisons, eternal pain—suffering

martyrdom and death; in the narrow part of the heart there are arrows, darts, bolts, fires, flames, ardors, jealousies, suspicions, spites, reluctances, angers and oblivions, wounds, injuries, sighs, madness, tongs, anvils, and hammers: 'the blind and naked archer with quiver. And then, the object of his love: 'my heart, my treasure, my life, my sweet wound and death, my divinity, my celestial deity, my leaning post, my rest, my hope, my fountain, my spirit, my north star, and my beautiful sun that never sets in my heart.' And on the flip side, 'raw heart, unshakable column, hard stone, diamond breast,' and of course, 'cruel hand that has the keys to my heart, my enemy, my sweet warrioress, target of all my thoughts,' and 'beautiful are my loves, not those of others.' You will see burning sighs in one of these celestial female glances, as well as watery thinking, terrestrial desires, and airy fornication: with reverence to chaste ears, this is one whose sheets remain white and unpenetrated. You will see her assailed by a lover armed with burning desire, a desire that cooks him, a charity that ignites him, love that inflames him, lust that flares up in him, and greed that flashes and shines up into the sky'' (*Candelaio*, pp. 32–33). For an analysis of the difference between this passage of *Candelaio* and that of the *Eroici*, see Bárberi Squarotti, ''Alcuni temi,'' pp. 81–85.

35. Bárberi Squarotti, ''Per una descrizione,'' p. 42.
36. Against Gentile's thesis of a pre-romantic Bruno, see Valerio Zanone, ''L'estetica di Giordano Bruno,'' *Rivista di estetica*, 12 (1967), pp. 388–89.
37. Bruno also distinguished between poets and versifiers, in *De umbris idearum:* ''I have spoken about creators of verse, not of poets'' (*Opp. lat.*, II, I, p. 16). In the *De monade* he again gives a negative connotation to versifiers: ''A vigorous sensation does not goad me, / nor reasoning, nor the honorable disposition of a cultivated mind; / what goads me is the eyebrow of a dishonest sycophant, / who is without the aid of a scale, a balance, or an eye, / but who is provided with the harvest of his miracles: / the encomium of a verse-fabricating grammarian, the glosses and the volumes of Hellenists, / who salute the reader of the book from the beginning, / as they bark in protest against the Zoïluses, the Momuses, and the Mastixes. / May such testimonials be absent from here!'' (*Opp. lat.*, I, II, p. 322). On the relationship between verse and mnemonics in Bruno's works, see Adriano Mariani, ''La negazione bruniana dell'estetica,'' *Rinascimento*, 23 (1983), pp. 314–16.
38. Numerous studies have analyzed Bruno's concept of images from a variety of perspectives. Without lingering on the various positions, I shall note a few of the more significant essays: Yates, *The Art of Memory*; Robert Klein, ''L'imagination comme vêtement de l'âme chez Marsile Ficin et Giordano

Bruno," in *La Forme et l'intelligible* (Paris: Gallimard, 1970), pp. 341–411; Mariani, "La negazione," pp. 303–27; Zanone, "L'estetica," pp. 397–98; Andrzej Nowicki, "Il pluralismo metodologico e i modelli lulliani di Giordano Bruno," in *Accademia Polacca di Scienze—Biblioteca di Roma*, fasc. 27 (1965), pp. 19–22. For a general survey of the relationship between painting and literature in the sixteenth century, see Klein, *La Forme et l'intelligible*; Mario Pozzi, "Note sulla cultura artistica e sulla poetica di Pietro Aretino," in *Lingua e cultura del Cinquecento* (Padova: Liviana, 1975), pp. 23–47 (also in the same volume, see "L' 'ut pictura poesis' in un dialogo di L. Dolce," pp. 1–22); Carlo Ossola, "Ut pictura poesis," in *Autunno del Rinascimento* (Florence: Olschki, 1971), pp. 33–119; and R. W. Lee, *Ut pictura poesis* (New York: W. W. Norton, 1967).

39. "And in this, you do exactly like a painter does, for whom making a simple drawing of history is not satisfactory; rather, he must fill the canvas and conform to nature with his art, he depicts stones, mountains, trees, springs, rivers, and hills in this painting, and he makes you see a royal palace here and a forest there, a strip of sky here, a part of a rising sun in that corner, and now and again a bird, a pig, a deer, an ass, a horse; while it is enough to show only a head of this, the horn of that, a piece of the rear of another, the ears of this, the entirety of that, this one with a gesture and a mien, that those others do not have. In this way, with great satisfaction, one would wonder, judge, and spin, as they say, a story about the picture. Thus, you should read these pages and understand what I mean" (*Cena*, p. 11). It is not by chance that the main protagonist in *Candelaio*, Gioan Bernardo, is a painter. On Bruno's insistent use of the term "seeing" in the comedy, see De Bellis, "Giordano Bruno: La parola e il vedere nei prologhi del *Candelaio*."

40. In *De vinculis*, Bruno tackles the central questions of aesthetic communication. See Zanone, "L'estetica," pp. 391–94; and Mariani, "La negazione," pp. 312–14.

41. In *De magia*, Bruno also confirms the relativity of aesthetic values through the proverb, *Asinus ad lyram*: "Just as in the proverb about the ass and the lyre, not all songs are suited to everyone, and just as different harmonists fetter different souls with their harmonies, so also different magicians fetter different spirits" (*Opp. lat.*, III, p. 444). See Mariani, "La negazione," p. 313.

42. On Mercury, see Rafael Lopez Pedraza, *Ermes e i suoi figli*, p. 21. On the ass, to the testimonies already given in chapter two should be added Mikhail Bakhtin's remarks. He considers the ass to be one of the oldest and most

enduring symbols of low, corporeal material (see Mikhail Bakhtin, *Rabelais and His World*, tr. Helene Iswolsky [Cambridge: MIT Press, 1968], p. 78). On the medieval *festum asinorum*, to which Bakhtin refers, and on the relationship between the ass and Mercury integral to the category of the "rascal," see Carl Gustav Jung, *The Trickster*, pp. 195–211; see also chapter three, note 6.

43. On the relationship between Mercury/Thoth and writing, see Jacques Derrida, "Plato's Pharmacy," in *Dissemination*, tr. Barbara Johnson (Chicago: University of Chicago Press, 1981), pp. 84–94. See also Paolo Rossi, "Thot inventore delle lettere e delle leggi," *Rinascimento*, 3 (1963), pp. 213–17.

44. Walter Otto maintains that it is Mercury's nature not to belong to any group in particular, to have no fixed domain, and instead to be constantly in motion (see Walter Otto, *The Homeric Gods*, tr. Moses Hadas [New York: Pantheon, 1954], p. 117).

14 Natural Science and Human Science: A "Nouvelle Alliance"

1. Ciliberto, introduction to *Lessico*, pp. xviii–xxi.

2. "Know that such a statement comes from Doctor Torquato, who I would like to believe has read all of Copernicus, yet has retained only the name of the author, of the book, of the printer, of the place where it was printed, the year, the number of signatures and pages; and since he was not unfamiliar with the grammar, he understood a certain epistle attached to it by God knows what kind of ignorant and presumptuous ass. This ass, who (as if trying to support the author by excusing him, or perhaps to enable other asses to find their herbs and fruits in this book, and not part with it starving) in this way, warned the readers before they started the book and mulled over its phrases. . . . Now, look, what a fine doorman! See how well he opens the door for you to that most excellent knowledge, without which the art of computations, measurements, geometry and perspective is nothing other than the pastime of ingenious fools! See how faithfully he serves the owner of the house!" (*Cena*, pp. 87–89). Osiander's epistle also elicited the anger of Copernicus's friends, one of whom, Tiedemann Giese, asked the magistrate of Nuremberg to order its abolition (see Alexandre Koyré's introduction to *Des revolutions* [Paris, 1934], pp. 12–13).

3. On translation, see chapter thirteen, note 27.

4. For an analysis of the motivations for antimathematical concept of nature in Bruno, see Biagio De Giovanni's astute observations, "Lo spazio della

vita fra G. Bruno e T. Campanella," *Il Centauro*, 11–12 (1984), pp. 5–19. See also Dino Fraccari's "L'impostazione antimatematica del problema della natura nella *Cena delle ceneri* di Giordano Bruno," *Rivista critica di storia della filosofia*, 5 (1950), pp. 179–93, though his findings are questionable.

5. Koyré's notion that Copernicus was not a Copernican because his universe was not one of infinite space is significant and is supported by Dreyer's studies. See A. Koyré's, introduction to *Des revolutions*, p. xxvii.

6. "Thus the first sky of the Peripatetic perishes, the beginning and the end of all things that exist in nature. That fifth substance perishes, too, able, by its nature, to move in a circle, which was the source and origin of all other movement, and that body perishes which was supremely perfect, embracing all other things through its virtue. That space and receptacle, now empty, shatter the imaginary enclosures of that body; and it expands on all sides in a great field in order to receive innumerable worlds: those heavenly motors, just as they are born from nothing, from the womb of a disturbed imagination, of a deprived disposition, with ignorance as their midwife, and are educated during the storm of a dark night, and become adults, so they vanish into nothing, as soon as the sun of intelligence rises. That infinite, insensible light is no more—that light which is intelligible, immaterial, infinite, superethereal, which fuels stars, the spark from which it makes the sun—as if whatever is said could be believed, and as if whatever drunken poets pour out originated from the decree of a superior intelligence. But it is necessary to recognize the same light, virtue, nature, dominion, power, and strength, thanks to which this space is not without form, but is, rather, adorned with such great variety, and then to recognize the infinite, which is beyond" (*Opp. lat.*, I, II, pp. 314–15).

7. De Giovanni, "Lo spazio della vita," p. 14.

8. De Giovanni rightly contests Yates's thesis (*Giordano Bruno and the Hermetic Tradition*, p. 155), in "Lo spazio della vita," p. 15. Yates's work, though extremely important to Bruno studies, errs at times toward a panhermeticism, ignoring themes and problems that could open up new directions in research. On the limitations of this English historian, see Ciliberto, "Giordano Bruno 1582–1583: Da Parigi a Oxford," p. 159.

9. Ernst Bloch, *Vorlesungen zur Philosophie der Renaissance* (Frankfurt: Suhrkamp, 1972), pp. 24–43.

10. Remo Bodei's synthesis of Bloch's categories is extremely useful. See his introduction to Bloch, *La filosofia del Rinascimento* (Bologna: Il Mulino, 1981). See also Bodei's *Multiversum: Tempo e storia in Ernst Bloch* (Naples: Bibliopolis, 1979).

11. A number of Renaissance authors have attributed various meanings to the theme *veritas filia temporis*. Even Bruno scholars diverge in their interpretations (ranging from the spiritualistic stance of Gentile to the cautious position of Garin). See Giovanni Aquilecchia's introduction to the *Cena*, pp. 56–59. For the history of *veritas filia temporis* in medieval and humanistic culture, see Franco Simone, "Veritas filia temporis: A proposito di un testo di Giordano Bruno," *Revue de littérature comparée*, 22 (1948), pp. 508–21.

12. See chapter nine.

13. This thesis seems to emerge, though the points of view are distinctly different, from the works of both De Giovanni ("Lo spazio della vita") and Ferrone (Siro Ferrone, "Il *Candelaio:* Scienza e letteratura," *Italianistica*, 2 [1973], pp. 518–43). On the close relationship between physics and morality in Bruno, see Ingegno, *Cosmologia e filosofia nel pensiero di Giordano Bruno*, p. 39.

14. I am referring to Ilya Prigogine and Isabelle Stengers, *Order Out of Chaos: Man's New Dialogue with Nature* (New York: Bantam Books, 1984). See also Ilya Prigogine, *La nuova alleanza: Uomo e natura in una scienza unificata* (Milan: Longanesi, 1979); on this last work, see Antonio Casella's review, "L'ordine e le fluttuazioni: *La nuova alleanza* di Ilya Prigogine," *aut aut*, 179–80 (1980), pp. 85–103. Though the complex scientific position held by Prigogine, who was awarded the Nobel Prize in chemistry in 1977, cannot be addressed here, it is worth pointing out that his theories are founded on an epistemology wherein the "science of things" and the "science of man" speak the same language inside a universe that is far from balanced (Prigogine is known for his studies of irreversible thermodynamics). He attentively observes the phenomena of intersections among different forms of knowledge: his "history of science" demonstrates how fecund the relations between philosophic interrogation and scientific research have been. In this light, Lucretius's position is reevaluated, held precisely as supporting this "alliance." With regard to Bruno, Paul-Henri Michel stresses that we should not underestimate the influence that the poetic descriptions of the universe given by a number of philosophers could have had on the progress of science (Paul-Henri Michel, *The Cosmology of Giordano Bruno*, tr. R. E. W. Maddison [Ithaca: Cornell University Press, 1973], pp. 296–97, 51–52).

15. Serres, *La Naissance de la physique*. For a detailed exposition of Serres's thesis on the *De rerum natura*, see my review of the volume in *Belfagor*, 37 (1982), pp. 238–42. For a comprehensive analysis of Serres's philosophical production, see two important monographs: "Michel Serres: interferences

et turbulences," *Critique*, 35 (1979); Ilya Prigogine, Isabelle Stengers, and Serge Pahaut, "Su Michel Serres," *aut aut*, 186 (1981). Serres's discussions of Lucretius have also been favorably received by Prigogine and Stengers. In addition to the *Critique* monograph, see *Order Out of Chaos*.

16. Lucretius's extreme importance for and presence in Bruno's works are undeniable. Tocco verifies this for Bruno's Latin works (see *Le opere latine di Giordano Bruno*); see also Fiorentino, *Al chiarissimo comm. Francesco De Sanctis*, in *Opp. lat.* For verification of Lucretius's presence in the Italian dialogues, the index in Gentile's edition is more than sufficient, and it is what I have used. Nearly all Brunian criticism recognizes Bruno's relationship to Lucretius, but there is as yet no detailed analysis addressing all its aspects.

17. Ezio Raimondi, *Il primo commento umanistico a Lucrezio*, in *Politica e commedia* (Bologna: Il Mulino, 1972), pp. 101–40; Garin's note "Commenti lucreziani," *Rivista critica di storia della filosofia*, 28 (1973), pp. 83–86; F. Papi, "Aspetti della tradizione lucreziana nel Cinquecento," in *Antropologia e civiltà*, pp. 107–25.

18. De Giovanni, "Lo spazio della vita," p. 19. In this regard, Nicola Badaloni offers a number of significant references; see his paper, "L'infinito nel Rinascimento: Giordano Bruno fra gli 'antichi' e i 'moderni,' " in *L'infinito nelle scienze*, ed. Giuliano Toraldo di Francia (Rome: Instituto Enciclopedia Italiana, 1987), pp. 257ff.

19. On the ass, see chapter two. The idea of fluidity and the importance of water recur often in Bruno's work. Bruno attributes to water the value of being the universal substance of things. Water is considered the principle of aggregation of atoms. The same vivifying power of the soul appears applicable to the function of water (see Tocco, *Le opere latine di Giordano Bruno*, pp. 277, 282, 284; Papi, *Antropologia e civiltà*, pp. 100–101, 280; Ingegno, *Cosmologia e filosofia nel pensiero di Giordano Bruno*, p. 105). In the Italian dialogues the terms "flux" and "to flow" appear often, and are the basis of the processes of aggregation and atomic disintegration (see Michel, *Cosmology*, p. 282). The terms *fluctuatio, exagitato,* and *vortex* are discussed by Badaloni, in "L'infinito nel Rinascimento." Along these lines, it is important to understand how much influence the hydraulic model of atomism had on Bruno, a model Serres recognized in Lucretius. Ernst Gombrich provides an extensive analysis of sixteenth-century hydraulic studies (with particular attention to Leonardo da Vinci's work). See Ernst H. Gombrich, *The Heritage of Apelles: Studies in the Art of the Renaissance* (Ithaca: Cornell University Press, 1976), pp. 39–56.

20. Mercury is the god of commerce: "herms" (the piles of stones left along the

streets) are also what served to delineate the markets (see Otto, *The Gods of the Greeks*, pp. 104–24). This is the sense in which Serres utilizes the symbol of Mercury as tutelary deity of exchanges between forms of knowledge (cf. Gaspare Polizzi, "Il parassita: Una 'randonnée' ai bordi del sapere," *aut aut*, 186 [1981], pp. 115–27.

21. On Bruno's tendancy not to oppose various methodologies, see Tocco, *Le opere latine di Giordano Bruno*, p. 358; Nowicki, "Pluralismo metodologico e i modelli lulliani."

22. "Colors are generally symbols of forms impressed in matter and, consequently, of the sensible universe. This is why one reads in the commentaries of the Hebrews, in which a Rabbi recounts to a Prince that the Messiah would arrive seated upon an ass. The Prince replies that were the Messiah to arrive in his lifetime, he would give him a palfrey. The Rabbi then replies, 'Could you possibly find an ass of a hundred colors upon which our Messiah would mount?' intending these words to mean that the Messiah is God, Lord of the universe, and therefore would not need the horses the Prince offers, precisely because the ass he rides is the symbol of primal matter, designated by Typhon, to which the Egyptians referred, and the hundred colors are the forms; the colors and the ass together are the whole of the universe" (Alessandro Farra, *Settenario* [Venice: Appresso la Minima Compagnia, 1954], p. 447 [copy used: BAV, Stamp. Chigi V 494]; the first edition of *Settenario* is 1571). On Farra's contribution to studies of the ass, see *La letteratura delle immagini nel Cinquecento*, ed. Savarese and Gareffi, pp. 6–7 and 174–75.

23. Otto, *The Gods of the Greeks*, pp. 104–24.

24. On the relationship between cabalistic combinatorics of the Torah's letters and Democritus's atomistic relativism, see Gershom Scholem, *On the Kabbalah and Its Symbolism*, tr. Ralph Manheim (New York: Schocken Books, 1965), p. 77; but on the notion of the Cabala as a particular typology of the labyrinth, see Umberto Eco's preface to Paolo Santarcangeli, *Il libro dei labirinti* (Milan: Frassinelli, 1984), p. x.

25. Bruno omits this passage in his final edition of the *Cena* (see Aquilecchia's edition).

INDEX